Albion Awakening

John Fitzgerald

&

William Wildblood

with an introduction by

Bruce G Charlton

Albion Awakening

ISBN: 9781708664954

Cover: The Westbury Horse by Eric Ravilious

NOTE

This book is divided into five sections relating to different aspects of the Albion story. The author's initials are given after the title of each piece and dates of composition are at the end in the few cases where that might be relevant. Photographs and images are credited where the copyright holder is known, and the authors would like to express their thanks for the use of these. We apologise for any omissions which, if made known, will be added in future editions.

Albion Awakening

CONTENTS

Introduction 1

Prophecies and Prophets of Albion 5
The Destiny of Britain 7
An Ancient Prophecy of England 12
William Blake 16
Auguries of Innocence 18
Dion Fortune and Glastonbury 21
The Magical Battle of Britain 24
England's Dreaming 28
The Jerusalem Suite 37
Taliesin – Bard of Britain 46
Journey to the Centre of the Earth 59
G Wilson Knight 72
The Inklings 77
The Eighth Narnia Book 80

Saints and Sages of Albion 85
Joseph of Arimathea 87
William of Glasshampton 95
The Betrayal of the Romanovs 104
King Charles the Martyr 107
King Harold Godwinson 112
Roger Lancelyn Green 116

Kathleen Raine 119
Colin Wilson 123
St Cuthbert 129
St Dunstan 133
Two Modern Saints 137
Is Albion an Angel? 140

The Land of Albion 143
The Old Country 145
Beachy Head and Albion 148
The British Myth 151
Albion Set Apart 153
Pilgrimage 156
Doorways to Albion 159
Christian Albion 166
Iona 172
Maumbury Rings 176
The Long Man of Wilmington 180
London 183
The Strange Ship 187
The Last of Logres 192
The Advent of Arthur 194
This Charged Land 203
Albion and Russia 208
Dwellers on the Threshold 213
Voyage to the West 219

The Decline, Fall & Possible Rise of Albion 223
The Vacuum of Leadership 225
The Glorious '50s 227
A Deeper Reality 229
The Old Port 232
Come and See 240
Another Chance? 242

England Led the World into Materialism 244
Empire and Albion 247
Albion Still Asleep 249
Albion Besieged 251
What are the Signs of Decline? 253
Deviations of Modernity 256
Brexit 259
Brexit and Religion 263
Those Whom the Gods Would Destroy 266

Awakening Albion 269
Awakening from Illusion 271
True Awakening Demands Deep Penitence 274
Inconsistency and Confusion 276
Fantasy and Reality 278
Intellect and Intuition 280
Mere Christians 285
Nationalism and Patriotism 290
Women Readers 292
An English Virtue 295
Where We Are Now 297
The Robin Hood Option 301
Redditor Lucis Aeternae 305
The Great Return 311
Beyond the Grey Havens 316
The Return of Constantine 320
The Sleeping King 324
When Britain Fell 327

Albion Awakening

INTRODUCTION BY BRUCE G CHARLTON

Albion Awakening was a blog which was shared between the triumvirate of myself, William Wildblood and John Fitzgerald. The theme is contained in the title: the blog was dedicated to the hope that 'Albion' - the legendary, mystical soul of 'Britain', would awaken and take-up her true spiritual destiny.

The blog was launched summer 2016, in the aftermath of the referendum vote in favour of Brexit; which we understood to represent a spiritual rejection by The People of Albion of the plan to subsume Albion in a European, bureaucratic super-state. Beyond that, we all agreed that leaving the European Union was - at best - only a first step; and that for any good to come from it the next step would need to be spiritual, not political. The blog continued for more than two and a half years, until it reached a natural close in spring of 2019.

The three of us brought different qualities to the blog. We are all Christian, all - indeed - inclined to a Romantic Christianity that sees a large and vital role for imagination, creativity and direct personal experience. We all, too, regard the Oxford Inklings group as spiritual mentors: in particular JRR Tolkien, CS Lewis, Charles Williams and Owen Barfield.

Beyond that - like the Inklings - we each have a somewhat different Christian emphasis. I was a lifelong atheist who converted in late middle age, and became an essentially unaffiliated Christian. My spiritual practice is rooted in a pluralist and evolutionary metaphysics deriving from sources such as Mormon theology, and the spiritual philosopher William Arkle.

William came from a Church of England background, and became a lifelong spiritual seeker - focused on Christianity; but at times including experience of Eastern, specifically Hindu, practices. He has a long experience of meditation and a vital period during young adulthood when he participated in direct contact with spiritual Masters.

John comes from a Roman Catholic, ultimately Irish, background - and sees his Christian life as rooted in the tradition, legend and myth of the British Isles. He is a story-teller as well as an historian; and sees a vital role for the imaginative arts in awakening Albion.

My contribution, as the blog administrator, was mostly to write a large quantity of mostly topical and off-the-cuff posts. I used the blog as something rather like a notebook, and produced something like a stream of consciousness of ideas relating to the main theme. Consequently, my posts were of essentially ephemeral interest, and we decided not to include them here.

William's and John's blog posts took more of a set-piece form; they contributed many rounded and polished mini-essays - also, in John's case, short imaginative fictions - on many topics relating to the Awakening theme. This volume is an edited selection of such pieces from Albion Awakening. Their value is of two main kinds: knowledge and inspiration.

In one sense, this book could be regarded as a 'crash course' in those people and events that make Albion - the phenomena that raise mere Britain to the mythic significance of Albion. In a second sense; this volume is a collection of potentially inspirational fragments of the Albion myth - which, we hope, will encourage (that is, give courage to) all lovers of Albion in sustaining and growing the reality of our national myth - from and within each of our-selves.

As arranged in this volume William and John's essays constitute a mosaic or collage of colourful reflections and suggestions on the subject of the spiritual nature of Albion: what we have-been, are, could be… and what we *should* be.

PROPHECIES & PROPHETS OF ALBION

THE DESTINY OF BRITAIN (WW)

In the late 1970s when I first became interested in spiritual matters I visited a place in Glastonbury called the Ramala Centre. This was really just a guest house catering mostly for people on the Glastonbury pilgrimage circuit and revolved around a husband and wife team who had recently published a book called The Revelation of Ramala (Neville Spearman 1978). The book purported to contain channeled teachings coming from a group of spiritual beings in the inner planes or higher worlds and, unlike many such, had a sense of authenticity to it. That does not mean everything in it had to be accepted as true. In a channeling experience one cannot assume that the communicator has all knowledge simply because he, she or it is communicating from the spiritual realm. As we have been told, 'in my Father's house there are many mansions' which means that the spiritual world can be conceived of as having many levels which, whether you think of them as planes of consciousness or actual localities, are discrete spheres of being in which spiritual knowledge, understanding and even holiness of character increase as one ascends. And one can only ascend these planes to the degree that one's inner state of being corresponds to them. Even if there are aspects of our being on these planes all the way up to supernal levels, these would be in the nature of a seed that requires to be opened and developed before it can be truly known or expressed. This means that any communicating spiritual being will only have the knowledge appropriate to its spiritual development and location which, in terms of the inner worlds, amounts to pretty much the same thing.

So, a channeling may be authentic in the sense that it comes from a genuine spiritually awakened being rather than a recently departed human soul or a piece of animated psychic detritus or even a demon or malicious spirit of some kind, but that does not mean the source is always right and cannot be mistaken. It all depends where it is coming from. There is also the matter of the channeler (medium) to consider. Is he able to bring through what is communicated without putting a personal slant on it, even if that is done unconsciously? In many cases I would say the answer would be no. In this case, however, I thought the process was fairly pure; that is, the source was a reasonably elevated one and the channeler brought through the communications with little personal interference. However, one still needed, as always, to use common sense, discrimination and intuition to sift out the objectively real from subjective opinion, belief and just plain error.

All this is to introduce one of the last chapters or talks in the book which was called 'The Destiny of Britain'. I felt a shock of recognition when I first read it, one of those moments when something you didn't know you knew is suddenly brought out into the sunlight of full awareness, and I'd like to give a few extracts from it here. With due acknowledgement and thanks to the authors, of course, who were David and Ann Jevons. The book was published anonymously back in the day but their names are on their website so I don't suppose anonymity matters much anymore at this distance in time. I've edited the extracts a little, but only in the sense of leaving sections out. I haven't added anything other than what is in brackets and that's only to make better sense of the piece in its edited form. When reading please bear in mind this comes from a book published in 1978.

> To many of her inhabitants it would appear that Britain is a declining country, set upon a path towards economic and moral collapse, but my purpose in speaking to you is to reassure you that she is indeed still great and to tell you of her purpose in the destiny of the Earth.
>
> Britain contains some of the most sacred points of divine power on the surface of this planet, and has always been the holiest of lands, kept apart, separate, from the other land masses of the World. It is true that the Nazarene (Jesus) came to Britain as a young man in order to prepare his physical body for overshadowment by the Christ (for) Britain is one of the great spiritual centres of the World.
>
> At the present time it would appear that Britain is on the verge of collapse (but) it is in Britain that the light of renaissance is being kindled. Britain is to be the leader of the World, not in the sense that she has led the World in the past through the conquering of countries but rather in the sense of a spiritual leader to whom other countries will look to for guidance. It has been written that Britain and America will be one (and) this is true. In the USA today you have much potential, much power but also a need for guidance. It is this

which Britain will provide for being prepared within this country now are the teachers of the New Age.

It is therefore unfortunate that at such a time Britain has chosen to attach itself in federation to other countries in Europe. As a nation she has free choice but through attaching herself to Europe she has delayed the destiny which she has to fulfil. She will in time overcome this obstacle, and find release from that federation, the motivation for joining which was trying to avoid that which was written in the economic future of the country. Nevertheless, in spite of this union having taken place, Britain will not avert an economic collapse.

At the present time Britain is preparing herself for her future role. Those of us of the Hierarchy who seek to forward the plan for this Earth are drawing very close to Britain at this time. Remember that Britain has had a glorious past and is a most holy and sacred land. In the future Britain is to play a role which is without parallel for which the people who inhabit these shores have to undergo a period of transmutation so that she may be ready to fulfil the true purpose of her being: the resting place of the Christ light.

As I say, this comes from a book published in 1978 and the talk may be from some time earlier. Ignoring the content for the moment, it is interesting to note that, while beings on higher levels may have some idea of a possible future, they are not accurate with regard to time. Most of the predictions here have yet to come to pass. Now that we are about to leave the EU (as correctly predicted here) matters may accelerate but it seems clear that a shorter timescale was envisaged by the speaker back then. Human free will is a factor that cannot be predicted perhaps and nor can the consequences of manipulations by the dark forces who obviously want to forestall and obstruct the plans of the spiritual Hierarchy (to use the language of the extract) for as long as possible. It seems that, so far, these dark forces have been highly successful in postponing any spiritual awakening. In the 1980s, shortly after this book appeared, they fostered materialism and greed on the one hand while, on the other, they debased much nascent spirituality by diverting it into the psychic dead-ends of New Age fantasies. They also spread social and moral attitudes totally at variance with any traditional Western ideas and we are stuck with these today. Of course, none of that would have been possible if we hadn't gone along with it and proved relatively easy to corrupt.

This talk and much of the book reflect the Age of Aquarius ideology popular in alternative spirituality circles in the 1970s but this was probably an unconscious imprint from the mind of the channeler. The substance of the talk will most likely have been transmitted in the form of ideas on a mental level and then clothed in words by the channeler so it will reflect his attitudes and opinions of the time in terms of its style and form. Nevertheless, if one filters these out, one is still left with a prophecy of the future spiritual importance of Britain. There is also the prediction of economic collapse which has been delayed for some time but which very possibly cannot be put off for much longer. Maybe leaving the EU will trigger it but that does not mean it is a mistake. Man does not live by bread alone and sometimes he has to give up his bread and his circuses in order to see that there is something more than this to life. I don't say that economic collapse is willed by the powers that be but it may be regarded as necessary, just as the delaying of economic collapse is not, in itself, wanted by the enemy but might be seen as useful in that it perpetuates our materialism and avoidance of spiritual responsibility.

From my perspective now I think that Britain has not been true to her calling. There was an opportunity but we were not equal to it at the time. I wonder if recent events mean that opportunity might come knocking again, another chance to fulfil our spiritual destiny? I even wonder if this second opportunity wasn't always seen as the real one by the true spiritual powers, and the earlier one was in the nature of a trial run or preparing of the way, a kind of false opening that nevertheless would serve to facilitate the future true opening. If that is the case we can expect the other side to redouble their efforts to delay, sidetrack and corrupt, and we should be alert to what takes place in our own psyches to make sure we do not succumb to these forces who will always attack where we are weakest in ways we do not expect.

Some readers may not like references to 'the other side' and 'the enemy'. Aren't we all supposed to be friends now and isn't everybody equal, all with the same rights to express ourselves and have our opinion regarded as valid if it's true for us? Oh, dear! Whatever happened to being wise as serpents? The fact is we are in a spiritual war and there is indeed another side. It is wise to know this even if we should not focus too much on it and start branding others in this world who might disagree with us as in league with the devil. Perhaps they are but that does not necessarily make them bad people in themselves. (It might, of course, but 'hate the sin love the sinner' is wise counsel.) Besides, there is nothing that will increase a sense of self-righteousness so much as considering oneself as enlightened and others as bad. It's one of the devil's classic tricks to catch out and bring down those who have made some spiritual headway. At the same time, there is no room for compromise in true spiritual understanding. Truth is truth and falsehood is falsehood and you cannot make any kind of compromise with the devil. You cannot extend tolerance to his ideas or you will end up adopting them in some form yourself.

The destiny of Britain is here linked to Christ. It is confirmed that he came to this country in his youth as part of preparing for his mission, and it is implied that in some sense Britain is a focus for what is called the Christ light which I would interpret as the spiritual light released by Christ during his lifetime or after his Ascension. Any individual can contact this light and enter into the Christ consciousness but first he must purify the physical, emotional and mental aspects of his being of all worldly stain and raise his inner sensibilities to the level of the soul. Perhaps this light is akin to the Holy Spirit and lies hidden in Britain waiting to be awoken and brought out into the open when a sufficient number of people have called it forth by equipping themselves to receive it? For those who might dismiss this on the grounds that this light is a spiritual thing so cannot have a physical location I would say, yes and no. Of course, it is spiritual but just as our soul is in our heart so a spiritual light can have an earthly focus when it is applied to the Earth.

September 2016

AN ANCIENT PROPHECY OF ENGLAND (WW)

Edward the Confessor was the last Anglo-Saxon king to have a full reign, from 1042-1066. As most people will know he was succeeded by King Harold but Harold's reign ended quickly and abruptly at the Battle of Hastings so it does not stretch the truth too far to say that Edward was the last real English king.

But Edward was not only a king, he was also a saint and it is in this capacity that we should take his prophecy about the future of England. Made (like many good prophecies) on his deathbed, it is to be found in the Vita Ædwardi Regis which was a biography of the king commissioned by his wife Queen Edith and written almost immediately after his death. The original text still survives in a manuscript dating to around 1100 which is kept in the British Library. So this prophecy has a genuine pedigree, something that can't always be said in similar cases.

Here it is rendered in contemporary English. I'm afraid I can't vouch for the accuracy of the translation but this seems to be the accepted version:

> The green tree which springs from the trunk
> When thence it shall be severed
> And removed to a distance of three acres
> By no engine or hand of man
> Shall return to its original trunk
> And shall join itself to its root
> Whence first it had origin
> The head shall receive again its verdure
> It shall bear fruit after its flower
> Then shall you be able for certainty
> To hope for amendment.

Like many prophecies this is somewhat obscure and so is susceptible to a variety of interpretations. For example, it was quoted by someone called Ambrose Lisle Phillipps in a letter to the Earl of Shrewsbury in 1850. These men were both Catholics and chose to interpret the prophecy in the context of the reestablishment of the Catholic hierarchy in England in 1850. But the letter is most interesting for the context it gives to the prophecy.

> During the month of January, 1066, the holy King of England St. Edward the Confessor was confined to his bed by his last illness in his royal Westminster Palace. St. Ælred, Abbott of Rievaulx, in Yorkshire, relates that a short time before his happy death, this holy king was wrapt in ecstasy, when two pious Benedictine monks of Normandy, whom he had known in his youth, during his exile in that country, appeared to him, and revealed to him what was to happen to England in future centuries, and the cause of the terrible punishment.
>
> They said: 'The extreme corruption and wickedness of the English nation has provoked the just anger of God. When malice shall have reached the fullness of its measure, God will, in His wrath, send to the English people wicked spirits, who will punish and afflict them with great severity, by separating the green tree from its parent stem the length of three furlongs. But at last this same tree, through the compassionate mercy of God, and without any national assistance, shall return to its original root, reflourish and bear abundant fruit.'
>
> After having heard these prophetic words, the saintly King Edward opened his eyes, returned to his senses, and the vision vanished. He immediately related all he had seen and heard to his virgin spouse, Edgitha, to Stigand, Archbishop of Canterbury, and to Harold, his successor to the throne, who were in his chamber praying around his bed.

You can see that the prophecy is given in a slightly different translation here, and in prose rather than verse, but the elements are the same.

So, we have the prophecy and we have corroboration as to its authenticity. What we need now is an interpretation. Some people say, quite reasonably given the historical framework of the prophecy, that it refers to the Norman Conquest and the fact that it took 300 years (3 acres) before the ruling hierarchy of England really began to be English again. But for Catholics, while the green tree represents England, the trunk from which it is severed is the Catholic Church. Again, the distance of three acres symbolises the three centuries during which the tree or shoot is separated from its trunk. After this period the shoot is reunited with the trunk and flowers afresh, and this is held to refer to the return of the Catholic episcopacy in 1850, three hundred years after the Anglican Church broke away from Rome during the English Reformation. The belief in this scenario is that the fruit that follows the flowering will come with the full-scale reconversion of the English to Catholicism, supposed to happen at some time in the future.

Assuming for the sake of interest there is something real in the prophecy what can we say about it now? First of all, I think we have to say that a prophecy of this nature is more of a symbol than a fact. That is, the prophet perceives an image in his imagination and expresses it as best he can. But this image is not an actual observation of a future event. It is something like a visionary representation of an idea that exists more in an abstract form than a concrete one, perhaps expressed through the medium of something familiar to the prophet like the two monks in this instance. Therefore, it is a symbol. Now one of the most interesting things about symbols is that they have different levels of interpretation, and a genuine prophecy may be the same. It may refer to different things and this is especially so if you believe that different events in the physical world can play out in similar ways. Consequently, Edward's prophecy can potentially refer to many things that happen to England. It could be the perception of a pattern that works itself out in different forms at different times. Thus, the Norman Conquest interpretation could be true and the Catholic interpretation could also have some truth to it (though not, I would say, in the over-optimistic and literalist way they choose to see it), and there might be other ways to interpret this prophecy too.

All this is highly speculative, of course, but I intend it more as food for thought or fuel for the imagination – just like a prophecy, in fact. So, what, acting on this principle of cyclical recurrence, or different outer events unfolding according to similar inner patterns, can we look to this prophecy for now? Might it be predicting a true Christian revival in England focusing on the reality of Christ, the original trunk or root, three centuries after its loss? Which would be when? Some might say the 20th century when fewer and fewer English people practiced religion, but others might point to the 19th which, though ostensibly Christian, was still thoroughly materialistic. This was also when the theory of evolution supposedly provided a theoretical framework for the rejection of Christianity. But I am tempted to go further back to the 18th century and the time of the Enlightenment when science began to poke holes in religion, and what religion there was became increasingly a matter of externals. Clearly there is no single moment as the loss of religion was an ongoing process but if you are looking for a point at which the balance shifted, and Christianity began to lose its power, then the 18th century, the age when reason overtook faith, is pivotal.

It might be objected that this sea change didn't only affect England but England played a central role through its scientists and philosophers of the time. It might also have been more deeply affected because its Protestant religion, though strong in a moral sense, was so spiritually dry. Besides, the prophecy doesn't just mention loss but also restoration, and was given in the context of England anyway.

WILLIAM BLAKE: A SLIGHT REASSESSMENT (WW)

William Blake is often taken as a kind of godfather of the Albion idea as it manifests itself in modern times, and his work is certainly very inspiring in that regard. When I was a teenager living in London I used to go to the Tate Gallery (as it was, Tate Britain now) to look at his pictures there. I was also given a book of his poems for Christmas one year and read many of these enthusiastically, even if uncomprehendingly in the case of some of the longer, more obscure ones which were frankly over my head at the time, and which I gave up on.

I was fascinated by Blake but something in me always held back from complete involvement. I liked his pictures for their imaginative vision, bold colour, energy and originality but at the same time I found them a bit crude and the human figures almost ugly. Despite the spiritual subject matter there was always something too earthy about the paintings for me to give them my unreserved appreciation. His shorter poems, the Songs of Innocence and Experience for example, were full of charm, insight and beauty but the longer ones were too dense even if some lines and passages were inspiring. But, as works of art, they didn't really move me. I felt that Blake was a visionary artist but not a particularly great craftsman and that sometimes his reach exceeded his grasp. Many people obviously don't feel that but it was my impression, and it reduced my capacity to appreciate his work as much as perhaps I should have done.

Looking back, I think what I found missing in Blake was a sense of the essentially spiritual nature of the spiritual. Let me explain what I mean by that. Both in his art and his poetry he seems to perceive the higher worlds very much in terms of this one. It's as though visions are raining down on him but are being interpreted in quite an earthbound way. I believe this is because, despite his extraordinary imagination and probable clairvoyance, he was still in many ways a product of 18th century materialism and the world of English nonconformist Christianity. That's not his fault but if we compare his spiritual outlook with that of a saint or devotional mystic of the Catholic church there is something quite materialistic about him. He received a vision but, like anyone, he interpreted this within the limitations of his own personality and that of the times in which he lived. I think his reception of the vision was partially deficient and that is why his work can sometimes be misinterpreted as political.

It might be said that Blake cannot be blamed if his work is taken to be something other than it really was but I would say that the deficiency of his receptivity is at least partly responsible. Maybe a purer soul would not have left himself open to such misunderstanding, but then God uses the vehicles that are available and none are perfect. By any criteria, William Blake accomplished a mighty work, and I write this not to criticise him but simply to point out that he was not perfect and his vision had its faults, most notably in that it tends to materialize spirituality. At least, in my opinion it does.

Perhaps if we regard Blake as a prophet but not a saint, we will have a clearer idea of him. I see him being welcomed into heaven and congratulated on his magnificent achievements, all the greater because of the time in which he worked, but then being sent off for a little purgatorial purification. May we all be so fortunate!

AUGURIES OF INNOCENCE (WW)

This is one of William Blake's most famous poems. It starts with the lines everybody knows.

> To see a world in a grain of sand
> And a heaven in a wild flower,
> Hold infinity in the palm of your hand,
> And eternity in an hour.

Yes, these are so well-known they are now almost hackneyed. They do capture the feeling that arises in a typical peak experience or transcendental state of consciousness, but that state can come to almost anyone seemingly at random, and even be stimulated (or perhaps simulated would be a better word) by drugs, and, though it may be called spiritual, it cannot be said to represent the spiritual goal at which we should be aiming. It is perhaps the goal of pantheistic mysticism but it is not the theistic goal.

That is revealed later with the last lines of the poem. Here they are.

> God appears, and God is light,
> To those poor souls who dwell in night;
> But does a human form display
> To those who dwell in realms of day.

With these words, Blake draws a clear distinction between two different kinds of spiritual approach, and he comes out in favour of the latter. The first approach is that of the philosopher who seeks knowledge or the Eastern mystic who wishes to dissolve his supposedly illusionary self into the greater Self for it there to disappear into the unmanifest ocean of light. This is a real state but to see it as our spiritual goal ignores the purpose of creation. If God is light and nothing more in his essence then he or it is abstract and impersonal, and creation, ultimately, is unreal. Nothing is real except the state of blissful unmanifest oneness. Now, reality does have an aspect in which there is simply pure light but that is not the whole of what reality is or what God in himself is, and it is not the aspect that we were created to fall back into. For it is rather like returning to the spiritual womb before we experienced this world of creation. But we were born, and we are meant to grow into sons and daughters of God, real individuals with real creative powers who can expand creation through love.

When Blake says that God has a human form he means that God is a person. He is saying that reality is personal and made up of beings not things, concrete not abstract. This is deeply unfashionable today but it is the truth taught by Jesus who stands for us as the human form of God, and to know it fulfils our spiritual purpose in a way that being reabsorbed by the light can never do.

Note that Blake says God is light to those who dwell in night. To say that God is light might seem to be the highest thing one can meaningfully say about him, but Blake says this is the case only for those who live in ignorance, whose spiritual darkness tells them that God must be light. Real seekers but not yet awake. However, to those souls who have risen from their spiritual slumbers and "dwell in realms of day", God is not just light. He is a person. Reality is personal, and that means that our individuality is a real thing. A thing given by God, self-evidently, but what God gives he does not take back. God is creative and he wants us to be too since we are his children. To be creative, you must have a self.

William Blake was perhaps the pre-eminent prophet of Albion. As I said in the previous chapter, when I was 16 I developed a real enthusiasm for him and asked for and received the complete works of his poetry for Christmas. I was also a regular visitor to the Tate Gallery in London which had a large collection of his paintings. To tell the truth, I was rather daunted by his longer poems and never read any of them all the way through. I certainly didn't understand what I did read. But I loved the Songs of Innocence and Experience, and found his pictures fascinating, partly, I think, because they depicted visions of a higher world of endless creative energy produced by someone who actually seemed to have seen what he was painting. Artistically, they are somewhat crude but the inspiration comes through and bursts off the paper or wood or whatever the material might be. Blake was not an orthodox Christian because his natural insight was too great to be confined by any framework of systemised thought. That doesn't mean he was right in everything he said or wrote, but he was undeniably authentic so, even when he might have been in error, I would say that was because the over-flowing abundance of his vision exceeded his mental capacity to express it.

In modern times, even the relatively few who do turn to a spiritual conception of the world are often more comfortable with abstract explanations of the God is light variety. A personal God just seems too childish. We've evolved beyond that anthropomorphic way of looking at things. We are now much more intellectually aware. But the funny thing about real evolution is that we often return to where we were before, but see it this time in a deeper way. God as person is not childish. It is real in a way that philosophical approaches to God can never be. Blake's vision in the Auguries of Innocence was true.

Albion Rose

DION FORTUNE AND GLASTONBURY (WW)

Orthodox Christians of a nervous disposition, please look away now. Dion Fortune (née Violet Firth) was an occultist. She delved into the unseen worlds, was a medium, practiced ceremonial magic and exercised psychic powers. She wrote books with titles like The Cosmic Doctrine and The Mystical Qabalah, occult novels such as Moon Magic and The Sea Priestess and founded a society called The Fraternity of the Inner Light. The Cosmic Doctrine purported to describe the formation of the universe and she claimed to have received it in trance from discarnate Masters, one of whom was supposedly Socrates. Unfortunately, this esoteric cosmology is long-winded and verbose, reading like a sub-Theosophical production with interesting bits but on the whole pretty dull. It is quite unlike her other works so probably was received in the way claimed. I doubt the source was as claimed though since its dense style and obscure content do not speak of a true member of the Communion of Saints to me. It's much more an intellectual product than a spiritual one, like most occult revelations, and probably came, like most occult revelations, from one of the denizens of the inner planes who over-estimated his spiritual status. Her novels are more entertaining though not quite as good as claimed by her apologists. They are well written but their spiritual content is limited.

Despite all this I have a great deal of respect for her. She exudes common sense and even wisdom in most of her writings, and undoubtedly helped clean up the sensationalist mess that was early 20th century esotericism. I think she also revealed or uncovered previously unknown truths, perhaps better described as symbolic realities, to do with Atlantis and the Arthurian stories in particular and the Western Mystery Tradition in general, and these have now passed into much wider circulation. She drew a clear distinction between magic used for benevolent or evolutionary purposes and the sort advocated by her deeply unpleasant contemporary Aleister Crowley, and on matters of sex she had a lot more insight than most modern pagans, seeing it in a not dissimilar way to the Church. Which, of course, gets her branded a prude nowadays. All in all, she seems to have been a no-nonsense sort of person, of great personal integrity, who worked tirelessly for what she believed in, possibly wearing herself out as a result and dying at the relatively early age of 55. She was also a Christian of sorts, albeit esoteric and unorthodox sorts, but still sincere in her love and respect for Christ.

One of her books which can be enjoyed by anybody, occultist or not, is Glastonbury, Avalon of the Heart. This is her love letter to the town and is a lyrical evocation of its special qualities. Dion Fortune was one of the first people to draw attention to Glastonbury as the spiritual heart of England, originally visiting it when Bligh Bond was conducting his psychic investigations of the Abbey ruins. She later bought Chalice Orchard at the foot of the Tor where she set up a retreat, and was eventually buried in St John the Baptist's church there. Her book describes the history of Glastonbury and the legends that surround it including those to do with the young Jesus, Joseph of Arimathea, King Arthur and the Grail. She seeks to harmonise the pagan past with the new and higher Christian way, seeing the former as fulfilled in the latter rather than just shown up as false, the correct attitude in my opinion. Here's an extract which shows both her poetical style and true Christian feeling.

> There is spiritual power in Glastonbury. To stand in the centre of the great nave, looking towards the high altar, is like standing waist deep in a swift mountain stream. Invisible force is rushing past with a streaming movement. Only in one other place and on one other occasion have I felt the like force - at Christmas communion in Westminster Abbey, when, coming out of the transept into the slow-moving file of waiting communicants it was as if one had stepped from the bank of river into swift-moving water when the central aisle was reached.
>
> What is this pouring power of holy places? Do we not miss the power of pilgrimage? The Reformation no doubt swept away many abuses in an age that had fallen on corruption, but with the abuses were destroyed also many good things. Some great truths of the spiritual life were forgotten when every man became his own priest.
>
> Whatever may be the explanation thereof, experience proves there is power in holy places, power to quicken the spiritual life and vitalize the soul with fresh enthusiasm and inspiration.

> Where strong spiritual emotions have been felt for long periods of time by successive generations of dedicated men and women – especially if they had had among them those who may be reckoned as saints because of their genius for devotion – the mental atmosphere of the place becomes imbued with spiritual forces, and sensitive souls capable of response are deeply stirred thereby when they come into it.

Before writing this essay I re-read Avalon of the Heart (it's quite short) and, in one of those odd little coincidences many people will recognise, I was struck by the similarity of the sentiments Dion Fortune expresses here and those in a piece on pilgrimage I recently wrote (see below). I include it for that reason but also because I think it shows that, whatever her other interests, her Christianity was genuine. I would recommend this book to anyone interested in the history and legends of Glastonbury even if some of it (it was published in 1934) has been superseded by more recent writings.

THE MAGICAL BATTLE OF BRITAIN (WW)

Dion Fortune was not just a theoretical magician. She practiced magic too and during the Second World War she put her knowledge of it to good use. That is, she employed her understanding of the way magic operates to aid in the defence of England. This might sound odd but what it amounts to is the power of thought, concentrated, focused and strengthened by ritual, directed towards a certain end. In a way, the Catholic Mass works on a similar principle though the Mass would work on a spiritual rather than magical level. I would say the minute's silence in wide use today is, potentially anyway, something along the same lines, though in matters of this kind the effect is determined by the motives and intensity of purpose of the participants. Naturally, success cannot be measured by any method at our disposal today but nor are we able to dismiss this out of hand from our present limited understanding of how the world works either.

Dion Fortune was a patriotic woman. She was probably what used to be called a High Tory in her political views, and one of her biographers describes her as aligned to the ideas of Winston Churchill. When the war came she, like most people, wanted to 'do her bit'. Her field of expertise was magic so that is where she thought she could best serve her country. What she did was to organise group meditations which were to take place every Sunday. These started in October 1939, just after the war began, and continued for three years until shortly after America entered the war when it must have seemed that the tide was turning. People on her mailing list, the members of her Fraternity of the Inner Light, were sent letters every week inviting them to participate in a meditation at exactly the same time. Thus, although it was a group meditation the group was not present in the same place. The letters elaborated the form the meditation should take, the instructions stating that "the work consists of certain well-defined stages, each of which must be carefully performed before passing on to the next. These stages are the steps of a stair on which the mind rises to a higher level of consciousness, performs certain work there, and then returns to normal." She stressed that "ethical principles are involved" and that the meditator should "invoking the Name of God, open your mind as a channel for the work of the Masters of Wisdom". The idea was to build up psychic force which could be used for the defence of the realm against the Nazi attack. As she makes clear, "success can only be achieved by single-pointed concentration". They must have thought they were on the right track when, shortly after they started their work, the Minister of War made a broadcast stating the same ideas and then a week later the Pope spoke in a similar vein. They did not claim to have influenced this trend but took it as evidence that all were responding to the same inspiration from the higher planes. In effect, it was a validation of their work and approach to it.

In February 1940 the group was told to visualise angelic forces guarding the coasts of Britain. The idea was that these forces were there but their power could only come through to the physical plane if it was assisted and called forth by meditators in this world who could, as it were, help to crystallise and solidify that power by their concentrated thought. A link between above and below could be constructed, almost like a funnel through which the power could manifest. The members of her Fraternity were also asked to repeat invocations when the Luftwaffe bombed Britain which would, it was hoped, summon those in the inner worlds who might help their earthly brethren in distress. This is magical thinking which might seem absurd to the materialist but is the basis of most religious ritual and practice.

The occult writer Gareth Knight has written an excellent biography of Dion Fortune in which some of this work is described. In 'Dion Fortune and the Inner Light' (Thoth Publications 2000) he relates how the group members were told to visualise a particular symbol which was a triangle linking three coloured spheres. In these spheres the imagination should place three figures who were King Arthur wielding a sword, Merlin holding a sceptre and Christ with the Holy Grail. This was later transformed into a pyramid with the Virgin Mary replacing Christ in his sphere as he rose to the apex of the pyramid, making it clear that the whole work was being carried out under his protection.

In her letter of September 8th 1940, quoted by Gareth Knight, Dion Fortune makes the following observation which I think shows her fundamental quality. "There is only one way to keep quiet and serene under bombardment - to be prepared to lay down your life for your country if necessary. Once that eventuality is accepted, one abrogates one's civilian mentality and the passivity and helplessness that go with it. Regard the warning wail of the siren as an 'alert' not as a 'retreat'...Try and make contact with (the Invisible Helpers), not in order that they may protect you, but that you may co-operate with them in helping those around you." Surely, we see someone here in whom the spirit of sacrifice and service was strong and sincere.

On one occasion her headquarters at Queensborough Terrace in London was bombed and the residents had to leave. In Gareth Knight's words "They drew consolation from the fact that although everything was thrown off the altar in the sanctuary, the statue of the Risen Christ remained standing on its pedestal, though shifted to the very edge". Who is to say that this is just a coincidence? Further on he writes, "As Dion Fortune remarked, she had often been alleged to be a Black Occultist but on this occasion the allegation could not be denied as she and the librarian looked like a couple of sweeps through the difference of opinion with the roof, which fell on them but tactfully refrained from hitting them."

Some people will accept that Dion Fortune's intentions may have been good but she was still an occultist which is a path forbidden to the Christian, certainly one fraught with risk, even danger. This is undoubtedly true. Anyone who opens himself up to the psychic realm needs to have an abundance of inner purity and common sense if he is to emerge unscathed. It is far easier to come into contact with demons, mischievous spirits or, at best, spirits that over-estimate their spiritual attainment than angels or true Masters if one follows the occult path. Moreover, occultism tends to distract from real spirituality because it is concerned more with the inner side of creation than the Creator. Even when occultists are sincere they can easily get lured down the byways of the spiritual path and that's where many of them do end up.

However, in my opinion Dion Fortune is someone who did possess both common sense and true dedication to the upward path, and I believe she performed a valuable service both for her country during the war and for the development of a certain branch of spiritual understanding in the 20th century. Whether the benefits outweigh the risks in occultism is another matter. Spiritually speaking, it is unnecessary and can easily be a diversion at best and sometimes something much riskier. But if the occultist works under the protection of Christ, submitting himself or herself to that rule at all times, then I think that he or she does have something to offer. How many do though? The temptation to pride and the love of power is always strong but I see Dion Fortune as someone who was definitely on the side of the angels and who worked with them, most of the time anyway.

The question now arises, does any of this have any relevance for us today? We may not currently be engaged in anything so obvious as the fight against the Nazis but there is still a spiritual war going on and it seems to be intensifying. It is no less powerful for not taking place in a physical form. Indeed, in some ways, it is more powerful because its effects are not directly observed and therefore more insidiously pervasive. Perhaps we can take a leaf out of Dion Fortune's book and dedicate ourselves to prayer and spiritual devotion because that is what all this amounts to. It may not be in so organised a form but every voice that is raised to God for his aid in this time of, let's be frank, spiritual tribulation adds to the power and effectiveness of the good. We need to make sure that our own hearts are pure though as the prayers of one saint are more effective than those of a thousand sinners.

ENGLAND'S DREAMING - WAYNE STURGEON'S 'ALBION AWAKE' (JF)

Brother Ninnias came with him to the end of the beanrows. Aquila had half expected that the monk would say something about what had happened, but, tipping up his head to look about him with a wide, quiet, all-embracing gladness, he said only, 'The storm is over, and it is going to be a glorious day.'
And Aquila, looking about him also, saw that the moon was down; but the dark had paled to grey, and the grey was growing luminous. The eastern sky was awash with silver light, and somewhere down by the stream a willow wren was singing, and the whole world seemed poised on the edge of revelation, about to spread its wings ...
'Do you believe in blind chance?' he asked, as he had asked it once of Eugenus the Physician, long ago. 'No, I remember that you believe in

a pattern of things.'
'I also believe in God, and in the Grace of God,' Brother Ninnias said. Aquila stood quite still, his face lifted to the light above the wooded valley that was setting the east singing like the willow wren. At last he stirred. 'I must be away to my men. Give me your blessing before I go.'

Rosemary Sutcliff, *The Lantern Bearers* (Oxford University Press, 1959)

It has often been said that in a time of spiritual and cultural disintegration (like our own) renewal will come not from the centre but the periphery. A society's institutions - government, media, churches, etc. - are so infected with the follies and miasmas of the age that they serve to stifle rather than engender creative thought and action. Wayne Sturgeon's collection of essays, *Albion Awake* (2013), belongs undoubtedly to the periphery, yet future historians, I feel, may come to regard it as an intellectual stepping stone towards the revitalised, spiritually-resonant centre that will soon - very soon, perhaps - replace the corrupted, crumbling centre we wrestle with today.

Albion Awake is not always an easy book to read. The essays - originally published between 1999 and 2013 in a variety of Anarchist and Third Position journals - are marred by spelling mistakes, repetition, and a patchy use of grammar throughout. This is not the author's fault. He has health conditions which leave him dependent on others to type up his work. But in actual fact these layout and presentation issues are quite striking in their own way. They give the book a certain *Samizdat*, 'underground printing press' feel. Whether the editor intended this or not I cannot say, but it did remind me of the anarcho-punk scene of the 1970s and '80s, which Sturgeon himself belonged to. There is the same DIY spirit and the same lack of respect for technical finesse, but also - and this is crucial - the same level of energy, commitment and artistic integrity. And this, ultimately, is what sticks in the reader's mind - not the typos or missing full stops, but the depth of the author's engagement with the political and social issues of our day, the mythical and religious dimensions this opens up, the breadth of his reading, and - most impressively of all - the joyful, heartfelt love he displays for his country - England - a love which shines out from every page like the 'countenance divine' shining forth upon 'England's clouded hills' in Blake's famous poem.

Wayne Sturgeon (b.1967) is not an 'establishment man' or a member of any political or cultural élite. He is an Outsider (in the Colin Wilson sense of the word), but he is also a humble and ordinary man with his own set of challenges in life. He lives in Brighton, has a family, supports people with learning difficulties, and lives with severe dyslexia and a chronic fatigue-type illness. Reading and writing do not come easily to him but he makes the effort because he knows he must. He is driven by an inner imperative, like the readers and writers of this blog, to do whatever he can to rouse Albion from the dreadful sleep of materialism and one-dimensional thinking he has fallen into.

Sturgeon's religious trajectory has also been far from smooth. He has, as it were, worn a lot of hats since becoming a born-again Christian in the late 1980's, veering from the extremes of liberalism (Quakerism) to the extremes of narrow literalism (the British Israelite movement) before finding his true spiritual home in the Orthodox Church. He has made mistakes along the way. This goes for his writing as well. He regrets, for instance, the essay in this volume entitled, *Anarcho-Illuminism*. But these are fertile mistakes, the kinds of errors and misjudgments that someone seeking seriously for truth and meaning - on both the individual and collective levels - often makes and sometimes needs to make if they are to learn, grow and develop.

Reading *Albion Awake* straight through, one can see how Sturgeon's thought has matured and become more well-rounded over the past two decades. It is a book, in my view, which works on four levels. The first of these is an analysis and understanding of where twenty-first century Britain is becoming dysfunctional. Sturgeon is extremely wary of mass movements and totalising forms of politics and religion. He values what the poet David Jones called 'that which is counter, original, spare, strange.' What he cherishes most of all is individual freedom, but this must not be confused with the two false conceptions of liberty - economic and social Liberalism - which the rulers of this age are currently foisting upon us.

Economic Liberalism sees the individual as an atomised consumer whose *raison d'être* lies in his or her spending power in an ever-expanding 'free' market which blindsides and bewilders us with its revolving door of constantly upgraded goods and services. This is the fake freedom the West told the peoples of Eastern Europe they had to have after the fall of Communism. It is a cause for rejoicing then that countries such as Poland, Hungary and Slovakia are seeing through such an impoverished vision of the human person and are turning towards a more rooted, organic understanding of politics, culture and society.

Social Liberalism walks hand in hand with its economic sibling. Just as, in classical Liberal theory, the removal of tariffs and trade barriers facilitates commercial growth, so too the undercutting of traditional (i.e. Christian) morality is said to liberate the individual from repressive and arbitrary social structures. The sexual revolution may well have been a liberating experience for certain well-insulated types who enjoy playing fast and loose with family structures, but it has had a devastating effect on those who cannot afford such transgressive fun and games and rely on family for emotional and practical support. It is my belief, for instance, that the economic warfare waged on working-class communities by Margaret Thatcher's government would not have wrought such havoc had those same family structures, which kept these communities strong throughout the Great Depression and the Second World War, not been undermined a decade before she came to power by the advent of the sexual revolution.

Social and economic Liberalism are every bit as destructive of the Personalism Sturgeon champions as were Communism and Fascism. Liberalism is more subtle, but just as lethal. It severs men and women from their roots; erases their ancestral memories; mocks their attachment to family, faith and flag; strips them of identity; promotes restlessness and confusion, and brings the chaos of the free market into every sphere of life, even the most personal. It aims to conquer and crush the personage David Jones calls the 'Tutelar of the Place': 'She that loves place, time, demarcation, hearth, kin, enclosure, site, differential cult ...'

This is exactly Wayne Sturgeon's understanding of individual liberty - a physical, emotional and spiritual state where we feel connected to something larger than ourselves - family, locality, religion, etc. - but where our identity is not subsumed into that wider whole à la Fascism (race-consciousness) and Communism (class-consciousness), nor stripped down and deconstructed as is becoming the norm under liberalism today. As Sturgeon writes in his essay, *The Matter of Britain*:

> At root, the problem is finding a balance between the

> individual and the community; we need both; if capitalism as a political ideology sacrifices the community to the individual and communist ideology sacrifices the individual to the group, the time has come to envisage a society where belonging is something that is not only understood in individualist western terms but on a deeper social significance, a holistic national/psycho spiritual dimension that seeks integration with the role of kinship and national identity. A "communal-individuality." This is beautifully expressed by the British myth of 'Albion' as found in the writing of the libertarian William Blake, Albion being the personification or archetype of the hidden soul of an alternative Britain not bound by the chains of Babylon and the New World Order.

Freedom, therefore, is a precious and a fragile thing. Sturgeon is very aware of how easily it can be corrupted by the big battalions of left and right. He cites the example of the Wandervogel movement in Weimar Germany; a youthful fellowship united by a love of Germany's forests, hills and rivers, which was hijacked by the Nazis and twisted into the Hitler Youth. An analogous fate, he reminds us, befell the UK's 'New Age Traveller' scene of the 1980s, which has been shorn of its anarchistic core by the far-left and is today little more than a mouthpiece for Cultural Marxism.

Establishing a 'third way' in British politics and society consequently becomes a very difficult thing to do. The second level of Sturgeon's book - how to make it happen - focuses chiefly on a number of economic measures, such as Mutualism, Social Credit and Distributism, which unfortunately fall outside my range of expertise. I do know, however, that these and similar concepts were highly influential during the inter-war period and remain key components of Catholic Social Teaching. They have enjoyed a renaissance in recent years thanks to Phillip Blond's book, *Red Tory: How Left and Right Have Broken Britain* (2010), and the work of his think tank, ResPublica. The Blue Labour movement, which leans heavily on the thought of the poet and theologian, John Milbank, has also been at the forefront of efforts to steer Britain in a less quantitative, more person-centred and tradition-friendly direction. Milbank's most recent collection of poems is called *The Dances of Albion* (2015) and Blue Labour would do well, perhaps, to focus more on this mythical aspect as it is here - at his book's third level - that Sturgeon's writing really starts to bounce and fizz. Behind the surface bustle of current affairs and culture wars stands Britain's spiritual dimension, which alone is real, though currently hidden. As Sturgeon says in *The Matter of Britain*:

> It is only when an individual has found his or her place in a society that has achieved and fulfilled its destiny in manifesting its national spirit that we can then begin to live in creative harmony with the green earth ... Such a concept of mythology (the poetic expression of the folk soul and collective national psyche) can be a valuable tool in helping to restore and heal communities torn apart by ethnical hatred, bigotry and cruelty. For indeed it is not just individuals who need healing or wholeness but sometimes a collective race or nation needs a restoration whether in culture or race memory.

This is a 'concept of mythology' which looks forward as well as back. In *Wyrd Albion* (an essay written in 2017, so not included in *Albion Awake*) Sturgeon hails Charles Williams' poetic suite, *Taliessin Through Logres* as:

> ... a highly imaginative psycho-geographic mind mapping for the revival and renewal of a prophetic vision of a Christian earth spirit, where lines of pilgrimage and correspondence activate spiritual centres throughout a feminised union of both pagan and Hebraic sites of historic importance. With the coming collapse of industrial civilization, will not the ancient practice of pilgrimage to sacred shrines, holy wells and points of healing power once again rekindle their mystical charm?

Britain's spiritual dimension goes by different names. Some, like Williams, call it Logres. Others, like Blake, know it as Albion. David Jones personifies the land and christens it 'The Sleeping Lord.' 'Does the land wait the sleeping lord?' he asks. 'Or is the wasted land that very lord who sleeps?' This brings Arthurian themes to mind, of course, and ties in nicely with what for me is the strongest essay in the book, *Anarcho-Monarchism*. Sturgeon portrays the monarch here not as some 'lord and master' type ruling over all, but rather as the servant of his subjects and the symbol and guarantor of their freedom:

> Monarchy can be reinvented as a concept to serve a distinctly libertarian ethos, if one can see in the monarch a symbol of sovereignty that is reflected in the absolute sovereignty of the free individual. The word "king" is derived from the word "kin" - so kingship denotes kinship, the king or queen being a symbolic guardian of the people's freedom and self-determination. Thus handed down generation to generation, the monarch carries the genetic inheritance of the people in a bond of mutual co-inherence. This is beautifully and poetically proclaimed in the tradition of British mythology that refers to King Arthur and the quest for the Holy Grail, in that the concept of kingship that is envisaged in the Arthurian mythos is interpreted as one of service and humility towards the people whom one 'rules'. A similar theme is found in the Christian Gospels where Jesus says to his disciples, "Whosoever shall be considered the greatest, let him first become the least and the servant of all." (And in this mythological context, Christ is the fulfilment of all archetypes such as Arthur, as well as the indigenous British and Norse mystery traditions such as Druidism and Odinism in particular.)

Sturgeon's reference to Christ leads us to the fourth and most profound level of *Albion Awake* - the specifically Christian resolution it proposes to the societal challenges outlined above. In 1989-90, shortly after becoming a Christian, he spent a year at the Monastery of the Holy Trinity in Crawley Down, West Sussex. The monastery belongs to the Community of the Servants of the Will of God, an Anglican contemplative order for men and women. The community recites the Jesus Prayer several evenings a week and celebrates a sung Liturgy of the Hours every day.

Sturgeon's year at Crawley Down proved a pivotal and formative experience. Holy Trinity's openness to Orthodox spirituality, particularly the Jesus Prayer, gave him an anchor and a bedrock - through good times and bad - which set him on the path to his eventual reception into the Orthodox Church in 2015. It is significant for the times we live in, I feel, that it should be a monastery rather than a parish church or a cathedral which played such a central part in his religious formation. This is exactly the kind of guidance and encouragement that monks and nuns gave to many 'sheep without a shepherd' in the chaos which engulfed Western Europe after the fall of the Roman Empire. The monasteries and hermitages of that time looked both forward and back - back to the classical civilisation of Greece and Rome, the remnants of which they single-handedly preserved; and forward to the great age of Christendom to come, setting minds and hearts on fire with their holiness, integrity and radiant love for God's creation. Brother Ninnias, in Rosemary Sutcliff's novel, *The Lantern Bearers* (1959), steers the hero, Aquila, away from a futile quest for vengeance for his slaughtered family and towards a more constructive way of fighting the Saxons - a life of dedicated service under the future High King, Ambrosius Aurelianus. Aquila's rage is channelled in a manner which brings him emotional healing and allows his talents and abilities to flourish. Brother Ninnias, like Julian of Norwich and many other contemplatives, has the gift of reading souls, and he uses this grace to point people in the direction that suits their nature and gives their God-given gifts the best chance to blossom.

Our own time, in many respects, is not dissimilar to this post-Roman *milieu*. I believe that a revival of monasticism, as in that era, could restore to Christianity the contemplative depth required to engage effectively with the spiritual needs of people today, which are not the same as they were in the High Middle Ages, the nineteenth century, or other periods of relative cultural stability. I also have the sense that Orthodoxy has a role to play here as well. Wayne Sturgeon definitely thinks so, and it could well be that the future of Christianity in Britain belongs neither to the heirs of the Protestant Reformation nor the advocates of a Catholic restoration. A turn towards Orthodoxy would, I feel, reconnect the country in a very profound way with the monks and nuns of the Dark Aged and with that host of British saints who gave such outstanding witness in the thousand years prior to the Great Schism of 1054. In this respect, Orthodoxy could potentially become the religious version of the third way Sturgeon has found so elusive in the political sphere. Certainly, it is hard to find fault with the sanity and balance of his personal *Credo*, presented to us in his introduction to *Albion Awake*:

> My personal Christian faith which informs and inspires all of this for me, is that of the traditionalist and ancient Orthodox and Catholic Christianity which existed before the Great

> Schism of 1054. I would, therefore, as regards my faith, describe my position as being Orthodox but not Eastern, Catholic but not Papal and Anglican but not Protestant, although I have always been open and sympathetic to the speculative and esoteric forms Christianity has taken, particularly in mystics like Jacob Boehme and Jane Leade and more recently Valentin Tomberg, etc.

Sturgeon hopes to set up a skete in the Sussex countryside - a small centre devoted to prayer, work, study and contemplation - informed equally by Orthodox spirituality and the Matter of Britain. The skete will take inspiration from Joseph of Arimathea and the earliest days of the Faith in this land, and look forward to the reanimation of those sacred lines of force - pagan and Christian - which Charles Williams hailed in his Taliessin poems and which lie like a string of jewels across this holy earth. That is a terrific vision to have, I think, and one which offers hope and encouragement to all of us who feel overwhelmed and paralyzed at times by the downward drift of the world.

It would be fitting at this point to let Wayne Sturgeon have the last word, except to say that 'first word' might be more appropriate. Having read *Albion Awake* and the author's more recent essays (plus an interview in *The National Liberal*) and spoken to him in person, I am sure that everything which has gone before on his spiritual journey can be considered a prologue and that, as the Italians say, *Il più grande è avanti* - the greatest lies ahead:

> Lastly, I do not see the future as closed. I am not a fatalist, I am not waiting for the "rapture"; my understanding of eschatology is that of a "conditional futurism" that is open both the verb and dynamic of grace and of human free will and agency. The choice is clear though - either we make and fight for a future or it will be made for us. The English punk band, The Sex Pistols, once sang that "there is no future in England's dreaming," but there is a future if we can dream it and so in my mind England is still dreaming, only this dream is the dream of Albion and one day this Albion will awake.

THE JERUSALEM SUITE (JF)

Looking back on my recent posts, I see I have referenced William Blake's *Jerusalem* on numerous occasions. Why this should be, I am not sure, but it has prompted me to return imaginatively to my childhood and the first time I encountered those veil-piercing lines.

It was July 1982, three weeks or so before our seven years at primary school ended. Seven years is a lifetime when you're a kid. I never thought, deep down, that I'd ever actually leave St. Catherine's. I knew in theory that one day I'd walk through those big green gates and never go back, but I simply couldn't believe in that day's reality. It didn't feel real. In my heart, I mean. I was too wedded to the place - the classrooms, the corridors, the library, the playground - the *mise en scéne* to so much childhood drama and adventure. More than anything, I felt emotionally bound to my peers - my companions, my comrades, my brothers and sisters in study and sport. I had no siblings of my own, and it upset me that my 'school family' would soon no longer come together under the same roof. September would see us all packed off to High School - the boys to St. Mark's, the girls to The Hollies, with interlopers from other South Manchester primaries - St. Cuthbert's, St. Kentigern's, etc - disturbing the unity and *esprit de corps* forged through more than half a decade of shared experience.

It was with some sadness then, that I contemplated the annual school concert, scheduled as always for the last Wednesday of term. The concert ran - year in year out - for an hour and a half. The orchestra played (including myself as a second violin) and the choir (of which I wasn't a member) sang. The programme was varied - theatre, spoken word, reminiscences from former pupils and a distribution of leaving certificates from the Bishop of Salford himself.

Every year, right at the end, the leavers would perform a special farewell piece. Twelve months before, we had been treated to the *Daniel Jazz*, ten minutes of bouncy choral speech recounting the story of Daniel in the lion's den. My year's offering (chosen by our Head of Year, Mrs. Elms) was shorter but possibly even more dramatic - the sixteen lines of *Jerusalem* in the setting made famous by Sir Hubert Parry, with piano accompaniment from our music teacher, Mr. Clarke.

I had neither heard nor read *Jerusalem* before. We ran through it for the first time in the School Hall on a sun-kissed Thursday morning. Ours was a humble little Hall, not much more than a wooden floor with a piano in one corner and a statue of Our Lady in the other. Mr. Clarke - a slim, sandy-haired chap - strode in, I remember, through the far doors, sat down at the piano and started to play. 'Morning all,' he hailed us, chipper as always. 'Just sing along with me for now please. As loud and clear as you like.' I picked up one of the lyric sheets he had left on the benches (which he expected us to stand on for what he called 'full-bodied amplification') and was instantly astonished. Before I'd even sung a note I'd turned to the lad next to me, Pat Finn, and whispered, 'This is great. This is what life's all about.'

I was right about that. *Jerusalem* was a joy to sing. It really was. Our raw but eager voices boomed, echoed and rebounded around the Hall, bringing (for myself at least) a marked sense of release, of vast spaces - inner and outer - opening up. The melody's dignified, gently rousing lilt soothed and settled my mind while triggering a powerful longing for a depth and quality of being - both individual and collective - which I suddenly and starkly realised I'd wished for more than anything else throughout my young life but had so far only partially experienced, if at all.

Blake's fantastic words - the molten lava of his language - 'countenance divine', 'clouded hills', 'burning gold' - had a poetic and spiritual potency which I had encountered in only a very few places - the Narnia books mainly, plus Roger Lancelyn Green's retellings of Greek, Norse, Egyptian and Arthurian legends. Mrs. Elms, to be fair, had told a few good stories in this mould too. She was from the West Country and had often held forth about Joseph of Arimathea and how he'd brought the Holy Grail to Glastonbury and planted his staff on Wearyall Hill, bringing forth the miraculous thorn tree which flowers every year on Christmas Day. All these tales played a pivotal role in my life, giving me that mythic, archetypal sustenance which the somewhat desacralised, post-Vatican II Catholicism of my youth believed the world no longer needed.

I was ready for *Jerusalem*, in other words, and when we sang it that morning it felt like I was coming home - to myself, to God, and to my friends - to that wider mystery I had always dimly perceived and had reached out for through both my reading and my yearning for camaraderie - a double-edged quest for a 'Round Table', if you like - all through my time at St. Catherine's.

'I will not cease from mental fight,' we sang, and the sun smashed through the windows, transforming the Hall into a golden bowl of warmth and light. I've always had a vivid imagination, it's true, but I swear at that moment I heard a voice in my ear. An old man's voice. Foreign. East European or Middle-Eastern. 'Before you leave this school,' it said, 'you will see the Holy Grail.' I was so shocked that I missed the next line - 'nor shall my sword sleep in my hand' - but made sure I was back on track for the last two - 'till we have built Jerusalem, in England's green and pleasant land.' It felt, all of a sudden, like a matter of life and death that I should sing those two lines loud and well. If someone had asked me why, I could only have replied, 'the old man expects it of me.' But who that old man was and why he had spoken to me, I had no idea at all.

There was a violin teacher who wasn't employed by the school but came in to give individual lessons to pupils who expressed an interest. One of those pupils was me - not, if I'm honest, because I had any huge enthusiasm for the violin but because my Mum and Dad were keen for me to learn an instrument. They saw it as a badge of distinction and a distinguishing mark for myself as a working class boy in a largely middle class school.

Miss Corcoran was the teacher's name. She was calm and grave, and though her name was Irish, like mine and many of my colleagues, she was actually Welsh - from Caernarfon - not far from the Castle, she said - and her voice was as musical as the instrument she taught. She was a smallish woman with brown straight hair and big silver earrings like hoops. Her eyes were brown and wide, her face as round as the sun in the sky, and the dresses and skirts she wore, unless my memory deceives me, were always blue or gold. She sometimes wore a headband too - usually green or purple but now and again white or pink.

Miss Corcoran's lessons were a definite boon as they gave you twenty minutes out of the classroom every week. I liked the little lamp-lit music room at the end of the corridor too and felt at home in her company. She exuded in her voice and bearing a watchful, unspoken spirituality, and I came over time (two school years) to see her as something of a kindred spirit.

My allocated time that particular year was twenty past two on a Monday afternoon, just before the afternoon break. I also recall that for reasons which now escape me I gave up 'private' tuition as soon as I went to St. Mark's. My lesson on the last Monday of term, therefore, two days before our concert, was the last one I ever had.

It was a damp and drizzly afternoon. Miss Corcoran sat facing me, as usual, on her three-legged stool. Rain rapped on the roof and trickled down the round windowpane behind her head. I can't remember the music we were playing but will never, ever forget Miss Corcoran saying about half-way through:

'I'm looking forward to Wednesday night, John. Mr. Clarke tells me you're singing *Jerusalem*. Is that right?'

'Yes, miss.'

'Do you like it?'

'I do, Miss, it's ace. It's the best song I've ever heard and I love singing it with the others.'

'Why?' she asked, leaning forward. 'What makes you love it?'

'I don't know, Miss. I feel real when I sing it. That's all. And I never feel real anywhere else, except in the playground or when I'm reading.'

Miss Corcoran's wide eyes widened some more. Encouraged, I carried on: 'I feel in tune with myself when I sing it, Miss. With who I really am, I mean. Deep down inside.'

Miss Corcoran nodded, grinned, adjusted her purple headband and stood up, her eyes fixed on my violin and bow. 'It makes me feel close to God as well,' I added in a quieter voice. 'Close to God and close to my friends.'

I expected her to say something in reply but all she did was point with her eyes to the instrument in my hands. 'Let me play it for you,' she said, and I handed her the violin and bow. Without further ado she started to play. *Jerusalem*, of course. And for the second time that fortnight I was astonished beyond measure.

She looked different. That was the first thing. Miss Corcoran usually played in the classical style, the violin jutting out from her chin at 90°. But a Gaelic fiddler stood before me now - violin slung low beneath her chin, bow clasped loosely in her hand. The tune was the same as the one I'd come to know. I recognised where the words went - 'And did those feet ...', etc. The feel of it was Celtic though, but hard to pin down. It felt like a lament in many ways, but one that was wild, exultant and savage all at once, its sadness caught, held, and taken up into a wide-ranging, all-embracing harmony and pattern - a visionary, healing tapestry of music.

Miss Corcoran played, I listened, and the fixtures and fittings around us - the stools, the piano, the lamp, the music stands - began mysteriously to blur, slide and fade. I rubbed my eyes but their solidity did not return. They wobbled and wavered, grew bigger, then smaller, then vanished altogether, leaving me in a new and very strange setting.

It was night and I was standing with a great throng of people around a roaring, leaping fire. The fiddler played on ('bring me my bow of burning gold') but out of sight now. I looked up. The stars were out in force. I picked out Cassiopeia and Arthur's Wain pinpoint bright against the inky sky. The air was cold and the warmth of the blaze welcome. Everyone was jostling towards it. I recognised a few faces - a couple of fellow-pupils - Billy Prince and Kath McQueen - one or two parents and even the odd teacher. But it wasn't the people around me that compelled my attention. It was the fire itself. I hustled my way to the front to see it more clearly. Everyone else just wanted to keep warm - rubbing their hands and turning up their collars - and that was fine, but I had seen something in the fire, something odd, something no-one else seemed to have spotted - figures moving about in the flames, little black silhouettes, about a score of them, at the heart and centre of the blaze.

Jerusalem was still going, at the line 'bring me my spear', but I'd lost track of time and wasn't sure if that was as far as Miss Corcoran (if it was still Miss Corcoran) had got to or whether she was playing it over and over in a loop. I concentrated on the fire itself - a mighty curtain of heat and light - and the more I looked the more I saw, like I was watching a film - forms coming into focus and a story taking shape. People in cloaks and hoods were walking up a hill and at the top of the hill was a great tower. Their leader was old and bent and walked with a stick but moved nonetheless with purpose, direction and speed. The woman behind him held something bright and quivering in her hands - some kind of jewel, I thought - but it was hidden in the folds of her cloak and I couldn't be fully sure.

The old man stopped at the tower, stretched out his right arm and touched it with his hand. As he did so he planted his stick into the ground and straightaway I was transported to another place.

At first I thought I thought I was back where I'd started, in the little music room at school. This room was similar in size and shape, but that, I swiftly realised, was the only resemblance. It was a chapel of some sort, with six wooden pews in front of me, three each side of a central aisle of roughened stone. Seven tall candlesticks burned on the altar, which was also made of stone and built into the back wall. An aged priest in silver vestments stood facing it in silence. A blossoming tree, with leaves of orange, gold and green, illuminated the back of his chasuble. Miss Corcoran, to my amazement, was standing to his right, minus her headband, and wearing a white alb with a yellow sun emblazoned on the front. But in her hands she held something brighter than both the candles and the sun - a luminous globe, constantly changing colour - from gold to silver to bronze and back again. The object's contours were concealed by its radiance and I couldn't tell exactly what it was - a chalice, a jewel, a plate or a bowl. But whatever it was, it filled the space - every square inch of it - with gold; a joyful, celebratory gold, which warmed and inspired my heart and mind, just as *Jerusalem* had stirred my soul so potently the day we first ran through it in the School Hall.

As soon as the hymn flashed into my head, I heard it again and realised it had been there ever since I'd come into that place, though up till that moment, for some reason, I hadn't been aware. It was a choir now, male and female voices singing with verve, passion and skill. I had no idea where they were. The sound seemed to come from all around, ringing and echoing through the room.

'Till we have built Jerusalem,' they sang, and the priest turned and bowed to Miss Corcoran as she handed him the Holy Thing. 'In England's green and pleasant land,' they concluded with a mighty gust of triumph and hope. And then there was silence, the priest standing before the altar again and Miss Corcoran kneeling beside him. I knelt down too and waited. Something stupendous was about to occur. I longed for it and was sure of it. The priest lifted the Grail (for surely that's what it was) high above his head and held it there for a long time. Miss Corcoran bowed down almost to the ground, but I kept my head up - watching, waiting, hoping. I expected a bell or a gong at least but nothing happened at all. The priest muttered a few words in a language I couldn't understand and that was it. I thought I'd copy Miss Corcoran and bow my head and close my eyes in the hope the miraculous would feel compelled to appear, but disappointment was already setting in and I began to feel tired in mind and body. Weary to the bone, in fact.

Maybe I fell asleep, or maybe I was already asleep and simply woke from a dream, because the next thing I knew someone was tapping on my shoulder with a stick. I opened my eyes and saw that it wasn't a stick but my violin bow. Miss Corcoran, wearing her usual clothes again, stood above me with my violin in her left hand and my bow in her right. Raindrops trickled down the round windowpane still, but there was high cloud and patches of blue sky now, as a shy, streaky sun splashed the music room with soft summer sunlight.

I was still kneeling down. I felt silly and embarrassed and stood up straightaway. Miss Corcoran smiled and tapped me with the bow again, this time on the other shoulder. 'Well done,' she said quietly, though her words were speech no more but song. 'You are a storyteller and a poet. Like calls unto like; deep calls unto deep. The Great Hymn called and you responded, like the Samaritan woman who encountered Christ at Jacob's Well.'

No-one had ever spoken to me like that before. Such things just couldn't be true. I shook my head sadly. 'I've a vivid imagination, Miss. That's all. Everyone says so.'

'Not so,' sung Miss Corcoran, shaking her head in turn. 'You will be a bard one day and sing your song at the appointed hour. I know it and swear it. I saw it in the music.'

The rain had stopped altogether. Absolute silence reigned. I held her eyes with mine. 'What was it, Miss?' I whispered. 'What happened?'

'*That*,' she replied, 'was The Jerusalem Suite.'

'The Jerusalem Suite?' I repeated. 'But what do you mean? What's the Suite? The music or the room?'

'Both,' she answered and undid her headband, letting it fall to the ground. Her hair fell down around her face and the sun streamed in through the window, circling her head with a halo of light which bathed the piano, stools, lamp, music stands and purple headband at my feet with the same warm, generous glow I'd seen suffuse every square inch of space in The Jerusalem Suite. I saw the glory of the Grail reflected in her eyes and wanted to ask a question about the old priest and tell her as well that a voice had told me I'd see the Grail before school ended. Was it Joseph of Arimathea himself then - as in Mrs. Elms' story - who'd spoken to me and who I'd seen in the heart of the blaze and in front of the altar?

Maybe it was, but I was young and confused and easily daunted. It's one thing when you're eleven years old to curl up in front of the fire and lose yourself in paperback myths and legends, quite another when the Grail Maiden, or one very like her, steps out of the book and into the pages of your own life. I dropped my gaze and mumbled something inconsequential - don't ask me what, I've deliberately forgotten - but whatever it was it wasn't the question I wanted to ask. I'm not sure how our conversation ended either, but when I closed the door behind me and looked down the corridor - ablaze from end to end with bars and shafts of golden sun - I understood that a door had shut on me in more ways than one. The bell rang for afternoon break and I knew that the moment had gone and I could never go back. I can't recall now if this filled me with sadness or relief or a mixture of both.

I saw Miss Corcoran at the concert, of course, and she smiled, shook my hand and said well done. But her congratulations were lost in a welter of back-slapping and hair-ruffling. We had sung beautifully, apparently, but the whole thing had fallen a bit flat for me, if I'm honest. And in truth, how could it have been anything other than an anti-climax after such an epiphany just two days before?

People, I recall, were pouring out of the Hall into the warm summer night. Not all at once though. As happened every year, some (mainly pupils) made a quick getaway while others (mainly parents) lingered. So that's how I came to be standing in the playground with a group of close friends - Pat Finn, Billy Prince, Kath McQueen, Harry Hanrahan and Cara O'Toole - all waiting for our folks. I had given up on the miraculous and was happy just to enjoy the chit-chat.

'We should all stand in a line when school ends on Friday,' said Cara, stretching out her arms, 'and bow down together and kiss the playground.'

'Definitely,' I assented. 'Let's do it.' I was impressed. That was exactly the kind of thought I could and maybe should have had myself.

From where I was stood I could see past the gates and onto the street. I spotted the Bishop, still in his mitre and robes, getting into a big car and disappearing into the night. Then I looked up. I hadn't noticed before how laden the sky was with stars. There, just above Cara's head, was Orion, there Cassiopeia, and there Arthur's Wain.

I tuned back into the conversation. Kath was suggesting that we buy the teachers presents. Harry agreed while Pat demurred. I wasn't sure myself, but then the extraordinary burst in and I heard the old man's voice again, loud and clear, but in my heart this time, not my ear, right at the core of my being.

'All true desires find their home,' he said. 'You must go your separate ways now and live and learn but you will be reunited at the appointed hour, all with your roles to play, when the waters break and the song is sung and the Grail is seen again and the High Tree of Albion blossoms into flame.'

Those, I perceived intuitively, were the words he had spoken in The

Jerusalem Suite that I hadn't been able to understand. Those words should, I suppose, have given me sustenance and support throughout my life, but for many years after that night, until about half-way through my time at University, I found them more of a burden than a blessing. I hurtled through one experience after another, wishing and hoping that the 'appointed hour' would come at once so I could experience a supernatural thrill to go with all the other thrills one searches for at that age.

Then, in my twenties and thirties, I switched tack and wrote The Jerusalem Suite off as wish-fulfilment and the product of an over-heated imagination. I don't know why, but I don't think that way anymore. Nor do I think about it the way I did as a teenager. Both stances seem simplistic and naive to me now. Things like this take time, you see. They can't be rushed. It's not for us to force the pace, not for us to know the times and seasons. Our role is to watch, wait, work, pray, and hold the flame aloft in a dark time. We are the lantern bearers - the watchers in the tower - the golden builders of Jerusalem. We hold in our hands the seeds of an all-encompassing renaissance - social, political, cultural and religious.

I'm coming to see that it's only when we're engaged at this level - living from the core and centre of our being - that a true Round Table can be built and a meaningful connection established with the Divine and with those around us. From there, all things become possible - renewal, restoration, healing and rejuvenation. Space is created and the secret voice is heard, listened to and acted on. The bells peal, the gong sounds, and the waters flow down onto the land, bringing fertility back to the barren places, illuminating hearts and minds, and filling the whole wide world with gold - a warm and generous glow, joyful and celebratory.

A person's life, in its innermost essence, is a quest for the Holy Grail - a voyage to the centre and a journey to Jerusalem. The Heavenly City will only appear, however, when we are ready and when the time is right. The dawn cannot be rushed. It comes at its own pace - when it's meant to and when it's most needed. At the appointed hour. The darkest hour. In the silence and the stillness of the night.

TALIESIN - BARD OF BRITAIN (JF)

'Time present and time past are both perhaps present in time future, and time future contained in time past.' So wrote the poet, T.S. Eliot, and I was by his side as he crafted his words. I guided the hands of Shakespeare, Blake and Milton too. I shouldered arms beside the great defenders of this realm - from Churchill and Nelson to Alfred and Arthur. I was a hod carrier when the Cathedrals soared heavenwards and a Master Druid when the stone circles were made. I lit candles with the saints - Cuthbert and Bede, Boniface and Hilda, Alban and Kentigern - exemplars of this holy isle. I was a guide, my lantern carving a path through the mist as Joseph of Arimathea - on his second visit to Albion - brought the sacred chalice to Glastonbury. For I had stood on St. Michael's Mount thirty years before, a wild Prince of the West, welcoming him as a trader (along with his nephew, the boy Jesus) to these rocky shores.

So much for the past. I shape the present and future as well. It is all one, as Eliot knew - a seamless robe, a unified field. I see, hear, feel and experience it all. Nothing under Albion's moon and sun is strange to my eye or foreign to my heart. It is a burden both crushing and exhilarating - a mixed chalice, a weight of glory.

It wasn't always like this though. My boyhood was simplicity itself. I was brought up in Deganwy on the Clwyd coast, midway between the Great Orme and Conwy Castle. Gwion was my name. My Mum and Dad (I miss them so much) were poor but loving. I wish those times would come back, I really do - throwing stones into the sea with my Mum at Llandudno, while my Dad carried me halfway up the Orme on his back.

I ran errands in those days, in exchange for stickers and sweets, for a lady named Ceridwen who lived in a big house behind the bay. I was friends with her son, Afagddu, who was my age and blind. I honestly don't think his blindness bothered him at all. He was able to play ball (the ball had a bell in it), build dens and run on the sand without any hardship. But Miss Ceridwen (I never caught sight nor sound of any husband) fretted and fussed continually. I heard her tell Mrs. Griffiths next door that Afagddu's blindness would hold him back in life and that she wanted to compensate somehow. He was a quiet boy too, you see. His words, though well chosen, were few. His mother thought he was withdrawn - walling himself off from the world. She would sit with him for ages - looking at him, hugging him, talking to him - trying to prise open the secrets of his mind.

As I say, I didn't think there was anything wrong, but Afagddu was my friend and I respected Ceridwen greatly. I was keen to help, so when she asked me to stay at the house for a year and a day and watch over a potion she was brewing for him I asked no questions but accepted gladly. She showed me a cauldron on the front room carpet - sapphire blue with a rim of pearls - then gave me a ladle and strict orders not to taste a drop.

That was an easy instruction, and I had no problem whatsoever until the last couple of days. The cauldron started to bubble and hiss, and no matter how much I stirred I couldn't calm it down. I was worried about the carpet getting wet, but what eventually happened knocked that into a cocked hat. It was the second last night, mid-summer's eve. I peered over the pearly rim to see if the ladle was needed when the water spat and leapt up, like it had a mind of its own, stinging my hand and splashing my thumb. 'Ow,' I exclaimed, 'that's hot.' I put my thumb to my mouth to cool it down and in that instant, there and then, saw and knew everything that ever was, is now and ever shall be - individually and collectively - my soul's journey through time and space and the whole history of this land, from the song of creation to the consummation of the age. Then Ceridwen appeared in the doorway, took one look and knew ...

Her scream rent the air as hands stretched out to tear my face to shreds. I saw the blow coming, jinked past and darted out the door onto the lamplit bay. I meant to turn left towards Holyhead and Ireland, but in my confusion turned right instead towards England. I ran by the light of the moon, Ceridwen gaining all the time, across the sand and shingle, until my legs turned to jelly and my knees began to buckle. 'If only I could change into a hare,' I thought, and as soon as I'd imagined it, there I was, a boy no more but a milk-white hare, bounding along the beach three times faster than before. But my spirits sank when I looked behind. Ceridwen had vanished but now there was a greyhound on my trail, sleek and slavering and four times as fast.

The chase continued for a night and a day, through wind and warmth and summer showers, under moon and sun and stars. Beyond Flint Castle, I grew weary. The dog snapped and snarled at my heels.

There was no way I could race her all the way to England. The Wirral peninsula loomed into view on my left. So I changed tack, turned into a salmon and sprang into the sea, only to be followed, swiftly and inevitably, by a gleaming, rapacious otter.

I reached Liverpool at dawn, hoping to shimmy between the ships, become a boy again and lose my pursuer in the harbour buildings or down in the crypt of the Catholic Cathedral. I glanced up, saw a seagull circling the Radio City Tower and switched plans on the spot, turning into a pigeon and soaring into the sky like the kites I used to see over Colwyn Bay. It wasn't long, however, before I heard the thrum of wings behind me. Blast! There was a hawk on my tail now, poised and regal, sizing me up and waiting for the first sign of fatigue.

The land drifted by below, a patchwork mosaic of rivers, motorways, medium-sized towns and parkland with more rugby posts - pointing up like white, accusatory fingers - than I'd ever seen before. By the time I got to Manchester I was flagging badly. I aimed for the city centre, thinking I could dive down into the throng, disguise myself as an ant and shake off my shadow in the urban mêlée. But the wind blew me off course, somewhere to the north and east. My strength failed. I could barely flap my wings. So I pinned them back and crash-landed into a haystack, changing at the last second into a grain of corn. I congratulated myself on my ingenuity. But not for long. A red and gold hen clattered through the hay, tossing yellow stalks aside with her scimitar-esque beak. I lay at the bottom, prostrate and forlorn. The hen saw me, stood over me, squawked in triumph, and swallowed me whole.

Darkness covered me. Warmth and wetness too. I no longer discerned the great themes so clearly - Albion's history, my own destiny and so forth - but I knew where I was - Ceridwen's womb - where we were - the Pennines - and what we were doing - wandering meditatively through the mountains, pausing often, sometimes for days on end, at wayside chapels and hidden wells, buried like treasure amidst the rocks and scree.

It was a quiet time - a time of rest, reflection and growth. I was an embryo, then a foetus, then an unborn babe, growing in awareness, strength and size, conscious of Ceridwen's sorrow and ongoing anxiety over her son. My intuition told me, however, that Afaggdu was doing just fine in her absence. Father Dafyd, the parish priest, would have taken him under his wing and he'd have Mrs. Griffiths' two sons, Pwyll and Arawn, to play catch with. But I felt bad on his account. as well. The potion was meant for Affagdu, after all, not me. But there was nothing I could do about it now, just wait to be born and trust that Ceridwen wouldn't kill me.

I didn't think she would, if I'm honest. I didn't expect any favours but the nine months in the mountains had clearly done her good, softening her heart, taking the edge off her anger and easing, if only a little, her maternal fears. And so I was born, tied up in a brown cloth bag and left to float down a winding, mountain stream.

I let the waters take me, ceasing to worry and even to think. Many was the waterfall I tumbled down and many the bumpy landing, until the hour came when I felt strong hands pulling me out, untying the bag and holding me up to the light of day for the first time in a year.

Sunlight smashed through leaf and branch, the river danced and glinted. The mighty tower of Durham Cathedral rose steep and sheer above, while before me I saw the face of a man - careworn but strong and lit from within with surprise and delight. 'Behold,' he cried. 'What do I see? A miraculous catch indeed. I will call the Taliesin - Shining Brow - for that is what thou art.'

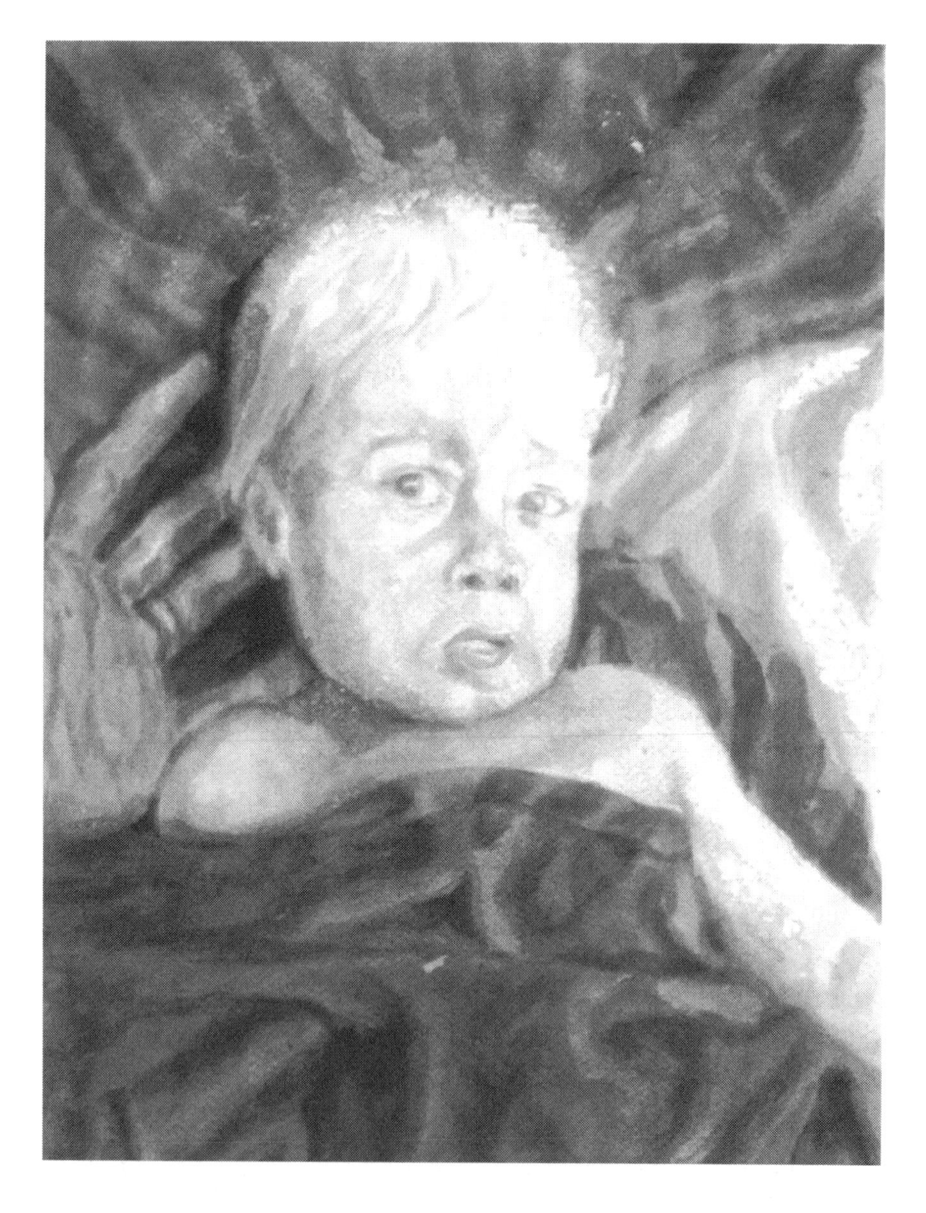

I was baptised in the Cathedral's great font a week and a day later, next to the tomb of St. Cuthbert. My new Dad, whose name was Elffin, carried me up the spiral staircase to the top of the tower straight after. His wife, Rhonnwyn, was there too. He held me aloft and I looked upon the land, rolling out before me like a magic carpet, all the way to Newcastle and the Silver Sea beyond. A light drizzle, like a second dose of holy water, splashed my bald baby head and my prophetic powers were instantly restored.

The story of Britain unfolded before my inner eye, unfurling like a tapestry or scroll. It was a magnificent tale, tainted here and there by materialism and greed, but powered in the main by courage and creative flair. I saw as far as the Dark Time and the light that shines beyond it - the spiritual blindness that beset the land, the implosion of the House of Windsor, then the War of Contending Flags - black and multi-coloured - that laid the Island of the Mighty waste. And then that winter dawn when a King of ancient line returned from the East, stepping down from his ship at Thanet as the Romans did of old. A universal shout of joy rang out across the realm and that night Arthur's Beacons were relit, from St. Michael's Mount to Flamborough Head. Next day the rumours began - from Devon and Cornwall - that Jesus Himself was back, walking along the rocky shore, telling stories, healing the sick, and giving bread and wine to rich and poor and good and bad alike.

A veil descends and I see these things no more, just Afaggdu and myself on Llandudno beach, throwing a shining, tinkling ball back and forth in looping, parabolic arcs. Ceridwen watches on contentedly while my old Mum and Dad wave and take pictures from the crowded pier.

I think again of Eliot and of that most pure and noble of English mystics, Mother Julian of Norwich. For I was a cobbler in the city while she dwelt amongst us, and it was after I had come to her window one Friday afternoon to pour out my heart (as we all did) and receive her blessing that she wrote those famous words of sustenance and grace:

'All shall be well and all shall be well and all manner of thing shall be well.'

And I, Taliesin, Bard of Britain, I who see, feel, sense and know it all - the power and the glory, the sorrow and the shame - can vouch and testify that her vision holds the truth.

Yea, and more than this. The fire and the rose, as the poet wrote, will be one again, and Jerusalem - that city of soldiers, saints and poets - will shine forth once more upon England's clouded hills - a beacon, a fountain, an iridescent jewel - the City of God and capital of the Golden Age to come.

All images in this piece come courtesy of my friend and collaborator Rob Floyd. Rob's art is rich in religious and mythological symbolism. His work, I am sure, will prove a source of stimulation and inspiration for readers of Albion Awakening. His oeuvre can be viewed in full at his website – www.robfloyd.co.uk.

JOURNEY TO THE CENTRE OF THE EARTH (JF)

I have been wanting to write an appreciation of C.S. Lewis's novel *That Hideous Strength* (The Bodley Head, 1945) for some time. I have been unable, however, to approach the book in any kind of conventional manner. I am not sure why, but there it is. The words refuse to flow.

The Irish sportswriter and man of letters, Con Houlihan (1925-2012), always avoided the press box at the Gaelic Football and Hurling games he covered. He preferred to stand on the terraces, slightly apart from the crowd, in a corner of the paddock by himself. His reply, when asked about this, was that 'a poet should approach his subject matter from an oblique angle.' *That Hideous Strength*, to my mind, is such an indisputably great book, such a wild, rambunctious, rough and tumble tale, shot through with fire and flair, that a review of my own to add to the million and one already written can never come close to capturing its singular essence. Only an oblique angle will suffice. But it isn't easy. I find it hard to even describe the novel's plot and basic themes. There's so much crammed into its pages - so much passion, drama and vision. You can't tame it. You'll be wrestling with thunder and lightning if you try.

The forces of evil - what St. Paul calls the 'principalities, powers, and rulers of the darkness of this world' - establish themselves in the sleepy university town of Edgestow under the guise of the National Institute for Coordinated experiments (NICE), a pseudo-scientific endeavour aimed ostensibly at eradicating disease and improving living standards. This cloaks its true goal, the abolition of humanity and its replacement by a disembodied artificial intelligence, wholly subordinate to the 'bent eldils' (fallen angels) who seek to keep men and women trapped in illusion and sin.

Opposing the NICE is the little community of St. Anne's on the Hill, an atmospheric, slightly rambling house and garden, brimming over with everything good - life, laughter, good conversation, honest toil, contemplative silence and serious thought. Presiding over this is Elwin Ransom, philologist turned interplanetary explorer, the hero of Lewis's previous 'space novels' *Out of the Silent Planet* (1937) and *Perelandra* (1940). Ransom, in his travels, has been honoured by the 'good eldils', angelic intelligences and servants of Maleldil (Christ), who inhabit the spheres of Mars, Venus and beyond, never ceasing to chip away at the blockade their corrupted brethren have set up around the

Earth. Ransom is open and receptive to their influence, and it is his patience and humility, his willingness to wait, watch and listen for guidance when instant physical action seems the only sane thing to do, that ultimately makes the difference and saves mankind from slavery.

That Hideous Strength has been compared by many to the 'supernatural shockers' of Charles Williams, but the two names that spring to my mind are Dostoyevsky and Joyce. It has the spiritual intensity of the former and the linguistic panache of the latter. Take, for instance, Lewis's account of Jane's first meeting with Ransom:

> Pain came and went in his face: sudden jabs of sickening and burning pain. But as lightning goes through the darkness and the darkness closes up again and shows no trace, so the tranquillity of the countenance swallowed up each shock of torture. How could she have thought him young? Or old either? It came over her, with a sensation of quick fear, that this face was of no age at all. She had (or so she believed) disliked bearded faces except for old men with white hair. But that was because she had long since forgotten the imagined Arthur of her childhood - and the imagined Solomon too. Solomon - for the first time in many years the bright solar blend of king and lover and magician which hangs about that name stole back upon her mind. For the first time in all those years she tasted the word King itself with all linked associations of battle, marriage, priesthood, mercy, and power.

Or this - the descent of Jupiter to St. Anne's:

> Upstairs his mighty beam turned the Blue Room into a blaze of lights. Before the other angels a man might sink: before this he might die, but if he lived at all, he would laugh. If you had caught one breath of the air that came from him, you would have felt yourself taller than before. Though you were a cripple, your walk would have become stately: though a beggar, you would have worn your rags magnanimously. Kingship and power and festal pomp and courtesy shot from him as sparks fly from an anvil. The pealing of bells, the blowing of trumpets, the spreading out of banners, are means used on earth to make a faint symbol of his quality. It was like a long sunlit wave,

> creamy-crested and arched with emerald, that comes on nine feet tall, with roaring and with terror and unquenchable laughter. It was like the first beginning of music in the halls of some King so high and at some festival so solemn that a tremor akin to fear runs through young hearts when they first hear it.

Lewis really lets himself go here. There is a bardic quality to the prose which the bourgeois conventions of the novelistic medium can barely contain. It struck me recently that certain passages towards the end of the book - the mayhemic 'Banquet at Belbury', the death of Feverstone in the earthquake, and the erotically-charged closing pages - represent exactly the kind of fiction that respectable opinion in 2017 would run a mile from. This, in my view, is entirely a good thing, redounding massively in Lewis's favour.

There is a freshness and vitality to his storytelling which seems lacking in British writing today, as well as in the country's wider spiritual and cultural life. The oft-cited decline in British Christianity, for example, is not primarily, as many claim, a crisis of faith. The high water mark of theological liberalism came and went a long time ago. There are plenty of believing Christians and a fair few pockets of energy and vigour across the denominations. The issue, rather, is one of integration and imagination. The Christian vision has lost its imaginative hold over the nation. What is required, therefore, I feel, is neither restoration nor modernisation, but deepening and reconnection. It is a matter of *ressourcement* - a return to the source - a rediscovery of the wellsprings of Divine inspiration within our own hearts, the heart of the land, and the heart of the Christian faith itself.

Engaging with *That Hideous Strength* would be a terrific start. No-one, surely, could read this book and persist in the atheist argument that Christianity is a mere crutch or comfort blanket and not, on the contrary, something shocking, scandalous and utterly thrilling that literally knocks one for six. In the words of Pope Benedict XVI, 'Christianity is not an intellectual system, a collection of dogmas or a moralism. Christianity is instead an encounter, a love story, an event.'

Part of this 'event' is the recognition that, as William Blake put it, 'everything that lives is holy.' Every person, every object, and every facet of the natural world is endowed and imbued with the Divine mystery. This is the meaning of sacramentalism - ordinary things transformed, made holy and given back to us alive with the light of

God. This is what happens to Jane on her way back from the encounter with Ransom described above:

> She saw from the windows of the train the outlined beams of sunlight pouring over stubble on burnished woods and felt that they were like the notes of a trumpet. Her eyes rested on the rabbits and cows as they flitted by and she embraced them in heart with merry, holiday love. She delighted in the occasional speech of the one wizened old man who shared her compartment and saw, as never before, the beauty of his shrewd and sunny old mind, sweet as a nut and English as a chalk down.

Without this 'eye of faith', this capacity to see the extraordinary in the ordinary, Christianity in this country will remain a dry and bureaucratic thing, ordered and respectable, unable to take flight and rise to the challenges of our time.

The final element is the land itself, the 'pleasant pastures', 'mountains green', and 'clouded hills' Blake evoked so powerfully in *Jerusalem.* There is a conspicuous absence in the UK, I think, of anything that might be called 'British Christianity.' None of the denominations, as far as I can see, seem interested in the powerhouse of mythic lore that animates our island and gives it such imaginative resonance and archetypal depth. There is no attempt to link the faith with the land and the aboriginal understanding that the land in itself (as Blake knew) is sacred and holy - qualitative not quantitative - hallowed ground, not a random collection of rivers, mountains and fields.

Despite the best efforts of Lewis, Tolkien, and one or two others, too many minds, on both sides of the divide, remain locked in a shallow Pagan v Christian dichotomy. They fail to see how Christianity relates to the mythic stream running beneath the surface of British history - how it builds on it and makes it complete. There is a vast reservoir of spiritual energy contemporary Christianity is missing out on here. Lewis, of course, makes no such mistake in *That Hideous Strength*, and this, I feel, is the book's key passage:

> 'It all began,' said Dr. Dimble, 'when we discovered that the Arthurian story is mostly true history. There was a moment in

the Sixth Century when something that is always trying to break through into this country nearly succeeded. Logres was our name for it - it will do as well as another. And then gradually we began to see all English history in a new way. We discovered the haunting.'

'What haunting?' asked Camilla.

'How something we may call Britain is always haunted by something we may call Logres. Haven't you noticed that we are two countries? After every Arthur, a Mordred; behind every Milton, a Cromwell: a nation of poets, a nation of shopkeepers ... Is it any wonder they call us hypocrites? But what they mistake for hypocrisy is really the struggle between Logres and Britain.'

He paused and took a sip of wine before proceeding.

'It was long afterwards,' he said, 'after the Director had returned from the Third Heaven, that we were told a little more. This haunting turned out to be not only from the other side of the invisible wall. Ransom was summoned to the bedside of an old man then dying in Cumberland. His name would mean nothing to you if I told it. That man was the Pendragon, the successor of Arthur and Uther and Cassibelaun. Then we learned the truth. There has been a secret Logres in the very heart of Britain all these years: an unbroken succession of Pendragons. That old man was the seventy-eighth from Arthur: our Director received from him the office and the blessings; tomorrow we shall know, or tonight, who is the eightieth. Some of the Pendragons are well known to history, though not under that name. Others you have never heard of. But in every age they and the little Logres which gathered round them have been the fingers which gave the tiny shove or the almost imperceptible pull, to prod England out of the drunken sleep or to draw her back from the final outrage into which Britain tempted her.'

This, I believe, is our role and sacred mission in this land today - to find the keys to Logres, render her visible once more, and join hands with the Pendragon in his quest to awaken England and all this holy realm from her drunken sleep.

'How can these things be?' Nicodemus asked Christ upon being told he must be born anew.

It's a question I often ask myself, counting down the hours at work, wondering if they'll notice if I take myself off the phones again and slip off to make a brew. My best bet, I decide, is to make one for everybody, so that's what I do. On my way back I notice a door that I've always seen closed standing slightly ajar. 'That's unusual,' I think. Once I've deposited the drinks I pop back. My head is sure that it's just a cleaning cupboard I haven't noticed before, but my heart keeps nagging at me, urging me to take a look. So I do, and find that both my heart and head are right. Yes, it is a cleaning cupboard, replete with all the stuff you'd expect to see - pails, buckets, detergents, etc. But my heart did not deceive me. There is indeed something more, right at the back, a spiral stone staircase, dimly lit, running down anti-clockwise.

I glance behind me. No-one watching. All locked onto their screens. I step into the cupboard, pull the door behind me, step over a mop and stand on the first step, looking down. I can't resist it. Anything to break up the morning. So down I go, intending to have a quick scout and come back up before I'm missed, but the further I go the more captivated I get, as if transported into some story or myth that feels more real, more true and more essential to who I really am than the upper world, which felt so imposing just a moment before but now seems thin and insubstantial in comparison.

The steps narrow as I descend. The further I go the more chipped and broken they become. Burning braziers lashed to the wall every twenty steps or so light the way. There's one to my left and one to my right and so on all the way down. Despite the momentary blast of heat as I pass them by, the air in the staircase is cool and fresh. I realise suddenly that I've no idea how long I've been going down for. Five years or forever, I've no idea at all. I look back up and see nothing but darkness. But there's a new smell in the air - fresh and wild and briny - like the sea, but it can't be, not here, not so far below the surface of the Earth.

The twists and turns of the stairway grow tighter. It's darker now.

There are no more braziers. I reach out to the walls for support and my hands touch moss and lime. I glimpse a light ahead, creeping around the steps. Then it's all over. There's a rough, arch-shaped doorway, and I'm out of the staircase and onto a lamplit jetty, fresh air smacking against my cheeks and the cool blue light of early morning slanting into the cave through a gap in the rock to the right.

Straight ahead of me is a boat, a small coracle wobbling on the dark, shiny waters, its oars at rest and its sole inhabitant standing on her deck, looking right at me. Light shines from his person. I'm not sure if it's the lamps or an inner radiance of some kind. He's a big man with presence and charisma. His hair and beard are golden, and he's in a sweeping robe of blue with a silver circlet around his head. I walk towards him. It's hard to tell how old he is. He seems really young at first - about twenty - then really old - sixty-odd or more. I settle in the end for around forty. He holds out his hand and pulls me aboard. 'Welcome,' he says in rich and resonant tones. He sits down on a bench and takes up the oars. I sit facing him, looking around and trying to get the measure of my surroundings.

'My name is Ransom,' the man says. 'You may already have read about me.' I nod. He smiles. 'Well done indeed,' he adds, 'for discovering the door.'

'But Sir,' I blurt out. 'How can all this be? We must be miles below the Earth yet everything's so bright and open.'

Ransom lets the oars rest. The boat glides on, propelled by the current. 'This is the centre,' he replies. 'The inside is bigger than the outside. More real too. You must take care here. You can cut your finger on a blade of grass, you know.'

I sit back, look about me again and start to relax. I see islands all around in the distance - some big, some small - with white jutting rocks and lots of grass. It isn't long before one of them looms up before us. Ransom turns, takes the tiller and guides the boat onto a yellow sandy beach. 'Follow me,' he says. We follow a winding, uphill path through the rough terrain. The air is so fresh, so invigorating. I drink it down in great gulps, thinking that it would be impossible now to feel distracted or sad or bored again, knowing that such a place as this exists - not light years away or in a parallel universe - but at the beating heart of our very own world.

We arrive at the top. I want to pause to enjoy the view - the waves glinting in the sunlight - but Ransom carries straight on, towards a grey stone building that looks like an abbey or a big church. Inside it feels cool, dark and atmospheric. We walk along a corridor. Small, pointy windows give glimpses of the sea and sky. Then the sudden, welcome smell of homely things - bacon, toast and coffee - the clink of spoons and the hum of happy voices. Ransom opens a door and we're in a round vaulted chamber with - wonder of wonders - the entire community of St. Anne's. I recognise them all. They're exactly like I pictured them in the book - Dr. Dimble and his wife, Arthur and Camilla Denniston, Grace Ironwood, Jane and Mark Studdock, Ivy Maggs and, last but not least, MacPhee, the irascible, bearded Ulsterman. Even the animals are there - Mr. Bultitude the bear, with a gold medal hung around his brawny neck, plus the jackdaw and the cat, whose names, in the rush and swirl of the moment, I can't recall.

Everybody looks utterly splendid with crowns on their heads and glittering clothes. Despite my workaday attire I don't feel out of place at all. I don't think I've ever felt more at home in my life in fact. I'm treated like a brother - one of the community - and it's the nicest, most convivial breakfast I've ever known. They ask me all manner of questions - chiefly about my family, but also about my own life: the kind of stories I like writing, my favourite books and films, who my biggest influences are, and so forth. I'm about to tell them about Mr. Aherne, my old English teacher, when a gong sounds from the depths of the building, a hush descends and everyone starts packing away. 'Come', says Ransom, and I follow them out of the room, down another corridor, up some steps and into a chapel with six tall candles ablaze on a stone altar built into the wall. The women, except Grace, peel off to the left and disappear into a side door. Ransom, Dimble, Mark, Grace, McPhee and myself walk to the front, turn right and kneel down in a pew. Mr. Bultitude, I note, stays half-standing, half-crouching at the back, as if keeping guard.

Through the window I see the waves crashing against the rocks below. It's the only sound that penetrates the chapel's deep, fecund silence. The rhythmic roar soothes and settles my spirit. I feel a sense of light, happiness and peace.

A fresco on the wall behind the altar glows and throbs with spiritual and artistic vitality. It looks so ancient - like it was painted before the dawn of time. Its gold and purple background is faded now but the images and shapes depicted on it stand out clearly still - three red circles arranged in a triangle, and in each of the circles a picture of a man. In the bottom left there's a crowned king with the word 'Artorius' written underneath. To the right is a wild-looking fellow in red called 'Merlinus', while above them both is an icon of Our Lord holding out a golden chalice. 'Christus' is His title.

The gong sounds again. I hear footsteps down the aisle. I turn my head and there's Mother Dimble in her flame-coloured gown with a jagged grey stone in her hands, like a misshapen rugby ball hewn out of rock. She passes through the little gate in the wooden altar rail, ascends a couple of steps, then lays the stone down reverently on the altar, next to the candle furthest to the left. She comes back down and sits in the pew behind us. Then Camilla approaches the altar, holding aloft a gleaming, jewelled sword. She looks fierce and regal in her silver robe and coronet as she places the sword blade-down between the two middle candles, before descending in her turn, sitting down beside Mother Dimble. Next comes Ivy Maggs in a green mantle, bearing a long white spear with a blood-red tip. She leans it between the wall and the right side of the altar, then returns to her companions below.

For a long while nothing else happens, just the waves, the silence and the peace. Then the footsteps come again, soft and suggestive, and everyone stands. There's a brightening in the air and a quickening in my mind. I look along the line of my colleagues and am astounded at how beautiful they appear - how royal, dignified and noble, one hundred percent themselves, yet at the same time infinitely more than just that.

The chapel becomes almost intolerably bright. I feel compelled to turn to my head and see, and that's when Jane comes sweeping by in a blaze of cobalt blue, with what can only be a miniature Sun between her hands, so dazzling and effulgent are its rays. She walks right up to the middle of the altar, turns, bows to the company before her and lifts the sacred object high above her head. Sparks fly. Her dark hair shines, soaked in light. I can make out little else, just the round contours of her face and the outline of the two chalices, the one held by Christ above, the other by Jane below. The rest is glory and gladness. The gong sounds, and I bow my head and close my eyes, hoping to be able to stay in this blessed place of peace and light for ever and ever.

When I open my eyes the light in the chapel is back to normal. The Holy Grail (for surely that's what it is) stands in the centre of the altar behind the sword - still radiant, still glorious - but in a more measured, manageable way than before. The sun outside seems higher in the sky.

It's obvious that some time has passed.

The women are sat behind me still, but there's only Mark Studdock sitting next to me. Everyone else is up at the front doing various things. Dr. Dimble and Arthur Denniston are standing just behind the altar rail, about a yard apart, each holding a candle. I see Ransom, with his back to me, kneeling down behind them. McPhee, to his left, drapes a golden chasuble emblazoned with the scarlet figure of a rampant red lion over his blue robe. Grace Ironwood, on the other side, replaces Ransom's silver circlet with a gold one. Ransom stands, bows to the Grail, turns, walks forward, takes his position between Dimble and Denniston, and starts to address us. But I can't understand a word of what he's saying! He's talking in a totally different language. Great syllables that sound like castles pour from his mouth. My heart leaps and quivers at them. The voice doesn't sound like Ransom's at all - it's like the words are speaking themselves through him from some strong place at a distance.

'It's the Great Tongue,' Mark whispers in my ear. 'The language spoken before the Fall.'

'Ah,' I reply, as the words start to make sense. I don't know why I understand them now when I couldn't before, but nonetheless I do. Here then, as best as I can remember it, is the gist of Ransom's speech:

'Brothers and sisters, the stairways between Britain and Logres are becoming rare and few. The nation continues along the broad and ample highway to destruction. Due to forces set in motion long ago, since the coming of the Tudors at least, our Kingdom of Logres, if Britain reflects on it at all, is dismissed as a fairytale or a relic of folklore, rather than welcomed for what it is - the underlying pattern and reality behind the national story.

'It is a call for celebration then, when one of the few remaining doors is discovered and a seeker finds his or her way to Logres. The potential for recovery - a national *ressourcement* - contained in such a discovery is incalculable. It could well be, as our resident sceptic MacPhee believes, that Britain is too far gone to be pulled back from the brink again and that a crash against the cliff face of reality is the only way to divest her of her illusions. My own view, certainly, is that what we achieved in 1945 would be nigh on impossible today. The bar of public opinion is increasingly hostile to what and who we stand for. Christianity, in those days, was deeply rooted in British life still, and that, sadly, is no longer the case.

'Nothing, however, is set in stone. It is a God of the living we serve, not the dead; a God of surprises, not a set of iron-clad laws. We do not worship the God of the Deists, who Blake raged against, that blind watchmaker who sets the world in motion a like a child's toy, then stands back and lets it wind down until the batteries run out. No, the God of Logres is not like that. Ours is a generous God, profligate even, continually sowing seeds and distributing largesse, always on the lookout for renaissance and renewal.

'The four Jewels of Logres that we see before us play a pivotal role here: the *Lia Fail*, the coronation stone of the High Kings of yore, and the precious relics Joseph of Arimathea brought to Britain and kept in the Grail Chapel until it was occluded in the reign of Artorius. We see the sword with which Simon Peter smote the High Priest's ear, the spear of Longinus which pierced Our Lord's side, and, at the centre of it all, the holy chalice of the Last Supper. These treasures have a deep and subtle power. They are continually at work, acting on the profoundest, most archetypal levels of the national psyche, bringing fertility where there is barrenness, quality where there is quantity, and a soulful, silent spirituality where is noise and empty chatter. Their restorative, salvific influence is keenly felt in both the visible and the invisible realms.

'The Vedic scriptures, as Grace reminded me at breakfast, make it clear that Heaven will never allow the world to disintegrate completely. Where the darkness appears thickest, that is where the messengers and avatars will appear. But it is up to us to recognise them. The avatars, in truth, are always with us. It is just that we fail to see them. The Grail Chapel, in reality, was never occluded. It was ourselves who lost the art of finding it.

'And now behold, the great wheel of the *Manvantara* comes full circle. The Dark Age draws to its close and the light of the Golden Age to come shines forth across the threshold of the future. The Sleep of Ulro is concluded, Albion awakes, the world is charged anew with the grandeur of God, and the Countenance Divine shines forth again upon England's clouded hills.'

His speech completed, Ransom bows to his congregation and strides back up to the altar. Denniston and Dimble accompany him briefly, laying their candles down. Ransom takes the Grail and comes down to the front. We all stand and make our way forward, kneeling down in a line along the length of the altar rail.

'Urendi Maleldil' says Ransom to each of us in turn, as we take the chalice and drink. He's coming from right to left, and I'm at the end of the line on the left, except for Mr. Bultitude who has shuffled up beside me. When Ransom presents me with the Grail it isn't wine that's there as I'd expected but sea water, clear and blue and flecked with splashes of foam like little waves. I look up, astonished. 'Urendi Maleldil,' he says again, and I take the Grail, which is warm to the touch, and drink. Then he places his hands on my shoulders. 'The splendour, the love and the strength be upon you,' he says in English. Then I go back with the others and sit down again. Ransom puts the Grail on the altar, exactly where it was before, and sits down with us too.

The water has a potent aftertaste - salty, raw and elemental. It has an effect on my mind as well. Everything seems to *mean* more. Everything's bursting with life - stonework and seats; sea, rock and sky; the faces and bodies of my companions. The three men in the fresco look so real now, filling out and becoming three dimensional, as if poised to burst out of their red circles and join us in the chapel. Merlin's black and grey beard appears to quiver in an invisible breeze, and that's the last impression I have, as the *mise en scène* shifts and I find myself sat at my desk again, the coffee I'd brought back from the machine warm to the touch still like I'd never been anywhere at all. Oddly enough, I don't feel disappointed to be back. It's good to see my colleagues buzzing around. The blinds flutter in the breeze and the sun slants in through the open windows. The symbols of my job I usually feel so much at war with - the screen, the keypad, the headset and the phone - look welcoming and homely, like old friends, imbued with light and depth and a personality, I feel tempted to say, all of their own. Normally I can't stand the sight of them; now I feel I could literally look at them all day. I'm reminded of Bloom in *Ulysses*, sitting in the pub, and captivated to the exclusion of all else by the red triangle on the label of his bottle of Bass.

Then, by association, the nimble figure of Mr. Aherne leaps into my mind again. I see him once more, thirty years ago now, in his red roll-neck jumper and wild salt and pepper hair and beard. He was everything an Irish man of letters should be - a compelling blend of mystery and fun - wholly devoted in his teaching to the transformative, salvific power of the Word.

Owen Aherne was a man out of time, standing at an oblique angle to his surroundings like Con Houlihan's ideal poet. He should have been Chief Storyteller to the High King of Erin, not cast out in the concrete jungle of a suburban '80s comprehensive. He wore it well though, like those White Russian émigrés in Paris after the revolution - Generals of the Tsar's armies eking out a living as housepainters, princes driving taxis, and so on. I remember him ripping up the curriculum and weaving his way between the desks - dancing almost - reciting great chunks of Shakespeare, Yeats and Joyce.

I recall one sun-dappled morning in particular, when lip service, on this occasion, was being paid to the curriculum and we were all supposed to be reading John Donne, who I've always found dull. Instead of reading the boring poem, *The Flea*, I was gazing at the drawing of Aslan my friend Mark had given me for my birthday at break. He had knocked it up in twenty seconds in yellow and red crayon on a loose piece of A5. I marvelled at the clarity and intensity of the image. He later went on to become an icon painter, which didn't surprise me, with a particular devotion to his namesake, St. Mark (St. Mark's also, by the by, being the name of our school), whose symbol, of course, is the lion.

I was so enthralled that I didn't hear Mr. Aherne approaching until he grabbed me by the shoulders and laughed out loud. I was sat at the back of the class. Everyone turned around, grinning. They knew a piece of classroom theatre was on its way. 'Well, well, well,' Aherne asked rhetorically, 'what have we here? Our very own Leopold Bloom, spellbound by Lewis's great tawny lion. We know what Malachi Mulligan said about this kind of fellow, don't we?'

'Yes Sir,' they replied in laughing unison, though no-one had the slightest notion. Aherne gave them the answer anyway. It was all part of the game. And I'll never forget that ringing, bardic voice of his as it echoed and resounded through the dour architectural modernism of Room A6:

'Go warily. That's what he said, my friends. Go warily. Preserve a druid silence. His soul is far away. It is as painful perhaps to be awakened from a vision as it is to be born. Any object, intensely regarded, may be a gate of access to the incorruptible eon of the gods.'

G. WILSON KNIGHT – SHAKESPEAREAN PROPHET (JF)

What is this
That rises like the issue of a king
And wears upon his baby-brow the round
And top of sovereignty?

Macbeth

I had a particularly inspirational teacher at primary school, between the ages of 10 and 11 - what used to be called Junior 3. Her name was Mrs. Hughes, and she introduced me to so much that has been absolutely central to my life since - literature, mythology, history, art and more.

I remember staying behind after class on our first day - a warm and hazy September afternoon - to fill in a form of some kind. My eye was drawn, I recall, to the pictures on the walls, scenes from myth and legend that I was encountering for the first time - Jason and the Golden Fleece, the Round Table, and the Rainbow Bridge of Asgard, to name but three. Raphael's *School of Athens* was there too, next to a picture of a man with a crown on his head. It was the crown, not the man, that captivated my mind. He had dark hair, a pinched face, and clenched white fingers. But the crown was gold and round and glowed from within with a light and fire of its own.

"Who's that, Miss?" I asked.

"Richard III," replied Mrs. Hughes.

I nodded vaguely, not yet recognising the name, but I view that episode now as a high and solemn moment - my first meeting with a Shakespearean king.

Years passed, and I forgot both crown and king, until the day I first read G. Wilson Knight, in the seductive lamplight of the Language and Literature Library in Manchester. It was twenty years on, the book was *This Sceptred Isle* and the words were these:

> Kingship is golden; and gold still exerts imaginative power. It is, after all, solid sunlight, and the sun remains visible king, and nothing, as Keats found when writing Hyperion can quite dethrone him.

I put the book down, stunned and overwhelmed. It all cascaded back - my teacher, the heat, the sunlight, the pictures on the walls - Jason, Arthur, Thor, Raphael, King Richard. There was no gap at all, it seemed, between the 'now' and the 'then'. I felt like I'd never been away, never left the classroom, that I was still there, that I'd always be there somehow. Why? Because it was my home and my truth. It was where I belonged, where I could be most truly myself and come closest to living the life I was created to live. I made a note of the writer's name - G. Wilson Knight. And that was my last encounter with a Shakespearean king. 'The wheel,' as Edmund notes in *King Lear*, 'is come full circle.

G. Wilson Knight (1897-1985), like my young self, was captivated and enchanted by the Crown. Like Mrs. Hughes, he was an inspirational teacher, chiefly at the University of Leeds. He was a poet, an actor, a theatrical director and a scholar of English Literature, best known for his works of Shakespeare criticism, such as *The Wheel of Fire* (1930), *The Imperial Theme* (1931) and *The Crown of Life* (1947).

He was no dry academic. His prose is electric - passionate, poetic and soulful - like a Dostoyevsky book or an El Greco painting in words - burning with spiritual and imaginative intensity. It was the poetry of Shakespeare's plays that obsessed him. Character, plot and theme held a lesser rank in his view. They grew out of the poetry, like the branches of a tree. And what Shakespeare's poetry contains, more than anything else for Wilson Knight, is an articulation of England's royal destiny and essence.

'Shakespeare's royalist thinking,' he writes in *This Sceptred Isle* (Blackwell, 1940), from which all quotations in this essay are taken), 'is, for the most part, patriotic, and his work from time to time spreads its wings in national prophecy. Royalty and England tend to involve each other, and these in turn involve strenuous themes of war and peace, order and disorder, conflicts of personal ambition and communal necessity, contrasts of tyranny and justice, the whole stamped by the chivalric symbol of Saint George and aspiring to Christian sanctions.'

The Crown is the key - the master symbol. It runs:

> ... as a golden thread through Shakespeare's drama,

> symbolising the nation's soul-life, which is also the greater self of each subject. In Shakespeare's human kings we watch different persons daring to identify themselves with this supreme value; and we can view each personal king as a prototype of national action, as England herself, fulfilling or falsifying her destiny.

The great image of this sacred royalty which Wilson Knight returns to continually is that of the crowned child - the 'baby peace', the 'Child Crowned, with a Tree in his Hand' - who appears to Macbeth in the witches' cauldron.

'Macbeth,' he says, 'is then further tormented by a vision of future Scottish kings blending, after the union of realms under James I, during whose reign this play was written, into a line of English kings too. This line of kings is descended from Banquo, secure in an integrity which, in the midst of suffocating evil, can yet say:

> In the great hand of God I stand, and thence
> Against the undivulg'd pretence I fight
> Of treasonous malice.

'In murdering Banquo, Macbeth tries to cut off Great Britain's future history at its root. But Fleance escapes.'

G. Wilson Knight was not a conventionally religious man. He was vice-president of the Spiritualist Association of Great Britain for many years. Yet his books are freighted with Christian sensibility and feeling. He had a profound, intuitive understanding of Christ as ultimate monarch - the King behind the kings - the Lord and Master of the universe. Christ, consequently, is the source and wellspring of Wilson Knight's royalist thinking. Contemporary Britain, I feel, would do well to take note of this, especially when liberal democracy appears to be losing its way so badly, less and less able, it seems, to connect with people and inspire them at the deepest, most essential levels - the levels involving truth, meaning and ultimate values - 'strenuous themes,' as Wilson Knight put it, 'of war and peace, etc ... '

I reflect on Wilson Knight's *oeuvre* often. When I do, an image comes to mind - my old school, the long corridors, Mrs. Hughes's room - empty now, save for the sunlight streaming through, the rough-hewn altar in the middle, and the golden, gleaming crown lying on top, waiting for someone - myself, perhaps - to touch it, feel it, weigh it, savour it, then draw a deep breath, take the leap of faith and place it on his head.

But that would be presumptuous on my part. That would be to turn my meditation on G. Wilson Knight - this noble Briton, this maverick, this prophet - into a fictional exploration of my own relationship with the Crown. That can wait. Forever, maybe. G. Wilson Knight, it has to be said, gives voice to the royal and Shakespearean position far better than I can. Let us leave him the last word, therefore, in the hope that his gem-like prose may be rediscovered and that his wisdom and vision might help this country regain her inner spark, reconnect to her inner sources of vitality, and, most importantly of all, restore her relationship with the Divine, from Whom, as with Shakespeare's poetry, all good things flow...

> ... Though we live in an age of rationalism and attempts to raise man as man, with little conscious admission of man as a crowned or crowning being, we go sadly astray if we forget them. In all matters engaging the most immediate and fearful problems of our existence we know that drama, the opposition of parties in Parliament and Court of Justice, is our first guide; but there is always also, as in a work of art, some symbol, some higher fusing power, or its emblem, to unify our opposites, or at least to suggest their unification. If we cannot resolve our conflicts, we must at least imagine a dimension in which they are, or might be, resolved; which perhaps means, in Christian terms, looking forward, or up, to the advent of Christ in glory. Such, then, is the symbolic function of the Crown, not only itself dramatic, but also signifying the resolution and the purpose of the drama within and beyond which it exists.
>
> This is, fundamentally why Shakespeare's work is so royally alive in our time; why it is acted, not only in Britain and America, but in Europe, in India and Japan; and in Russia. Shakespeare's drama, with its fanfares and ceremonial, abounds in kingly ritual; and his people speak, move, act royally. Villains or heroes, it is no matter; it all lies deeper than ethic. We have for long talked of the Crown as the link binding

an empire of free communities; that is true, and it is a great conception, herald and pattern, it may be, of a yet greater. But meanwhile we can speak of another, and related, link, which may indeed prove to have some bearing on that greater conception as yet unshaped; a link, or rather a golden thread, putting, as Puck has it in A Midsummer Night's Dream, 'a girdle round the earth'; the golden thread of Shakespeare's poetic royalism which, despite all barriers, yet binds, as does nothing else, the world.

THE INKLINGS – HERALDS OF THE COMING CHRISTIAN RENAISSANCE (JF)

I once claimed, in response to a post on *Bruce Charlton's Notions*, that J.R.R. Tolkien and C.S. Lewis could be viewed as twentieth-century incarnations of the 'two witnesses' referred to in the Book of Revelation. That was silly and hyperbolic, yet my sense remains that the Inklings in general, and these two in particular, were sent by God to carry out a great creative work which would echo and resound and have long-term repercussions for good in the world.

At first sight this might appear questionable. *The Lord of the Rings* and the Narnia books were published in the 1950s. Since then, the materialist worldview, ably assisted by social and economic liberalism, New Age 'spirituality' and post-modern vacuity, has made great strides in hollowing out the deposit of faith and culture that the West still possessed, albeit in diminished fashion, immediately after the Second World War (when Lewis's *That Hideous Strength* and Charles Williams' *All Hallows Eve* were published).

'What use were Lewis and Tolkien then?' a cynic might quibble. One could equally turn the question around, however, and ask, 'But what if they never existed? What if they never wrote a word? What if their words went unheard? How much more precipitous might the decline have been?'

It's staggering when you think about it, the amount of people - young people in the main - who, without Lewis and Tolkien, would have been deprived of such a fine and noble imaginative vision, such a potent alternative to the drab secularism masquerading as freedom which sets, it seems, so much of the world's agenda today.

I say 'seems', because its power base is dissolving as I write. Its hold over the imagination is weakening. Liberal humanism has become shouty and shrill. It no longer motivates, unshackles or inspires. Its future appears limited, and the Inklings, I feel, have played a significant role in challenging and undermining its flat, one-dimensional, increasingly joyless manner of experiencing the world. But that's just the start. The Inklings story will run and run. Because what their writings point towards is nothing less, to my mind, than the great Christian renaissance to come - the 'Age of the Holy Spirit' prophesied by Joachim of Flore in the twelfth century and Nicholas Berdyaev in the twentieth.

The reformers of the Second Vatican Council, to take the Catholic perspective I know best, sensed something of this approaching change, I think. They realised that what had become a sometimes rather rules-obsessed Tridentine Church might struggle to inspire hearts and minds in the modern era. Their (or their interpreters) mistake, however, was to throw the baby out with the bathwater, sidelining the sacred and casting off tradition in a doomed attempt to appear 'relevant' to a *Zeitgeist* which was already, in the late 1960s, shifting and morphing into something quite brazenly anti-Christian.

The reformers, unlike the Inklings, lacked imagination. Their 'Spirit of Renewal', one feels tempted to conclude, has enjoyed its greatest successes only in de-mythologising large swathes of Catholic life. The body of work left behind by the Inklings, on the other hand, has helped re-mythologise the world and baptise the contemporary imagination. The Christianity of the future prefigured throughout the Inklings' *oeuvre* is different to post-Vatican II Catholicism. Like the Tridentine Church, it revolves around the sacred and is faithful to tradition, but is guided more by imagination than legalism, consecrating and making holy God's great gift of creativity - the 'flame imperishable' that Iluvatar, in Tolkien's *Ainulindale*, hurls forth into the void at the beginning of the world to bring life and light to all things.

Let us conclude, on that note, with a passage from Philip and Carol Zaleski's outstanding Inklings biography, *The Fellowship* (Farrar, Strauss and Giroux, 2015). These two paragraphs, in my view, illustrate and explain exactly what the Inklings were (and are and will be) all about:

> Fan fiction, derivative fantasy novels, and sophomorphic imitations aside, it is plain that Tolkien has unleashed a mythic awakening and Lewis a Christian awakening. Tolkien fans are often surprised to discover that they have entered a Christian cosmos as well as a world of Elves and Hobbits; fans of Lewis's apologetic writings, on the other hand, are often discomfited when they learn about their hero's personal life, his relationship with Mrs. Moore, his hearty appetite for drink and ribaldry, and his enduring affection for the page and planetary gods. But Tolkien's mythology was deeply Christian and therefore had an organic order to it; and Lewis's Christian awakening was deeply mythopoeic and therefore had an element of spontaneity and beauty often missing from conventional apologetics.

The Inklings' work, then, taken as a whole, has a significance that far outweighs any measure of popularity, amounting to a revitalisation of Christian intellectual and imaginative life. They were twentieth-century Romantics who championed imagination as the royal road to insight and the 'medieval model' as an answer to modern confusion and anomie ... Even when they were not on speaking terms, they were at work on a shared project, to reclaim for contemporary life what Lewis called the 'discarded image' of a universe created, ordered, and shot through with meaning.

THE EIGHTH NARNIA BOOK (JF)

But for them this was only the beginning of the real story. All their life in this world and all their adventures in Narnia had only been the cover and the title page: now at last they were beginning Chapter One of the Great Story which no one on earth has read: which goes on for ever: in which every chapter is better than the one before.

C.S. Lewis, *The Last Battle*

Theologians of the Orthodox Church talk often about the Eighth Day - the great day of Eternity that will dawn at the consummation of this age, once the seven Biblical days of creation are completed. The light of this Eighth Day to come shines on and around us even now, but our spiritual vision seldom seems sharp enough to sense it. Sometimes, however, it bursts through into human consciousness, the Transfiguration of Our Lord on Mount Tabor being the outstanding example, a prefiguration of the Heavenly City and the regenerated, phoenix-like world to be revealed at the end of time.

It's no overstatement to say that C.S. Lewis's Narnia books played an analogous 'Eighth Day' role for me as a boy. Between 1979 and 1982, from the ages of 9 to 12, I lived and breathed the rich, suggestive air of Narnia. It felt like home; my natural element. Before I'd even read a word of Lewis I had stood enchanted in our suburban South Manchester bookshop, captivated by the cover of *The Last Battle* - the bonfire, the stable, Jill's bow and arrows, Eustace's sword, and the mighty red lion emblazoned on Tirian's shield. One Friday night as well, in January or February 1981, I had a particularly numinous dream, which saw me personally involved in *The Lion, The Witch and The Wardrobe,* playing my part in the battle to liberate Cair Paravel. Afterwards, Aslan sat us all down in the courtyard and told the most fantastic story, which I was sure I'd be able to remember when I woke up, but which, by breakfast time, was already escaping my memory. It was a bright blue late winter Saturday, and in the afternoon my Dad took me to Old Trafford to watch United play Leeds. We got caught up in a spot of hooliganism, I recall, on the Mancunian Way after the game, but for all the excitement - both the football and the fisticuffs - it's the afterglow of Aslan's story in my young mind that makes that day so memorable.

It's clear to me now, thirty-five years on, that the Narnia stories plugged a huge spiritual hole in my life. Together with Roger Lancelyn Green's mythic retellings (especially his King Arthur book) they filled the sacred space that my ancestors had known since time immemorial but that had been left empty for me by the abolition of the Latin Mass in 1970. And what Lewis did for myself - a Romanised Gael from the North West corner of the Empire - he did for countless boys and girls around the world, with all kinds of backgrounds and all manner of circumstances, and goes on doing today. He is a storyteller and a witness, a prophet and a bard, a princely, and surely heaven-sent counter-presence to the demythologised, dechristianised temper of our times.

The early-1980s, in Britain, felt like an especially intense time to be a pre-adolescent. It was an era of style and colour, but also of riots, recession, and the ever-present threat of nuclear catastrophe. A local newspaper ran a series of articles on Nostradamus, and I was convinced that the end of the world was at hand. I also believed, at that time, that there existed an eighth Narnia book, not a continuation (as in Neil Gaiman's *The Problem of Susan*) nor fan-fiction, but something on an altogether different level - a secret, hidden text that contained the essence and magic of Narnia, distilling it into a story, like to the one that Aslan had told us in the courtyard, setting off in its readers and hearers a reaction akin to Jewel's in *The Last Battle*: 'I have come home at last! I belong here. This is the land I have been looking for all my life, though I never knew it till now. The reason why we loved the old Narnia is that it sometimes looked a little like this.'

I was certain that before the final conflagration took place this book would reveal itself and make its holy yet homely presence felt in the world. I hoped and prayed that I might be present when it did, and often I would imagine our school's classrooms and corridors dissolving and giving way to the stone passageways, cavernous halls and lantern-lit chambers of the Grail Castle itself. In a tiny chapel, I was sure, at the top of a spiral staircase, the Grail and the eighth Narnia book stood between the candles on the altar, waiting for the appointed hour - the *Kairos*, the supreme moment - to roll around at last.

It's interesting, looking back on it all now, to see how much has changed in our world but also how little. We live, after all, in equally uncertain times, and many's the moment when I see, or think I see, the *mise en scene* of my current working life - the computers, the drinks machines, the carpeted stairs - collapse and reconstitute themselves into the form and fabric of Carbonek Castle. And I'm there -sprinting through the echoing throne room, then up the spiral staircase, starlight glinting through the narrow slits of windows. At the top I find a wooden door, closed but with a soft and radiant light spilling out onto the floor at the bottom. I turn the handle - push, pull and shove - but there's no give and the door stays shut. I bang my head on the wood in frustration, then stiff my mind and pray: 'Oh God, if ever I've done anything good in my life, give me a glimpse please of that which I've always seeked.' The door swings open and next thing I know I'm kneeling down, gazing into the heart of the Grail's golden blaze as it fills the room and bathes my soul in its healing, transfiguring light.

There are six tall candles on the altar, three to the Grail's left and three to the right. I see flowers as well, and a flicker and swish in the air like the beat of angels' wings. An ancient, bearded priest in green - Joseph of Arimathea himself, perhaps - sits on the right, while three men kneel with heads bowed low right in front of the altar. I can't see their faces, but I know who they are - Galahad, Percival and Bors - the three Grail knights. Standing on the left is a female figure robed in red with a face like the sun, holding an open book in her hands, silver in colour with a mighty red lion emblazoned on the front. She reads aloud - sings rather - in a language I don't know but for some reason am able to understand as well as if it's my own. Her chant - high, strange and wild - reverberates around the chapel and I recognise and remember what it is she's singing - the long lost story, no less - the story Aslan told us in the courtyard, the self-same tale, I realise now, that Lucy read in the Magician's Book in *The Voyage of the Dawn Treader*, the one about the cup and the sword and the tree and the green hill, the one she rates as the loveliest she's ever read and that Aslan promises to tell her again and again for ever and ever.

Over-excited and carried away, I scramble up and dash into the room, arms outstretched. But a puff of wind laced with flame blinds and singes my eyes, and I'm ushered out of the room by a host of invisible hands and bundled down the stairs. Darkness engulfs me and when I come to I'm somewhere else altogether. A fresh, briny, morning smell, probes and pushes my mind awake. I'm met by lapping waves in front, white cliffs behind, and a canopy of pale blue, seagull-flecked sky high above. There's sand beneath me, rough and bristly to the touch. I stumble to my feet. The sun, rising behind the cliffs looks huge, five or six times its normal size. That's when the other smell hits me - familiar and reassuring - the smell of breakfast - fresh coffee and roasting fish. Something catches my eye, small and bright, towards the sea and to my right. It's a lamb, tending a cooking fire and a burnished bronze coffee bowl. 'Come and have breakfast,' he says in his milky voice.

'This is all a dream,' I say to myself. 'Like the one I had about the fight at Cair Paravel when I was a kid.' I look behind me again, fully expecting to see the big sun vanished and the fixtures and fittings of the office restored to their habitual reality. But no, it's still there, even bigger than before if anything. I can look straight at it too, without even needing to shield my eyes.

I crouch down, pick up a fistful of sand - spiky and spongy at the same time - and watch it trickle down and stick to my fingers. It's unmistakably real. And there's a brightness in the air and on the ground and a joy in my heart which assures me that this is no dream. Then I start to understand. The dream, in fact, is over. This is the morning. The dawn. The Eighth Day has begun.

I stand up, turn and face the sea, and walk towards the Lamb.

SAINTS & SAGES OF ALBION

THE STORY OF JOSEPH OF ARIMATHEA (JF)

Painted by a monk of the Brotherhood of St. Seraphim of Sarov in Norfolk, England

Hear the tale of Joseph of Arimathea, who brought the Chalice of Christ to this land. Listen now.

Joseph was a merchant, the younger brother of Our Lady's father, Saint Joachim. He was a great seafarer and was often away from Judea, sometimes for months on end, voyaging up and down the Middle Sea to the Pillars of Hercules and beyond, now and again as far North as the mist-shrouded island of Britain.

Because it was so distant, Joseph wasn't able to visit Britain as often as he would have liked. Without knowing why, he felt a warmth and affinity for the place - for the wildness of her rocky shores, the greenness of her hills, the depths of her forests, the songs and incantations of her people, and the constant interplay of wind, sunshine, rain and mist, chasing each other this way and that across the mottled sky.

The Britons were good hosts. They knew how to entertain visitors and make them feel special. So when Joseph the carpenter - the father of Joseph's great-nephew, the boy Jesus, Mary's son - spoke to him one day about taking the lad on a trip, Joseph immediately thought of Britain. It would be good for Jesus, he thought, to experience a really long voyage, and good for him too to explore a country with a climate and landscape so different from his own.

Joseph had always enjoyed Jesus's company. He liked him so much that he wanted their times together to go on forever. He wasn't quite sure why he was so drawn to him. Jesus was nine years old now, and though he played happily with the other boys and was a good and dutiful son, there was clearly something different about him, something hard to pin down - a stillness, a waiting, a sense of space and peace. Just being close to Jesus - not necessarily speaking to him - had a good effect on Joseph, refreshing his mind and making his body feel lighter and younger. So he was delighted that Jesus's parents had entrusted him with his care for the three month round trip.

On arrival, thirty days later, at the South West tip of the island, Joseph and his party were joyously received by Conor, King of Dumnovia, who had come to know Joseph well over the years. There was a fine night of feasting and storytelling in the Royal Pallisade and the next morning it struck Joseph that Jesus might benefit from a day alone with nature, far from the hubbub of the market-place. So he left him on Looe Island, under the watchful gaze of Conor's men, while he went into town to sell his linens and spices. And when he returned towards sunset, he saw a sight that imprinted itself on his mind and stayed with him for the rest of his life. For there was Jesus sitting on the sand, with the sea and the sun at his back, and all around him - sitting, standing, lying down - was a circle of fishermen, the lame and the crippled, the old, and tiny little children. Jesus was talking animatedly and gesturing with his hands. All eyes were fixed on him. Conor's soldiers stood by on the rocks, leaning on their spears, but they were watching him too. So were the seagulls that circled the sky. Joseph saw Jesus pick up a pebble. It was small, about the size of the tin cup his mother had given him for the voyage. He took it with both hands and lifted it high above his head. And the rays of the setting sun caught the pebble and it shone forth with a mingled light of flame-flecked red and gold. Everyone gazed at it. Then Jesus saw Joseph coming and let the pebble fall. He waved happily to his uncle, like any nine year old boy, and the moment was gone.

Joseph never forgot it though, until the moment came again twenty-four years later on the night Jesus blessed and shared the bread and wine. Joseph was there, as always, watching, wondering, and waiting. For twenty years there had been nothing. Then, out of nowhere, so much so quickly - miracles, crowds, disciples, disdain, acclaim. And now this supper in Simon the Leper's upstairs room.

A fire crackled on the hearth. Jesus's Apostles sat around him at the table. Some looked perplexed. Joseph noted Peter's furrowed brow. Judas, for some reason, was no longer there. But John, sitting to Jesus's right, seemed as calm and serene as ever. Joseph was waiting at the table, along with Mary Magdalene, her sister, Martha, and her brother, Lazarus. He saw a winespill on the floor and went to get a cloth. And when he came back, there it was again - the moment at Looe Island. 'Take this,' said Jesus as he lifted the golden chalice (which Joseph had bought at Capernaum Market), 'and drink from it. This is the Chalice of my blood, the blood of the New Covenant, which will be poured out for you and for many.' He paused, then raised it above his head. 'Do this in memory of me.'

Joseph dropped the cloth. Past met present in the person of his mesmeric, unpredictable great-nephew, and the scales fell from his eyes. Yet just one day later Jesus was dead, and his followers (save John, Jesus's mother, and Mary Magdalene) scattered like chaff. Joseph himself had stayed the course. It was the least he could do, he told himself, to make up for the years he had spent hiding his discipleship for fear of the Chief Priests. Joseph cared nothing for them now, but when the Temple Guards seized Jesus in the garden he had fled with the rest, running back across the lawn to Simon's house. When he got upstairs, he saw the fire burning low and the Chalice still there on the table, blazing fiercely with an intense, red-tinged glow of its own. Just standing there watching it shine somehow warmed Joseph's heart and helped restore his spirits. So he picked up the chalice and took it with him into the night.

Hours later, Joseph found himself at the foot of the cross with John and the two Mary's. When, in the midst of driving rain and hail, Jesus bowed his head and died and the Centurion plunged his spear into his side, Joseph leapt forward on an impulse and held up the Chalice, catching the blood and water that poured forth. He ran to the Governor's palace and asked Pilate if he, Joseph, could take Jesus down from the cross and bury him. Pilate, who knew and respected Joseph, said yes. So Joseph wrapped him in his finest linen shroud and buried him in his own tomb and Peter and James rolled a heavy stone across the entrance. But the Chief Priests were furious. 'You'll never trade again,' Jacob the Fox roared.'You were one of his followers. You'll let those Gallileans steal the body so that this liar's boast of rising from the dead will seem true.' And they put an armed guard around the tomb. But Joseph went home and stayed there two days until the Temple Guards kicked down his door and dragged him off to a dank and stinking cell at the bottom of the High Priest's palace. They chained his arms to the wall and left him there in darkness. He knew why too. Mary Magdalene had told him earlier that day. 'Jesus is risen,' she had cried as she danced a jig on his doorstep, her face transfigured with joy. 'It's true, Joseph. I've seen him. I've spoken to him.' And Joseph was sorry now that he hadn't believed her and had put her story down to wish-fulfilment and an over-active imagination.

Then, as he was thinking of Mary, the cell pulsed with light and Jesus himself was there, dressed in white and blue, with red, raw wounds on his insteps and wrists. His left hand held the Chalice, while with his right he touched Joseph's chains and instantly they snapped apart. Joseph stood up. Jesus embraced him. 'Peace be with you,' he said, and Joseph felt a power and richness surging through him and a sense of peace and wholeness that was too deep for words and too much to take in. He fell to the floor and lay there weeping, curled into a ball. Jesus lay beside him and put his arms around him and held him tight.

When Joseph felt ready, they stood up again. 'Soon,' said Jesus, 'my Angel will lead you back to the city. He will tell you what to do and where to go.' Then he handed Joseph the Chalice and taught him how to say the Mass. Joseph knelt down and Jesus placed his hands on his head and made him his first Priest. Then Joseph looked up and Jesus was gone. But so was the darkness. The Chalice shone as it had on the night of Jesus's betrayal. Joseph saw the stone walls of the cell surrounding him. He walked around for a while, then sat back down, watching, waiting and praying.

The Angel, when he came, came quietly and not all at once. A red spot in mid-air, just at Joseph's eye level, pulsated and expanded and took on shape and form until a mighty winged being with a flaming sword stood before him. 'I am Michael the Archangel,' he said in a voice like a trumpet blast. 'Come now.' The cell door opened at the

Angel's touch. Joseph picked up the Chalice and followed him along the corridor. It was night. The guards were lying on the ground, fast asleep. The Angel led Joseph to the High Priest's courtyard. The palace gates swung open as if in response to an unspoken command. Michael walked the length of one street with Joseph, then turned right into a little alley. 'Go now,' he said. 'Gather those close to you and sail West to the Pillars of Hercules, then North to the shores of Britain. You must make your way into the mountains from there, following the star which the Most High will send you. Where the star stops, there you shall build your church - the Church of the Grail - and you will be the first Grail King.'

Joseph was so astounded at everything that was happening that the Angel's words about becoming a king made no sense whatsoever. Then Michael vanished and Joseph was alone. He clasped the Chalice tight and ran to the house of Mary Magdalene.

By twilight next day, Joseph had gathered his company - his wife, Anna, and their twelve year old son, Josephus, along with his brother, Bron, his wife, Enygria, and their baby son, Alain. There was Nasciens too, a prince from the East who had come to Jerusalem on business and had seen Jesus and spoken with him and become his disciple, giving up the throne waiting for him at home. Mary Magdalene was there as well, together with Lazarus and Martha. Mary had told the Apostles Joseph's story, and John the Beloved came to the harbour that evening to give his blessing. Then they set sail. The ship had one sail and it was white, but Mary had spent the afternoon drawing a picture of the Archangel Michael on it, red and gold in colour with a flaming sword in his right hand.

They voyaged West for fourteen days and fourteen nights. Joseph had placed the Chalice in a little chamber below deck and the pilgrims gathered around it as often as they could in silence, prayer and song. They found they needed neither food nor drink. Just being in the presence of the Chalice gave them all the sustenance, both physical and spiritual, that they needed.

They came to the port of Massilia in Southern Gaul, where they stopped to rest awhile. Mary, Martha and Lazarus went into the town to see what was there and when they came back Mary's eyes were ablaze and her face was shining like the sun. 'I must stay,' she told Joseph. 'I am sorry. But I know in my heart and soul that this is my work: to bring the grace of Our Lord Jesus Christ, the love of God, and the fellowship of the Holy Spirit to the people of this place.'

Joseph was sad beyond reckoning to lose Mary and her family, but he recognised in her words and demeanour the unmistakable marks of God's calling. So he gave her his blessing and Mary gave him her blessing and Joseph and his family sailed on to the South West tip of the island of Britain.

They were within sight of Dumnovia when Nasciens committed a grievous sin. The Angel had instructed Joseph that only himself and Mary Magdalene were to hold the Chalice, but one day, when no-one else was about, Nasciens felt an overpowering desire to touch it. 'If I can touch the Chalice,' he thought, 'it will be the same as touching Jesus.' But as soon as he did, he fell to the floor and a mighty voice, which Joseph recognised as that of the Angel, boomed around the ship. 'Nasciens,' it said, 'for the great love you feel you will be rewarded, after Joseph is dead, by becoming the second Priest of the Chalice, which shall henceforth be known as the Grail. But the punishment for your presumption today will be to live far beyond the lot of mortal men, until the day the third Grail Priest succeeds you, so that every minute of your life becomes a weariness and only the grace and presence of the Grail will keep you from losing your mind in despair at the endless cycle of birth and death and the loss of so many loved ones gone before you to the Seat of Judgment.'

So Nasciens changed his clothes to black and stayed below deck, kneeling before the Grail in silence and penitence for the rest of the voyage.

King Conor was long dead but Joseph and his party were royally welcomed by Caradoc, Conor's son, who was now King. He asked Joseph and his family to live with him and his Queen in the Royal Pallisade, but Joseph looked up at the night sky, saw no sign of the promised star, shook his head sadly and continued on his way.

On the third night, the star appeared before them like a throbbing, radiant ball of red and gold. Their journey was long and hard and they travelled far, high into the mountains of Gwynedd. But everywhere they went, the poor and the lame and the little children came to greet them and receive a blessing. Anna had turned their ship's sail into a flag and she walked at the head of the company each day, through the mountains, hills and valleys, holding Mary's drawing of the Archangel like a banner before her. Behind her, Joseph carried the Grail, veiled now in a cloth of white samite.

At long last the star stopped above their heads in a valley sheltered by four mountains, where a spring of bright, clear water bubbled and flowed. So the company built their church - the Church of the Grail - on that very spot.

They stayed there years and years. In time, the Church became a castle known as Dinas Ffaraon - the Fortress of the High Powers - with the Grail King ruling the surrounding lands. Joseph was the first Grail King, as the Angel had prophecied, and when he died his son Josephus succeeded him as King and Nasciens as Priest. But Josephus was killed in battle shortly afterwards and the Kingship passed to Alain son of Bron. Alain's royal line exists today, though it is hidden now until the coming of the fourth Grail Priest, he who will restore all things for a season before the advent of Antichrist and the second coming of Our Lord.

Alain, while he was King, made contact with Mary Magdalene's community in Gaul and with the Sisters of Saint Brighid in Ireland, those holy women who watch and guard the sacred flame night and day at their monastery in Kildare. For hundreds of years a great round of chant rang out from all three sites, one following on from the other - from dawn till mid-afternoon in Gwynedd, from mid-afternoon till midnight in Gaul, and from midnight till dawn in Kildare. A triangle of numinous force was established - a musical mirror of the Holy Trinity - from Britain to Gaul to Ireland and back to Britain again.

Nasciens had been Grail Priest for over four hundred years when one night Blaise, the Chief Druid and teacher of Merlin, came to Dinas Ffaraon and advised him that because the times had grown so evil it would be prudent to partially remove the castle and neighbouring lands to the Otherworld. Those with a questing, sincere heart might still stumble upon the Grail, but Dinas Ffaraon would no longer be a place to be found on a map and the Grail would therefore lie out of reach of maraudering Irish pirates. And so it fell out and so it remained until the time of Arthur and the coming of the third Grail Priest, Galahad. But by then the spiritual sight of men and women had become so dim and occluded that even if the Grail Castle had still been a physical place in the world they would have been unable to perceive it.

If it was like that then, it is a thousand times worse today. Yet stories are told and rumours abound and whispers run wild that the fourth Grail Priest is among us and is about to show his hand. Some even claim to have seen him - a man I know, for instance - a mountaineer who was out climbing with his nephew one bright March day. He got lost in the foothills trying to get back to his car and stumbled on an old stone church near a spring of bubbling water in a valley ringed by four mountains. It was almost dark and golden lights were shining in the church. There was singing too, some kind of chant in a foreign language. My friend and his nephew crept closer and peered in and saw a company of men and women - a dozen or so - standing in a circle around a candlelit table, and on the table was a golden chalice which seemed to shine and vibrate with a red-tinged glow all of its own. Standing behind the chalice was a man, but neither my friend not the boy could see his face because of the light radiating out from the chalice. But they did see him lift it up above his head. Three times he did it, while bells rang and everyone in the church knelt down and bowed their heads. The mountaineer and his nephew were so moved by what they saw that they knelt down too and bowed their heads and closed their eyes. And when they opened them the mountains and spring were still there but the church had gone and what they saw instead, about two hundred yards off, just discernible in the gloom, was the familiar outline of my friend's Ford Escort, parked beside the same oak tree he had picked as a good parking spot early in the morning.

They drove back to Manchester in silence he said, but it was the happiest, most restful, most inspiring silence he had ever known. 'I had the sense,' he told me, 'that tremendous events, way beyond the scope of our minds to comprehend, are close at hand. A radical reorientation, despite appearances, is on its way. Redemption and renewal are nearer to our world, nearer to our country and nearer to our hearts than we think.'

WILLIAM OF GLASSHAMPTON (JF)

The Hermit possesses the gift of letting light shine in the darkness. He creates light, he creates silence and he creates certainty ...

Valentin Tomberg, *Meditations on the Tarot*

Father William Sirr (1862-1937) was an Anglican priest whose cherished hope of founding a contemplative community did not manifest in his lifetime. Yet this apparent failure has served as an inspiration to many, and his example continues to guide and enlighten today.

Fr. William discerned a vocation to the priesthood early in his life, but his family's straitened financial circumstances meant that he had to work for several years before starting theological training. He was employed for eight years as a confidential clerk at a wine merchant's in London, a role which sounds like it was pulled from a Grahame Greene novel and which gave him a Greene-like insight into fallen human nature. This education in the elasticity of business ethics served him well as a priest and made him virtually unshockable. Once ordained, he accepted a curacy in Vauxhall before entering the Fransiscan Society of the Divine Compassion in 1902. He was made novice master a year later and elected superior in 1906.

Fr. William spent the next decade ministering to the poor in the East End. He did this with distinction and devotion but gradually came to feel that the Church was failing to connect, at the deepest level, with the people who most needed her. This, he believed, went back to the dissolution of the monasteries under Henry VIII and the subsequent absence in the Church of England of the enclosed, contemplative life. He held that for the Church to impact positively on society, her practical ministry needed to spring from the hallowed and ancient soil of stillness, prayer and contemplation. Increasingly, he felt that God was calling him to renew that tradition and provide the Church with the bedrock of silence and recollection she would need if her societal mission was to flourish.

In 1918, Fr. William was given permission to found a monastery in Glasshampton, Worcestershire, in the stable block of a derelict country house. He converted the premises admirably - no easy task for a man in his late fifties and early sixties - but was unable to find men willing to stay and build the religious community he felt called to establish. Many came to visit and spend time discerning their vocation, but the life was austere, Fr. William's culinary skills poor, and his recitation of the Daily Office so slow that it irritated rather than inspired. Temperamentally, he was perhaps more suited to the solitude of a hermitage than communal living, and he died in 1937 having failed to make his vision a reality.

Yet on a deeper level, he was anything but a failure. Two of the men who came to him at Glasshampton, Fr. Robert Gofton-Salmond and Fr. Gilbert Shaw, were instrumental in the establishment of the Community of the Servants of the Will of God, based at Crawley Down in West Sussex and still flourishing today. Here is an icon of Fr. Gofton-Salmond (right), Fr. Shaw (centre) and Fr. William (left). These three are regarded as the founders of the community and their memory is celebrated each year on August 18th.

The monastery built by Fr. William became a house of the Society of St. Francis in 1947, so his many years in Glasshampton of prayer, waiting and patient building were not in vain in the end. Glasshampton Monastery, according to its website, was named by *The Sunday Telegraph* in 2011 as one of the eight best places in Europe for a retreat, so the foundations laid by Fr. William were obviously robust, both spiritually and materially. Below is a picture of the monastery chapel as it is today.

Alongside this physical legacy, there is also Geoffrey Curtis's biography, *William of Glasshampton*: *Friar - Monk - Solitary* (1977), and two more recent essays I have drawn on for this post: Peta Dunstan's, *Fr. William's Baton*, which can be found in *Oneness: The Dynamics of Anglican Monasticism* edited by Stephen Platten (2017), and a 2014 article on the excellent *Desert Spirituality in the City* blog. – www.citydesert.wordpress.com.

Reading and reflecting on this literature, there are two things in particular which strike me about Fr, William. The first is his realisation that action needs to be grounded in the life of the spirit and not the other way around. This insight is all the more impressive as it was arrived at while experiencing at first hand the material deprivations of the London poor. Despite the grievous hardships he saw, he understood that the assistance offered by the Church would have no value unless it was grounded in prayer and contemplation. Practical help could be given just as effectively, if not more so, by a whole raft of non-Church organisations. Spirituality, after all, is the Church's *raison d'être*. Everything else flows from that. Fr. William would have concurred with his contemporaries in France - the 'non-conformists of the 1930s' - and their rallying cry, 'Primacy of the Spiritual.' Thinkers like Emmanuel Mounier (1905-50) believed that men and women can only flourish in a society which puts their spiritual needs first and places the political and the economic realms at the service of the spiritual.

This was exactly Fr. William's understanding, a worldview which he lived out at Glasshampton with great faith and single-mindedness for nigh on two decades. This is the second thing which stands out - his ability to first of all discern his contemplative vocation, and then stick with it and continue to believe in it despite a lack of tangible success. One can imagine the inner voices which must have assailed him from time to time - accusations of folly, egotism, and a dereliction of duty in the face of so much deprivation, which he had been in a position, in the East End, to alleviate. Happily, it was the 'still, small voice' which he chose to listen to, and today - 81 years after his death - we can recognise very clearly the deep wisdom that spoke to his heart and prompted him to go to Glasshampton.

It sounds counter-intuitive to suggest, but Fr. William might have had more immediate success in building his community had he lived in our day rather than the inter-war era. Christianity was much more prominent in Britain at that time, with church attendance generally high. Despite poverty, strikes, and high unemployment, there was, on the whole, a far greater degree of national and social cohesion than now. But this very cohesiveness might actually have worked against Fr. William's project rather than for it. People, in those days, felt like they *belonged*. Whether it was the family, the neighbourhood, the church, the workplace, the union, or the guild - often all of these and more - Britons felt at home in a variety of settings and contexts, which all interlinked and related to each other like the circles of a Venn diagram.

With the exception of those First World War veterans who were either unable or unwilling to adapt to civilian life, men had so many support networks and places they could call home that everything Fr. William was offering they could probably find elsewhere. His offer was so extreme and so intense that most likely it would only have appealed to those with a real hunger and desperation for God, contemplation, and fraternal, religious community. Such individuals would have searched in vain for years for these things and found only meaninglessness and rejection. Such individuals would have been few. It was not so hard, generally speaking, to find meaning and depth in the 1920s and '30s, but the situation today is very different. The institutions that brought us comfort and belonging are in varying stages of disarray and dissolution. We feel, as a result, increasingly lost and disorientated, groping blindly for contact with something real and true, but searching all too often in all the wrong places and ending up more alienated and confused than before.

It hasn't quite kicked in yet, but despite (or because) of all the above, I feel we might be standing at the dawn of a new religious epoch, an epoch analogous to that which flourished across Western Europe in the fifth and sixth centuries. At that time, holy men and women like Saint Kevin of Glendalough turned their backs on the crumbling Roman Empire and the collapse of everything stable and known, and retired to remote and rocky places to live lives of prayer and solitude. To their surprise, others follow them there, seeking refuge from the chaos and finding a joy and a sustenance that were fast disappearing from the dominant culture. St. Kevin (below) and others like him lived lives of depth, simplicity, integrity, and sacramental devotion. They spoke to the hearts and minds of others because they themselves were imbued and aflame with the heart and mind of God. So the pilgrims stayed and new communities were born - fellowships of radiant love, which would go on to shape and transform culture and society - locally, nationally, and internationally.

The great archetypes often surge to the surface of human consciousness in times of change and turmoil. The figure of the hermit is undoubtedly one of these. The very existence of the ninth card of the Tarot deck tells us as much:

Hermits abound in European literature and mythology. Nasciens, the Hermit of Carbonek, is an excellent Albion-related example. Thomas Malory, in his *Morte D'Arthur,* tells us that Nasciens, as a young man, committed some unspecified sin against Joseph of Arimathea when the latter brought the Holy Grail and the Christian faith to these lands. His punishment was to live far beyond the span of mortal men as Priest of the Grail until the advent of Galahad, the Grail Knight, some four hundred years later.

There are echoes here of Simeon in Chapter Two of St. Luke's Gospel, who is told by the Holy Spirit that he will not die until he has seen the Redeemer. Ramandu and Coriakin in C.S. Lewis's, *The Voyage of the Dawn Treader* (Geoffrey Bles, 1952), also spring to mind - two stars, currently earthbound and living on remote islands in the Eastern Sea. Ramandu is awaiting rebirth, when he will, as he puts it, 'once more tread the Great Dance', while Coriakin has been given the unruly Dufflepuds to govern by Aslan in response to another unspecified offence. When Eustace enquires of Ramandu what that crime might be, he is rebuffed with a magisterial, 'My son, it is not for you, a Son of Adam, to know what faults a star might commit.'

It is the Hermit of the Southern March, however - another profoundly archetypal figure - who reminds me most of William of Glasshampton. Chapter Ten of Lewis's *The Horse and His Boy* (Geoffrey

Bles, 1954) is named after this character, and he appears nowhere else in the story nor in any of the other Narnia books. By the end of the chapter we have learned that the Hermit (Lewis uses a capital 'H') has 'lived a hundred and nine winters in this world', and has extensive knowledge of present events but limited insight into the future. He keeps goats, is a skilled medic, and has 'the hugest and most beautiful tree that Shasta had ever seen' at one end of a pool in a 'wide and perfectly circular enclosure protected by a high wall of green turf.' We are told nothing about his spiritual life, yet the chapter glows with a quiet, restful luminosity, which leaves the reader feeling as refreshed from his or her encounter with the Hermit as do the four protagonists.

Shasta and Aravis, along with their horses, Bree and Hwin, are racing through Southern Archenland with a Calormene army on their trail and, more pressingly, a great lion - 'a huge, tawny creature' - snapping at their heels:

> Shasta looked forward again and saw something which he did not take in or even think about. Their way was barred by a smooth green wall about ten feet high. In the middle of the gateway stood a tall man dressed, down to his bare feet, in a robe coloured like autumn leaves, leaning on a straight staff. His beard fell down to his knees.

The Hermit tends Aravis's wounds, sends Shasta out on the next stage of his mission, rubs the horses down, and feeds them with grass and goat's mash. His words to Bree, the proud Narnian warhorse, are very much in keeping, to my mind, with Fr. William's spiritual approach. Bree is feeling shame and remorse that he did not try to fight the lion off but ran as fast as he could for the safety of the Hermitage. 'I've lost everything,' he complains. 'Slavery is all I'm fit for.' The Hermit, gently but firmly, pops the bubble of wounded *amour propre* and restores a proper perspective:

> 'My good Horse, you've lost nothing but your self-conceit. No, no, cousin. Don't put back your ears and shake your mane at me. If you are really so humbled as you sounded a minute ago, you must learn to listen to sense. You're not quite the great Horse you had come to think, from living among poor, dumb horses. Of course you were braver and cleverer than them.

> You could hardly help being that. It doesn't follow that you'll be anyone very special in Narnia. But as long as you know you're nobody very special, you'll be a very decent sort of Horse on the whole, and taking one thing with another. And now, if you and my other four-footed cousin will come round to the kitchen door we'll see about the other half of that mash.'

This little speech, in many ways, conveys the essence of Fr. William's theology. As a spiritual director, he was not so much interested in what one believed or which denomination one belonged to. He focused instead on clearing away the barriers that were blocking the life-giving, restorative action of the Holy Spirit in a person's life. Then the real work could begin - a patient, peaceful waiting on God in silence of heart and quietness of mind. Like the mute boy in Andrei Tarkovsky's film, *The Sacrifice*, who sets about watering his dead father's tree in faith and hope that one day it will miraculously bloom.

Or like Shasta in the very next chapter of *The Horse and His Boy*, who hears the Voice of Aslan while riding wearily to Anvard, following the Hermit's instruction to warn King Lune of the coming Calormene attack. As with Bree, Shasta is lifted out of self-pity and narrow, self-defeating horizons and shown a wider, truer perspective. It is a miracle. It is what we all long for, and it will happen to us just as it happened to him, be that during our lives, at the end of our lives, or at the end of time itself. It is the 'one thing needful' - heart to heart contact with the Living God - and it is what Fr. William spent so long, and so successfully in the end, trying to restore to the life of the Church. He knew how much his country needed it. And if we needed it then, how much more so now?

> The High King above all kings stooped towards him. Its mane, and some strange and solemn perfume that hung about the mane, was all round him. It touched his forehead with its tongue. He lifted his face and their eyes met. Then instantly the pale brightness of the mist and the fiery brightness of the Lion rolled themselves together in a swirling glory and gathered themselves up and disappeared. He was alone with the horse on a grassy hillside under a blue sky. And there were birds singing.

William of Glasshampton, pray for us.

LOGRES, BRITAIN, AND THE BETRAYAL OF THE ROMANOVS (JF)

The French astrologer and religious and political thinker Charles Ridoux has just published a 64 page essay commemorating the massacre of Tsar Nicholas II and his family by the Bolsheviks in Ekaterinburg one hundred years ago on July 17th. It can be read on his website – www.ridoux.fr.

The martyrdom of the Romanovs formed the third and most devastating part of a trilogy, which began with the regicide of Charles I of England in 1649 and continued with the execution of the French king Louis XVI and his wife Marie Antoinette in 1793. Each of these murders marks a step on the way in the dechristianisation of Europe, a process which appears very near to completion today.

Ridoux argues that this slaughter would not have occurred had Britain not reneged on a promise to welcome the Tsar and his children as exiles. Permission was denied, not by the UK government - as previously thought - but by George V himself, the Tsar's own cousin. Ridoux quotes the Romanian esotericist Jean Parvulesco (1929-2010), who in his 2005 book *Vladimir Poutine et l'Eurasie*, claimed that the

King's refusal leaves the British monarchy open to what he calls a 'choc en retour', in the same way as many in France came to see the death of Louis XVI as payback for the burning at the stake of the Templar Grand Master Jacques de Molay at Philip IV's command in 1314.

One is reminded, reflecting on this exile that wasn't, of Dr. Dimble's reflection in C.S. Lewis's *That Hideous Strength* (The Bodley Head, 1945) on the battle for England's soul between the holy realm of Logres (or Albion) and the mercantile, rapacious global power known as Britain:

> 'But in every way they (the Pendragons) and the little Logres which gathered round them have been the fingers which gave the tiny shove or the almost imperceptible pull, to push England out of the drunken sleep or to draw her back from the final outrage into which Britain tempted her.'

It would appear that on this occasion, unfortunately, Britain was too strong for Logres.

That Hideous Strength springs to mind again in Parvulesco's description of Lenin as a shell of a man, a walking zombie, wholly under the influence of malign occult powers: '*He became something increasingly inhuman, a being with a centre of gravity in a reality outside this world, totally subservient to and dependent on his non-human masters.*'

This is exactly what happens to Wither, Frost and Straik in Lewis's novel, as the Bent Eldils subsume their personalities, leaving them desiccated automatons of the evil they chose to embrace when they were still capable of human responses like choice.

Even in the direst of situations, however, God will find a way for good to flourish, and the murder of the Tsar and his children is no exception. The life of Father Nicholas Gibbes (1876-1963) stands as a wonderful witness of the Divine capacity to respond creatively to evil and defy conventional expectations. Gibbes, the son of a Rotherham banker, was a spiritual seeker of seriousness and depth, who, after much wandering, found himself at the Imperial court in Russia, where he taught English to the Tsar's children. He became a close friend of the Royal Family and was deeply marked by his years in their presence, seeing them as exemplars of holiness, sacrifice and right living.

After 1918, Gibbes travelled widely throughout the East, praying and reflecting on the meaning of his encounter with the Tsar and his family, until in 1934, at the age of 58, he joined the Russian Orthodox

Church, becoming successively monk, deacon and priest. He returned to England in 1937, and became the first English priest of the Russian Orthodox Church Outside Russia (ROCOR) and the founder of the first Orthodox church in Oxford. Many were struck by his piety and prayerfulness, and before he died in March 1963, an icon given him by the Imperial family was miraculously renewed and began to shine. So maybe Logres - in that mysterious, unpredictable fashion so suggestive of God's hidden hand - proved stronger than Britain in the end!

Archpriest Andrew Phillips has written beautifully on the life of Fr. Nicholas Gibbes on his *Orthodox England* site. I would urge as many of us as possible to read and reflect on his essay today, as an act of reparation, first and foremost, for the part played by this country in the death of the Romanovs, and also as a spiritual riposte to the dark powers who engineered that act of infamy and remain so active in our world, capturing and enslaving hearts and minds at an increasingly rapid rate. Without a Tsar on the Russian throne, as a living symbol of Christ the Universal King, their task becomes so much easier. Holy martyrs of Russia, pray for us. May you rest in peace and rise in glory.

THE HIDDEN SHRINE OF KING CHARLES THE MARTYR (JF)

There are other places
Which also are the world's end, some at the sea jaws,
Or over a dark lake, in a desert or a city -
But this is the nearest, in place and time,
Now and England.

T.S. Eliot, *Little Gidding*

Today, January 30th, is the anniversary of the execution of Charles I in 1649. The painting above by Augustus Egg (1816-63), *Charles I Raising His Standard in Nottingham*, hangs in the Walker Art Gallery, Liverpool. What I find striking in this picture is its absence of triumphalism, expectation, or even hope. The ragged, storm-laden sky says it all. The musicians go through the motions, but the atmosphere is tense and sombre, as if the outcome of the English Civil War, which hasn't started yet, is already known in hearts and minds.

The King's body language is far from Churchillian, yet there is little sign of fear on his face. Resigned to his fate he may be, but he is clearly determined to take a stand, defend his crown, his country and his people, and go down fighting if need be. The painting, I think, sums Charles up well. He succeeded his father, James I, in 1625, and at his execution the ancient principle of the Divine Right of Kings was buried with him, seemingly forever. The Monarchy was restored in 1660 in the person of his son, Charles II, but the great days of English kingship - when the monarch led and Parliament followed - were over. The Royalist defeat set the nation's course for centuries to come - an agenda dictated by mercantile, bourgeois interests to the detriment, in my view, of both the aristocracy and those on the margins of society. The reward was wealth and empire, but the price, as William Blake (himself no monarchist) understood, has been the diminution and fading of a higher, national vision. England's spiritual identity has been compromised, and it may well be that we have only started to feel the reality of this loss and blurring in very recent years.

Charles I had his flaws like all of us. He was prone to bouts of vanity and conceitedness, but he was clear and firm in his principles and had a rock solid sense of who he was and what he stood for. He retained the affection of his people throughout, seeing himself as their servant as much as their ruler. He curbed the iconoclastic excesses of the Reformation and inspired a widespread renewal of the spiritual life, a prime example being the contemplative community set up at the church of St. John the Evangelist, Little Gidding, Cambridgeshire, by Nicholas Ferrar in 1626.

This is the church made famous by T.S. Eliot in *Little Gidding*. 'You are here to kneel,' he writes, 'where prayer has been valid.' Charles paid the last of his three visits to St. John's in 1646, in an attempt to elude the victorious Parliamentarians. 'If you came at night like a broken king', remarks Eliot in memoriam. Charles' subsequent capture, imprisonment, trial and execution are events which hang heavy over England still, I feel, like the clouds in Egg's painting. They seem somehow unresolved, at least to me, and sometimes it appears inevitable to my mind that the nation is due an almighty chastisement for allowing it all to happen. I take comfort, however, in the thought that Charles, by the example of his life and death, has found a home now in the great Arthurian lineage of returning kings - those 'once and future' sovereigns who will spring forth from the national imagination to lead their repentant people and thrust back the powers of evil at their country's hour of need.

I had something of an epiphany last week *a propos* of this. In Didsbury, the Manchester suburb where I live, there's a lamp-lit bookshop on a little cobbled street behind the tram line. I was leafing through a book last Saturday afternoon (the 21st) called simply, *A History of Didsbury*. The frontispiece was a two page map dating from 1929. The book itself was published in 1978. I noticed some handwriting in blue ink on the right of the map, over to the East, between Didsbury Cricket Club and Fletcher Moss Park. The ink had faded a bit but the script was neat and elegant - an **X** accompanied by the words, **Shrine of King Charles the Martyr**.

I've lived in or around Didsbury for most of my life and had never heard of such a place. Didsbury Library has two blue plaques commemorating the Royalist army's brief stay here in 1644 en route to the Battle of Marston Moor. But I had never heard of a shrine or anything like it. It was an intriguing discovery, nonetheless - though odds-on a joke or a spot of wishful thinking - and I set off at once to explore, intending to come back to the shop later to buy the book.

The area between the park and the cricket club is occupied by a business park now. It's a nice, tree-lined part of town, but I had never visited the business park and never seen any reason why I should. I walked around for a good half-hour in the mist and drizzle. I thought I'd hate it but I actually found it quite a peaceful, almost Zen-like, place. Apart from the security guards sat listlessly at their desks and a few men in suits strolling about, I saw no-one at all. The squat glass buildings seemed to have fallen asleep, lulled by the soft rain and the rising fog.

The business park is bisected by a wide driveway, which branches off into a network of paths and lawns. I saw nothing anywhere to suggest the existence of a shrine. The only old-looking thing I found was a small, chapel-like structure on a grassy roundabout with a triangular roof and an arch-shaped door of dark and heavy wood. I tugged the round, iron handle. The door didn't budge. I walked around to the other side and peered through the window. Nothing to see though - just flip charts, whiteboards, and so forth - the usual business paraphernalia. I found neither plaque nor inscription on the lime-washed walls, so shrugging my shoulders I went on my way, feeling more let down than I'd expected, given that I hadn't really, deep down, expected to come across a shrine at all. 'Maybe it's hidden' I mused,

'Maybe it's always been hidden. Maybe you can only see it with the eye of faith and imagination.' I was disappointed, I recall, that I didn't appear to have much of either.

I bumped into an old friend in Didsbury Village on my way back and by the time I got to the shop it was closed. I decided to leave the matter there, and that was how things stood until three days later - Tuesday evening to be precise. I had arranged to meet my friend for a pint in the Dog and Partridge after work, so I got off the train at East Didsbury, one stop earlier than usual. I walked to the bus stop by the cricket club. It's only three stops from there to the Village. It was almost fully dark and the lights were on everywhere. The sky was clear and the air mild.

The bus was busier than I'd anticipated. I had to sit on one of the sideways-facing seats next to the space for wheelchairs and prams. I tried to remember if there was football on, but I hadn't got very far when the bus stopped at the traffic lights next to the business park. Then, where the squat glass buildings should have been, I was blessed (and wounded) instead by the most extraordinary sight - a colossal edifice - a Cathedral or Abbey of some kind - with tall high windows all ablaze in golden light. The roof was a giant triangle, with the thick silhouette of a cross standing out on top against the Western sky. I glimpsed a lawn, a bonfire, a ring of people and a flash of red. Then the lights changed and the bus rolled forward. Someone was playing a violin. I stood up on tiptoe and saw a girl with a fiddle in front the fire. She had dark hair and a red bandana, and the music I heard through the open window will sustain and inspire me, I swear, through this world and the next - mournful and fierce, exultant and yearning - a funeral dirge and a triumphal march at one and the same time. It was cut from a different cloth - that's all I can say - music from a higher level - a sphere of beauty and intensity that was all too soon behind me as the gears whirred and the bus gathered speed, powering on into the night.

I looked around but could tell straightaway that none of my fellow passengers had seen or heard a thing. They were all too ensconced in their papers and phones. One or two had even fallen asleep, worn out, like myself, after a hard day's work.

And that's where I left it. I toyed with telling my friend in the pub but decided against in the end. Maybe I will one day. Perhaps he'll read this blog. He said he might. I've not been back to the business park or bookshop either. I'll go to the bookshop again, of course, but probably not the business park.

Some things, I reckon now, are hidden because they're meant to be. They rest in the invisible realm - accessible only to the eye of imagination and faith - until the time for their appearance (or reappearance) in this world is ripe. We're graced with glimpses from time to time and these give us strength, but the King will return when he's ready - when Heaven and Earth are ready - and when *we're* ready to return to the Truth, take off our shoes and socks, and let our feet be bathed by Christ the High King, in whose Name he rules and serves.

30th January 2017

KING HAROLD GODWINSON (JF)

Today, October 14th 2016, is the nine hundredth and fiftieth anniversary of the Battle of Hastings. With a surname like Fitzgerald, I must have had an ancestor who fought on the Norman side that day, yet I've always felt a strong dislike for Duke William and a profound affinity for his opposite number, King Harold II, the last of the Anglo-Saxon kings. As a boy, I read everything I could on this period of history and I remember how affected I was by the English defeat at Hastings and the death of Harold. The only other episode in my reading which upset me as much was the slaying of Hector by Achilles (with a little help from Athene) in the *Iliad*, another example of outrageous injustice and misfortune.

To say that Harold was unlucky in his short reign from January to October 1066 would be an understatement. He did as much, if not more, as Winston Churchill did in 1940 to maintain his country's independence, yet the dice didn't fall his way and he had no allies overseas to distract, pressurise and push back the enemy. On September 25th, Harold crushed an enormous Viking army at Stamford Bridge near York in one of the most spectacular military triumphs of the Medieval era. Three days later, Duke William landed on the South coast. Harold could, and maybe should, have bided his time in York, resting his troops and gathering reinforcements. He couldn't bear, however, to remain in the North when the Normans were ravaging his own Earldom of Wessex. Such was his confidence in his men and his leadership that he raced hotfoot down to Senlac Hill and faced the invader with a footsore army at about half its optimal strength. Even so, the Saxons dictated terms for the first three hours of battle, until over-excitement led some of the soldiery to chase the struggling Normans down the hill, fatally compromising the defensive solidity which was central to Harold's strategy.

Harold has also suffered from the artistically sublime but politically biased Bayeux Tapestry. This famous picture of Harold swearing a solemn oath ...

... that he would allow William to assume the throne on the death of the childless Edward the Confessor (1042 - 1066) creates a very slanted impression of what most likely happened. The precise reasons why Harold found himself shipwrecked off the coast of Normandy in 1064 remain obscure. But he was rescued by William's men and stayed in the Duchy for a number of months as a guest (or prisoner, a cynic might claim) of the Duke. Harold's vow was almost certainly made under some kind of duress. It is barely conceivable, considering the circumstances, that it could have been a freely given decision. History, sometimes, is indeed written by the winners.

When Edward died on January 5th, Harold - despite being the son of an Earl (Godwin) rather than a King - was clearly the only man capable of inheriting the Crown and preserving the integrity of the country. During the second half of Edward's reign he had shown himself to be a first class leader (especially in his campaigns against the Welsh) and a highly competent administrator. He had the character and personal attributes, once the threat of invasion was quelled, to become one of the great English Kings, in the lineage of Alfred, Athelstan and Edgar. But it didn't happen for him, through no fault of his own, and Norman propaganda has done its best ever since to airbrush him out of history.

Harold, in this respect, could be viewed as England's 'missing' King, the *Grand Monarque* the country never had. Certainly, in my view, *Harold II* is the great play that Shakespeare never wrote. For a long time after the Norman Conquest, stories and legends circulated that Harold hadn't died at Hastings, that he was hiding, biding his time before returning at the head of a mighty host to beat off the oppressor. Harold plays his part and finds his place, therefore, in our nation's great Arthurian tapestry.

I have always felt as well, in a way which I can't quantify but which I feel to be vitally and existentially true, that Harold's death - even though it took place on the battlefield and not on the executioner's scaffold - in some way prefigures and foreshadows the terrible stain of Regicide, spreading across Europe, from our own Royal Martyr, Charles I, in 1649, to Louis XVI in 1793 and Tsar Nicholas II and his family in 1918. On this note, it is worth mentioning here that Fr. Andrew Phillips of St John's Orthodox Church, Colchester, will be celebrating a memorial service for King Harold and all his companions at the Church of St Mary Magdalene, Whatlington, East Sussex, on Thursday October 27th at 11 am.

There is certainly a belief in some quarters that Harold was the last Orthodox King of England, the victim of a stitch-up between William and the Pope to impose the Roman rite once and for all on the country and banish the remaining elements of Celtic Christianity. How true this is I cannot say, but what is interesting is that Harold's daughter, Gytha, later married a prince of Smolensk named Vladimir Monomakh, who later became ruler and Grand Prince of a united Kievan Rus, a vast realm, stretching from the Baltic Sea in the North to the Black Sea in the South. They named their son, Harald, after his maternal grandfather, so there is a connection with the Orthodox world here and something of a happy ending too in that Harold's name and achievements lived on and took flourishing root overseas.

Harold's is a legacy, a story and a mythology, which can, and should, be tapped into today, here in his native realm. Those who voted 'Leave' in the June referendum, for instance, could do a lot worse, to my mind, than look to Harold as a symbol and exemplar of what fighting for independence really means and what it potentially costs. It is a spiritual aspiration, first and foremost, with absolutely no guarantee of worldly success, a thriving economy or material prosperity. You might even be forgotten. Airbrushed out of history. Traduced in a contemporary rehash of the Bayeux Tapestry. It is a risk and a leap of faith, but if you do it for the right reasons and in the right way - nothing to do with markets and trade deals, but everything to do with passion, heart and soul - then the people who matter - the poor, the weak, the humble, the little children who Christ welcomed into his arms - will cherish and bless your memory, until the wheel spins round and you come again - in Russia, France, England and everywhere else - Arthur, Harold, Charles, Louis, Nicholas - the Once and Future King.

14th October 2016

ROGER LANCELYN GREEN – STORYTELLER AND BARD (JF)

Roger Lancelyn Green (1918-1987) was a man of many parts - school teacher, stage actor, children's writer, biographer and librarian. He was also the hereditary lord of the manors of Poulton-Lancelyn and Lower Bebington in Cheshire. He studied under C.S. Lewis at Oxford, later becoming his close friend and biographer, and though Green was very much a lesser-known member of The Inklings, that famous circle of creative Oxford Christians, I would argue that his books have had a wider readership, at least in Britain, than any other Inkling, save J.R.R. Tolkien and Lewis himself.

Green's lasting legacy lies in his storytelling, or in his retelling of stories, to be more exact. It is an impressive list of classics, his books appearing at regular intervals throughout the 1950s and '60s, including *The Adventures of Robin Hood*, *King Arthur and His Knights of the Round Table*, *Tales of the Greek Heroes*, *The Tale of Troy*, *Myths of the Norsemen*, *The Luck of Troy* and *Tales of Ancient Egypt.* I remember how popular these books were during my primary school days in the 1970s, and no matter how much has changed in England since then, that fact remains. Green's tales are as much in demand and just as available now as in 1970. You will find one or more in nearly every bookshop and library across the country.

This, surely, is a sign of great hope. As noted in previous *Albion Awakening* posts, recent decades have seen an unprecedented diminution in levels of spiritual integrity and vision in British public life. Roger Lancelyn Green's continuing popularity, in the face of such frantic levelling, shows the extent to which children (and adults) are naturally, and always will be, drawn to the sacred drama of myth. This attraction and receptivity is the essence of Albion - our island's saving grace - deeply embedded in the national consciousness and far beyond the reach of corrupting forces. Viewed in this light, Greens *oeuvre* can be seen as high quality raw material - a touchstone and first point of contact for any upcoming spiritual renaissance in this land.

Green's prose style is limpid and fluid, charged, like that of many other children's writers, with atmosphere and narrative tension. Yet for me there is something more, something almost holy about his books, some kind of numinous sheen that glimmers on the page as I read. Certainly, when I look back on times of alienation and spiritual aridity in my life, it was often the recollection of a line or a passage from *King Arthur* or *Myths of the Norsemen*, as much, it seemed, as any prayer, Bible reading or religious observation that reorientated me towards the Divine and the 'still small voice' of Christ. Balder's funeral in *Myths of the Norsemen* springs immediately to mind - the burning ship, the Western ocean, the blood-red sky, and Odin's one word whispered into his dead son's ear: 'Rebirth'. Then, after *Ragnarok* and the Twilight of the Gods, the emergence of a new world - clean, fresh and pure - and the return of Balder from the Houses of the Dead to a new heaven and a new earth. I remember how tremendously moved this made me feel, and I remember too how astonished I was, years later, to find C.S. Lewis articulating the self-same boyhood passion in *Surprised by Joy* (Geoffrey Bles, 1955):

> But then, like a voice from far more distant regions, there came a moment when I idly turned the pages of the book and found the unrhymed translation of Tegner's Drapa and read -
>
> I heard a voice that cried,
> Balder the beautiful
> Is dead, is dead ...
>
> I knew nothing about Balder; but instantly I was uplifted into huge regions of northern sky. I desired with almost sickening intensity something never to be described (except that it is cold, spacious, severe, pale and remote) and then found myself at the very same moment already falling out of that desire and wishing I were back in it.

My sense is that it was Green's proximity to The Inklings, and to Lewis in particular, that gave his mythic retellings their distinctively spiritual feel. As with Lewis, Tolkien, Charles Williams and Owen Barfield, Green points us towards a wider, deeper, truer reality than that expounded by the cultural, media and educational establishments of our day. We should give thanks therefore for his witness and his role in our times as storyteller and bard. We live, after all, in a confused age, where the eye of spiritual vision has been dimmed and the Grail has passed up into Heaven and vanished from our sight. Or so it seems. Prophecy and poetry dare to suggest, however, that the Grail will come again, possibly to this very patch of earth, this 'jewel set in a silver sea', where it revealed itself so spectacularly in former times. How then will we recognise it? How will we perceive it? How will we discern its presence and hear its still small voice in the midst of our daily circus of commerce and distraction?

'Remember the signs,' says Aslan to Jill in The Silver Chair (Geoffrey Bles, 1953). 'Here on the mountain the air is clear and your mind is clear; as you drop down into Narnia the air will thicken. Take great care that it does not confuse your mind. And the signs which you have learned here will not look at all as you expect them to look when you meet them there. That is why it is so important to know them by heart and pay no attention to appearances. Remember the signs and believe the signs. Nothing else matters.'

Reading, enjoying and reflecting on the work of Roger Lancelyn Green would represent an excellent step on the path to true discernment. Green guides us away from appearances and towards the essential - the recollection of the things that matter - the signs and symbols that will survive whatever *Ragnarok* awaits us, that heal and bring life to the Wasteland, that turn winter into spring, death into life and old worlds into new ...

'Then Galahad held the spear so that the drops of blood fell into the wounds of the Maimed King; and at once Pelles was healed of his sufferings, and his flesh was as whole and unscarred as if Balyn had never struck the Dolorous Stroke.' (*King Arthur and His Knights of the Round Table*)

KATHLEEN RAINE – POET, PLATONIST, PROPHET (JF)

I discovered Kathleen Raine (1908-2003) in the Language and Literature Library on the top floor of Manchester's Central Library. It was December 1995 or thereabouts. I was in my mid-twenties then and am obviously a lot older now, but at least I'm still alive, unlike the Language and Literature Library, which exists now as a mere shell of its former self. The Central Library was closed for refurbishment between 2006 and 2010. When it reopened it was still the same circular city-centre landmark and a very attractive space, particularly for those with young children. But what a price to pay! The refit saw the Library lose something like two thirds of its book stock. There are computers aplenty now and lots more individual and group working spaces, but the chances of a young person wandering in and stumbling on a life-changing book have been greatly diminished. That, to my mind, represents a real loss and diminution, and seems somehow emblematic of our era's spiritual and intellectual poverty.

Technically, as I say, the Language and Literature Library still exists, but it's been reduced in size from two levels to one, and has been completely divested of its glamour and mystique. It was a very romantic and seductive place in the '80s and '90s. The lamps hung like little moons and time stood still as you perused the upper and lower levels, pausing here and there to revel in old favourites (Shakespeare, T.S. Eliot and C.S. Lewis in my case) or to make new discoveries, most notably Kathleen Raine and Colin Wilson, the subject of my next piece.

If you stayed there long enough, the spines of certain books would seem like they were speaking to you, urging you to pick them up. I had refrained for a long time in looking at the book with the golden spine and the title in red italics on the upper floor. I feared it for some reason, as if it might be some kind of Siren, luring me to a rocky and storm-tossed death. I only took it down, I remember, one evening about six o'clock when I was in a particularly desperate state of mind, adrift on the sea of life and spiritually and emotionally lost.

I took it down, opened a page at random and immediately felt, for the first time in ages, that I was breathing clear and healthy intellectual air. It was like the spell for the refreshment of the spirit that Lucy finds in the Magician's Book in *The Voyage of the Dawn Treader*. The book was by a woman I'd never heard of - Kathleen Raine - but it spoke to me of things that were once familiar and second-nature but that I'd somehow lost on my journey through teenagerdom and young adulthood. The book was called *The Lion's Mouth* and I later found out that it was the third volume of Kathleen Raine's autobiography, published in 1977.

What struck me most emphatically was the authority and confidence with which the writer expressed her vision. Jesus 'spoke with authority' says St. Mark's Gospel, and the onlookers were 'astonished.' It's a grand comparison to make but I felt much the same way, so long had it been since I had heard or read anyone talk with conviction about spiritual truth. Raine spoke of the Imagination (with a capital I) and the absolute necessity of following the promptings of her 'Daemon', a kind of guiding spirit or guardian angel, always there to orient her towards her intuition and instinct and away from the calculating rationalism of the world. For Raine, this meant placing poetry before all else, and *The Lion's Mouth* is unsparing in its account of how such dedication to the Daemon caused tremendous human unhappiness, for herself and those closest to her. Eliot, in *Little Gidding*, refers to such bitter self-realisation as:

> ... the rending pain of re-enactment
> Of all that you have done, and been: the shame
> Of things ill done and done to others harm
> Which once you took for exercise of virtue.

Despite this, the poet's insistence on the existence of a higher order than that which we can touch, taste, see, feel or smell, served to inspire me. Her willingness to stake her life on it and her sheer faith in the Platonic archetypes and the multi-layered nature of reality was exactly what I needed at a time when I had lost sight of the Divine in the madness of the city, the poundings of popular culture and the pressure to do something worthwhile with my life.

I have been reading and reflecting on Kathleen Raine ever since. She is best known today, perhaps, as a poet and a scholar of William Blake, who she always regarded as her master. Her poetic *oeuvre* is undoubtedly fine but the nature poetry she specialised in is not quite my taste, so I'm probably not best placed to comment. Her two-volume *Blake and Tradition* (1965) is a masterpiece of both scholarship and spiritual insight, showing that the two need never have become mutually exclusive. In it, she debunks the materialist literary theory then gaining ground in academia and directs us towards the true sources of Blake's inspiration in Plato, Plotinus, and the hidden esoteric traditions of the West. *Defending Ancient Springs* (1967) is a similarly astute book, which studies a range of creative figures who, like both Raine and Blake, placed the Imagination front and centre in their lives and work - Edwin Muir, Vernon Watkins, W.B. Yeats, S.T. Coleridge, Percy Shelley, and St. John Perse.

In 1981, along with a handful of like-minded individuals, Raine founded *Temenos: A Review Devoted to the Arts of the Imagination*. The journal's aim was to to transform and reverse the premisses of Western civilisation, from the materialistic to the imaginative. *Temenos* still exists today under the title *The Temenos Academy Review* and its website can be viewed here - www.temenosacademy.org.

I'm not convinced, speaking plainly for a moment, that *Temenos* has moved in the right direction since Raine's death fourteen years ago. I have had some contact with the group and they seem disappointingly uninterested in fighting what Raine called the 'Great Battle' between darkness and light, beauty and ugliness, God and the Devil. It has become a very genteel, London-centric organisation, and reminding its 'top table' of Raine's *cri de coeur*, as I once did in a letter, can seem almost rude or improper, like passing the port the wrong way or hearing the vicar swear in church. But for whatever reason, the *Temenos* board has decided that its *raison d'être* is not so much 'Albion Awakening' as flying the flag of the esoteric in high academic circles. I have to respect that and acknowledge that without *Temenos* the British cultural landscape would be even more barren than it already is. *Temenos*, at its best (e.g. the Audio Archive on the website), is a real light shining in darkness, even if at times I'm tempted to think that 'Don't Frighten the Horses' should be its motto.

I subscribed to the *Temenos Academy Review* for two years. The best thing I received was a book called *Lighting a Candle*, a collection of reminiscences of meetings with Kathleen Raine from about twenty-five people. What comes across most forcefully, reading and rereading this excellent book, is the sanctuary-like ambience of her flat at 47 Paultons Square, Chelsea. It was as if a deeper, purer air could be breathed there than elsewhere. The word 'temenos' means 'sacred space' and that is what her home was to her many visitors.

Her life and work have been a sacred precinct for me too and I hope and pray that the candle she lit will go on burning - bright and strong - even as the world grows darker and colder, so that that which is good, beautiful and true might be salvaged from the wreckage of this age, which is passing away, and sent across the sea to the shores of the Golden Age to come, a Golden Age which Kathleen Raine foresaw and did her level best to serve in word and deed as a witness and exemplar of the highest order.

COLIN WILSON – ENGLAND'S JOHN THE BAPTIST (JF)

Portrait of Colin Wilson by Rob Floyd (2009)

www.robfloyd.co.uk

As discussed in my previous post, I discovered both Kathleen Raine and Colin Wilson (1931-2013) in the Language and Literature Library on the top floor of Manchester's Central Library. For a long time, during the summer and autumn of 1997, I had become increasingly aware of a book called *Colin Wilson: The Man and His Mind*. I wondered who this Wilson was and what was so intriguing about his mind. I walked past the book and asked myself the question many times but didn't take it from the shelf. I mustn't have been ready for it at some level. At that time, I was just beginning to emerge from a long black hole of aimlessness and bereavement. So I read George MacDonald's *Phantastes* instead, which healed and re-baptised my imagination in a similar way to how C.S. Lewis describes his encounter with the book in *Surprised by Joy*.

That was September. In the October I came across Wilson's name again in a book about David Lindsay, the author of *Voyage to Arcturus*, but again, I didn't take down *The Man and His Mind*. When I eventually picked it up, it was for no particular reason on a Monday evening in early December, about half past six. I took the book from the shelf, flicked through it for five seconds, knew straightaway that I had to take it out, looked in my pocket for my library ticket and found that it wasn't there. Without any hesitation I put the book back, raced downstairs and caught the bus home, five miles to the suburb where I lived, got my ticket and jumped on a bus straight back. It was a quarter to eight when I got there, fifteen minutes before closing. I was terrified that someone might have taken the book out while I'd been gone, but no, it was still there, thank God. There had been no question whatsoever of waiting until the Library opened the next day. I had to read about Colin Wilson there and then. His ideas leapt and burst off the page. They had an immediacy - a ferocity even - that compelled my attention and focused my mind like a laser beam, banishing in an instant (or so it seemed) all the fears, inhibitions, doubts and anxieties that had formerly assailed me.

Colin Wilson: The Man and His Mind was published in 1990 and written by an Australian pastor and academic, Howard F Dossor. I find it a terrific book still and highly recommend it as an introduction to Wilson's work. I remember how impressed I was by the chapter headings - 'The Philosophy', 'The Fiction', 'The Literary Criticism', 'The Criminology', 'The Sexology', 'The Psychology', 'The Occultism'. I was astonished at how wide-ranging Wilson's *oeuvre* was and at the clarity and directness of his message - we are asleep, we can wake up if we choose, we are capable of far more than we currently think or imagine, we only need to make the effort and concentrate our minds fully on what we are doing right this minute.

Wilson's philosophy worked on me like a tonic. I had been feeling adrift on what Pope Benedict XVI later called the 'dictatorship of relativism', where one thing is as good or bad as another and nothing has ultimate value or significance. Well, here was a man who had none of that, a man of passion and conviction who believed that finding meaning, pattern and purpose was the most important thing a man or woman could do. It isn't enough to be free *from* external forces -

oppression, poor living/working conditions, etc - life has to be *for* something as well. It has to have an inner direction and focus, two factors which the modern and post-modern worlds mitigate decisively against. But only then will our inner energies become sufficiently sharp for higher levels of consciousness to awaken and unfold within us. What is more, it is those among us who feel most trapped and alienated in our contemporary, un-heroic *milieu* - Wilson's 'Outsiders' - who are most likely to develop into the standard bearers for evolution's next leap forward - not a materialistic advance - better technology, more mod-cons, and so forth - but an intellectual and spiritual surge, the continuing and ongoing conquest of matter by mind.

It was a heady brew. Intoxicating even. No wonder I had been wary of picking up the book. But now I was ready, and the next half-decade saw me plough through more Wilson titles than I can recall now - *The Outsider, The Occult, Mysteries, Beyond the Occult, The Black Room, The Mind Parasites, The Philosopher's Stone*, and many more. Around the mid-2000s, however, I started to realise that even though I regarded Wilson as the most important writer alive, my life didn't actually appear to be all that much better than it had been in 1997. I didn't share his natural optimism for one thing, and I began to get frustrated at my inability to find meaning simply by willing meaning to be there. I grew increasingly irritated with his approach. His continual deference to science annoyed me, the way he tried to express what were essentially spiritual realities in scientific terms (such as his 'ladder of selves' theory) as if those were the only terms that mattered. What I once found dynamic and counter-cultural I now found repetitive and one-dimensional. I continued to admire and respect Colin Wilson, but he was my 'North Star' no longer and I perceived that I needed to dig deeper and more thoroughly if I was to effect the root and branch changes required to purge me of my ego and properly orient my life towards goodness, truth and light.

'Metanoia', it's called in the Gospel's original Greek - turning one's life around - the English 'repent' being a rather weak translation. This 'turning around' was to lead me back at length to the Christian faith I had fallen away from, via a rediscovery of the writers I had loved most as a child - C.S Lewis, J.R.R. Tolkien, Roger Lancelyn Green and Rosemary Sutcliff. In Christ, I began to sense and feel everything I had yearned for but hadn't been able to locate in Wilson's philosophy - a personal God, warmth, tenderness, tradition, and an emphasis on silence and listening - waiting on God - rather than making repeated attempts to instigate change through will power alone. Taking the Kingdom of Heaven by force, in other words.

So it was a real eye-opener, earlier this year, when I read *Religion and the Rebel* (1957), Wilson's sequel to his wildly successful début, *The Outsider*, for the first time. To the same extent that *The Outsider* had been lauded by the critics, so *Religion and the Rebel* had been panned and derided. I think, looking back, that this negative reception must have influenced me subconsciously. How else could it have been that I had devoured so many Wilson titles down the years and never felt tempted by this one?

It is rich fare indeed, a survey of religious Outsiders - including Blaise Pascal, John Henry Newman and Soren Kierkegaard - which showcases a different Wilson altogether - mystical, intuitive, and strongly marked by the poetry and esoteric thought of William Blake and W.B. Yeats. What makes the book extra special in my eyes is that it contains a wider, civilisational element, which is almost entirely lacking from his later work. Wilson links the emergence of the Outsider to the ongoing (and now precipitous) decline of the West. Then he goes further by stating that the Outsider stands as both symptom and remedy of our civilisation's spiritual and cultural malaise. He or she is capable of bringing a new religious revelation to the table, or at least of injecting a fresh burst of impetus to the existing revelation. This is particularly germane in 2017, I feel, especially in Europe, where we are beginning to see how a people who have ceased to believe in God might start to cede place to a people for whom God is still active and real.

As Bruce Charlton has pointed out, Colin Wilson appeared to be on the brink of becoming a Christian at the time he wrote *Religion and the Rebel.* He did not do so, and his writing took on a different hue. I was given a clue as to why this might have happened when, together with my friend, the painter, Rob Floyd (see portrait above), I visited Wilson at his Cornwall home in 2009. Wilson and his wife, Joy, were most hospitable and generous hosts, but I remember him saying at one point how disappointed he was that his 2004 autobiography, *Dreaming to Some Purpose*, had been so poorly received by the critics. This surprised both Rob and myself as Wilson always gave the impression in his books that he was utterly impervious to the broadsheets' attempts to marginalise and belittle him.

My guess is that just as the critical hostility to *Religion and the Rebel* impacted on me in ways I didn't realise, so it impacted subconsciously on Wilson himself, diverting him from a spiritual approach to a more science-flavoured one, which might, on paper at least, have stood a greater chance of finding favour with the establishment that had lifted him so high then cast him so brutally down. It's just a theory, as I say, and I might be completely wrong, but my sense is that it accounts for a lot and that there's potentially more than a grain of truth there.

Might have been. Could have been. Should have been. Wilson's life, like all our lives, is littered with what ifs and maybes. But whatever his shortcomings, they pale into insignificance when weighed against his largeness of spirit, his breadth of vision, and the sheer ambition and scale of his intellectual project. For twenty years now, since that night in the Library, I've regarded him as the foremost British thinker of the age, even during the period when I distanced myself from his work. It's a national scandal that UK academia views Wilson as a crank at best and a crypto-fascist at worst, while life-denying, nihilistic pseudo-thinkers who can't or won't express themselves clearly such as Foucault and Derrida are held up as paragons of cutting-edge thought. I'm convinced that that if young people were encouraged to read and think about Wilson's ideas then the mental health crisis currently engulfing our country would be greatly ameliorated. Unless that isn't what the authorities want? Maybe they don't want any more Colin Wilsons. Perhaps they've never forgiven him for daring to step beyond the role prescribed for him as a working class boy from Leicester, which - despite the reburial of Richard III and the recent success of its football team - remains one of the most deeply unfashionable and looked down-upon cities in England.

A prophet, as we know, is never accepted in his own country, and certainly Wilson has received a warmer welcome overseas than here, especially in Eastern Europe, the Far East and parts of the Middle East. As we enter Advent, it seems natural to me to see him as a kind of John the Baptist figure, standing alone in the wilderness, calling us to Metanoia, a radical reorientation and restructuring of our lives in preparation for the One who is to come.

Advent also urges us to reflect on the second coming of Christ, and that could occur at any time, of course. Before it does, however, I suspect we might be granted one last shot at redemption - one more revival and rebirth - the end, as Blake put it, of Albion's long sleep on Britain's rocky shores - a resurgence of religion, creativity, beauty and nobility throughout the land. On that day, Wilson's true status will be plain to see - as clear and bright as the lightning blazing across the sky - a herald and forerunner of a new level of spiritual and imaginative intensity in this realm.

'Come the three corners of the world in arms,' says Faulconbridge in Shakespeare's *King John,* 'And we shall shock them. Naught shall make us rue, if England to itself do rest but true.'

Colin Wilson shocked many, from all corners of the world, out of mental slumber during his career. He will carry on doing so as the years and decades ahead unfold.

Thank you, O Lord, for his life and his work. Grant him, we pray, some well-deserved rest from his labours. Welcome him into the light of your face, and may he find in your presence a place of light, happiness, refreshment and peace.

ST CUTHBERT (WW)

I have a book, inherited from my great uncle, called The Book of Saints and Heroes by Mrs Lang who was the wife of Andrew Lang, the well-known Victorian compiler of fairy tales. My copy was published in 1912 and it's the oldest book I have. It has twelve beautiful coloured plates and many more black and white illustrations, all by someone called H.J. Ford of whom I haven't heard but who was clearly a master of his art. I never met my great uncle as he was one of the generation killed in the 1st World War but I feel the book gives me a small link to him and I value it for that reason. But that's not the only reason I have kept it when so many other books have gone to the great library in the sky. The stories of the early saints are so inspiring and so beautiful, and they are told here in such a way that brings them vividly to life. The dedication of these men and women to God is total and though that does put one's own efforts into rather sad perspective, it is also an encouragement to set your shoulder to the metaphorical plough.

One of the stories is called 'The Apostle of Northumbria' and it's about St Cuthbert. It tells how in the 7th century the young Cuthbert, who was living in a monastery, though not yet a monk, had so damaged his knee that he could no longer walk. One morning as he was lying at the edge of a forest, trying to forget his pain, he saw a man dressed in white and riding on a white horse coming towards him. The man stopped and talked to Cuthbert, asking why he did not get up to greet him. Cuthbert explained the problem with his knee at which the stranger made some suggestions as to how it might be cured and then departed. The cure worked and Cuthbert was persuaded that he had been visited by an angel. This inspired him to become a monk and devote himself entirely to God. He then spent several years as a priest travelling around the north of the country doing missionary work and spreading the word of the Gospel which at that time was still fairly shallow-rooted in those parts. He was much respected for his asceticism and loved for his kindness to the sick and the poor. He even gained a reputation for healing to such a degree that he became known as the Wonder Worker of Britain.

St Cuthbert by Henry Justice Ford

At one time when Cuthbert was giving instruction to the nuns at a place called Coldingham he was seen going out at night. A monk, curious to know where he was going, followed him down to the seashore where, to his astonishment, he saw Cuthbert enter the water and walk out until it reached up to his neck. There he remained until dawn, chanting the praise of God. When he came out of the sea two seals swam towards him and breathed over his cold feet to warm them after which they rubbed him dry with their bodies. The monk confessed to Cuthbert that he had spied on him and told him what he had seen. But Cuthbert asked him to keep it secret because he did not want to be thought holier than he was. The fact the story has come down to us rather implies that the monk failed in this duty!

In 664 Cuthbert was sent to the island of Lindisfarne to teach the monks there the rules of the holy life for they had grown careless and each followed his own will. Although he was resisted at first his patience and example won the monks over and they eventually returned to proper practice. His work in Lindisfarne completed, Cuthbert yearned for the solitary life and with the consent of his Abbot he withdrew to Farne Island to dedicate himself to prayer and contemplation. However, duty called again and in 684 he was made Bishop of Lindisfarne. He travelled far afield in that capacity, serving his flock tirelessly but eventually with advancing age he was allowed to resign his office and return to Farne Island where he eventually died, much loved and venerated by all. His body was brought back to Lindisfarne where for 11 years it was left in its coffin in the church so that the people might pay their respects. After that time the monks wished to transfer his bones to a specially built tomb near the high altar but when they opened the coffin they fell to their knees in astonishment. The saint lay as if asleep, his body uncorrupted, and all the funeral vestments in which he had been wrapped were still fresh.

Two hundred years later the monks at Lindisfarne had to flee from their island as Vikings attacked the northern coasts. They carried the body of Cuthbert and his relics with them and these they took first to Ripon and then to Durham where in 1104 Cuthbert's body was placed in the new cathedral where his relics are still kept today. According to Simeon the Chronicler, even though the saint had died more than four hundred years previously, his body still bore the semblance of life.

There was also found in the coffin a copy of the Gospel of St John and this is supposed to be the oldest Western book that still keeps its original leather binding.

This is just one of twenty three stories in The Book of Saints and Heroes. There was a time when all children would have been brought up with tales about such inspiring figures as these, either in literary form or else told as stories by their grandmothers or other older relatives and teachers. It's a sad time when the young are denied access to examples of spiritual heroes whom they might be inspired to emulate or, if not that, then at least know that there are such people in the world.

Note 1: When my 11 year old son saw the picture here he commented "That looks like Gandalf" at which I thought "Maybe it was, or his equivalent."

Note 2: Regarding the uncorrupted state of Cuthbert's body, if I was asked if I believed in that I would have to say yes. The resurrection of Christ proves that the inner spirit can master the outer body and I don't see why a soul of sufficient purity and holiness might not have a body that reflected that. There are too many accounts in spiritual history just to discount this as a pious fiction.

ST DUNSTAN (WW)

The saints are men and women sent by God to call human beings back to him. They are all very different but united in a love of God that is not just felt but is all-consuming in their lives. There are no better patterns for humanity and it is a woeful age that does not recognize this.

In the previous chapter I wrote about a Northern saint so this time I will choose one from the South. I have a fondness for early saints who lived at a time when Christianity was fresh and vital and who also manifested or had manifested in their lives rather more of the supernatural than many who came after so my chosen saint comes from a thousand years ago. Once again, I am going to use as my main source The Book of Saints and Heroes by Mrs Lang because I think this captures the aura of saintliness better than many more academic studies, which can tend to the intellectual, or overtly religious ones, which can tend to the sentimental. Presumably Mrs Lang was a practicing Christian but she seems more concerned with the holiness of her subjects than using them as a means to proselytise. As she tells the stories of these saints, it is the true love of Christ and utter dedication to his work that is their distinguishing feature.

Dunstan was born in Glastonbury around 910 when King Athelstan was the ruler of Wessex which at the time comprised most of the South West of England. An auspicious event took place just before his birth when all the candles held by the congregation during a service at Candlemas went out, but then the one held by his mother was miraculously re-lit by a tongue of fire descending from heaven. The story, even if apocryphal, is charming. What better way could there be to announce the coming of a saintly child?

Dunstan's parents were noble and he was given a good education by the Irish monks of the local monastery. He studied the Bible, naturally, but also the Latin poets and historians, and English ones too such as Caedmon, the 7th century Northumbrian poet. He learnt music, becoming an excellent harpist, arithmetic and geometry and also something of the stars. Practical matters were not neglected and he was taught how to design vestments for the priests and metalwork, making crosses and other items for church use. As late as the 13th century, there still existed bells made by Dunstan in the church at Abingdon.

All in all, he had the best and most rounded education you could at that time and I dare say it wouldn't be too bad nowadays either, though naturally a little limited as regards the sciences. Eventually Dunstan was taken to live with the King at his palace but his talents and intelligence aroused jealousy amongst the courtiers and he found himself accused of witchcraft and condemned to a test of innocence known as the ordeal of cold water. This was one of the milder tests of the time but even so the victim was thrown into a pond (or cesspool some accounts say) to see if he would sink or swim. Dunstan survived the ordeal and his life was spared but he was exiled from the court anyway so went to Winchester where he sought refuge with the Bishop who was his uncle.

After some time, the bishop had him ordained priest and he was sent abroad to a Benedictine monastery to study. When he returned to England he had clearly become something of a fanatic for he built himself a tiny cell too small even to stand up in and resolved to spend the rest of his life there, contemplating God. He fasted to excess and it may be this that gave him visions of the devil who mocked and tempted him so much while he was at his devotions that eventually an exasperated Dunstan seized the devil by the nose with a pair of tongs and sent him on his way. This may sound like another apocryphal story but it is a fact that those who seriously set their feet on the spiritual path are the subject of attack by dark forces who seek to derail their attempts to come closer to God. Nowadays this may not take such an obvious form, so no need to buy a set of tongs just yet, but nonetheless it still exists.

Though Dunstan's intentions were undoubtedly sincere this was not a healthy way of life to sustain for very long. It is not untypical for a spiritual neophyte who is trying to take the Kingdom of Heaven by storm to become a little fanatical but growing experience should bring one to the realisation that a more balanced approach brings better results in the long term. Luckily for Dunstan, in a story reminiscent of one from the life of the Buddha, who was similarly saved from excess by a young girl who gave him some milk when he had fasted almost to death, a lady of the court persuaded him that it was his spiritual duty to help others rather than concentrate entirely on himself.

While still a young man Dunstan was appointed abbot of Glastonbury. He also came into great wealth as a result of some inheritances, and he used this to develop the abbey, building a new church and drawing up a set of rules for the monks based on that of the Benedictine order. Once again, he became so respected for his wisdom and intelligence that his advice was sought by King Edmund and then, after Edmund's assassination, by Edred his successor. But when the 15 year old Edwig came to the throne Dunstan fell out of favour and was obliged to flee to Flanders before being summoned back when Edwig's brother, Edgar, became King of Mercia.

Dunstan was now held in such high regard that when the incumbent Archbishop of Canterbury died he was made Primate of England. He used his power and influence with the king to bring about many reforms, both spiritual and temporal. Monks were encouraged to dedicate themselves properly to the holy life, something that had not always been the case at a time when becoming a monk was often used as an excuse for an easy life of indolence, simony (buying and selling of ecclesiastical privilege) was outlawed and so was the nepotism that had been rife amongst the clerical community. Dunstan also ensured that the poor were able to seek justice before the king, and that copies of the Bible were written and placed in the churches so that priests could more properly teach their congregations the facts of the Christian religion. He even required the king, as an act of penance, not to wear his crown for seven years and the king actually submitted to this, such was his respect for the archbishop. At the end of this time Dunstan devised a new coronation for the king and the form this took is still the basic pattern for the coronation of British monarchs today.

After Edgar's death Dunstan's influence at court waned and he retired to Canterbury to spend his time in prayer and good works of a more mundane nature. He built churches and set up schools, worked to improve the lot of widows and orphans and practised the crafts in which he had always shown great skill. He made bells and organs and illuminated manuscripts. Overleaf is an example of what may be his work from the Glastonbury Classbook now held in the Bodleian Library. But on the eve of Ascension Day 988 he was told by angels in a heavenly vision that he had just three days left to live, and to prepare for his passing. Sure enough, three days later Dunstan died. He had served numerous kings and had contributed much to the wise running of the country. Unlike many saints, he lived his life in the public eye, making laws for the good of the Church, trying to heal division, reform religious practice and bring together the warring English factions of the time. His is not a life like Cuthbert's, filled with miracles and wonders and largely devoted to contemplation, but one lived serving God in the outer world just as the lady who had persuaded him to leave his cell when he was still a young man had suggested he should. There is room for both sorts of saint.

An image of Christ. The monk at bottom right has been identified from the inscription as Dunstan and the whole drawing may be by him too.

TWO MODERN SAINTS (WW)

John Fitzgerald writes in his piece about the Inklings that "the body of work left behind by the Inklings has helped re-mythologise the world and baptise the contemporary imagination". This set me thinking. I haven't read much by any of the other Inklings and I hadn't even heard of them when growing up, but that sentence sums up the effect that Tolkien and CS Lewis had on me as a child. I'm sure they had a similar effect on countless others too. Indeed, I sometimes think that without them (and a few others but them principally), children growing up in the mid to late 20th century would have been left almost completely spiritually bereft. Most of us had very little exposure to real spiritual truths and what we did have seemed formal and remote. But the stories of these two writers brought the spiritual world alive and, importantly, did so in a way that not only opened up the imagination but was also Christian. The world was re-enchanted and done so in the light of Christ.

Modern Christianity often seems like a fire that has burnt itself out. Whether that is because of the paucity of real saints (saints are the lifeblood of any religion) or because it has lost touch with its roots or because it has become infected with social and political ideologies or because it is now more concerned with the letter than the spirit or because it has desacralized itself or because it frequently denies the truth and power of its own mythology and symbolism or because it has severed its connection with the imagination or because it focuses too much on this world and not enough on the next, is almost beside the point. (Actually, all these things are linked). The fact is it has lost its glowing and full-bodied colours of yore, its sense of being lit from within, and become a black and white thing of two dimensions. And with its truth attacked from the outside and its vitality sapped from within, as well as a tendency to accommodate itself to what is trying to destroy it, it is now in many ways a faint shadow of its former self.

But, as John Fitzgerald pointed out, Tolkien and CS Lewis helped revive Christianity by re-establishing it in the world of the imagination. The former covertly, the latter more obviously but they both did it and they did it in a way that many people either didn't notice or didn't much care about if they did, thus getting beneath the prejudices instilled in the modern mind. Furthermore, they brought back a sense of Tradition which after the Second World War appeared to have been completely abandoned by all the clever people intent on building their soulless world of modernity. I mean by Tradition a connection to real things, both natural and spiritual, that humanity had established over centuries but which was in danger of being swept away by those, more or less the entirety of the intelligentsia in the West, who preferred ideology to truth.

Running parallel to this idea of the restoration of poetry and imagination to religion was something else. Both Tolkien and Lewis recognized the reality of evil and taught the necessity of fighting it. In a way that's what their books were all about. At the time, they were writing even many Christians were embarrassed by the idea of the devil, preferring to see good and evil in terms of psychological principles. But our two writers knew better and in this, as in many other ways, they were prophets. Now, anyone who is serious about trying to understand the spiritual world knows that dark forces, demons, call them what you like, exist and have tremendous power in this world which must be resisted. They cannot be compromised with. The best way to fight them is through handing oneself over to God and doing his will but this is not a passive thing as it was not for Gandalf or Frodo or any of the sons and daughters of Adam sent into Narnia to help restore it when things were going badly. It requires trust and hope and love of the good, and soldiering on doing one's duty as Frodo and Sam did even when all seemed lost. Pacifists don't fight and they don't win either. Obviously, I'm not saying that one should never turn the other cheek but resist not evil does not mean giving way to it.

I said they were prophets. Much of what Tolkien and Lewis wrote can be seen to apply to the present-day demonic assault on mankind. I'm thinking of Saruman and the Scouring of the Shire, already started in Tolkien's day but now everywhere and seemingly irreversible, or even the whole of The Lord of the Rings, and, in particular, The Last Battle and That Hideous Strength. The Ring can be many things but it is certainly not inappropriate to relate it to modern computer technology which gives us great power but at what inner cost? I also regard the depiction of a small band of men and women of true hearts and good will working with the inner powers against the demonically inspired forces of a corrupt Establishment, as depicted in That Hideous Strength, to have more than a touch of truth to it.

I mentioned to Bruce Charlton that these men were probably saints but that they, especially Tolkien, would almost certainly reject that title and look with extreme displeasure on any fool who gave it to them. Well, they're not here to do so and I don't suppose they care from where they are now. But if saints are those who faithfully carry out the will of God and work for him on this Earth then I don't see why not. These two men performed a great work and are surely responsible for bringing many people to, and, just as important, keeping them in, the way of Christ over the last half century or so. They re-illuminated a light that was in danger of going out and did so in a way that inspired millions. In their stories, and Lewis's religious writings, they not only provided lifeboats for sensitive souls drowning in a sea of atheistic materialism, they also gave us spiritual weapons to fight ignorance and evil. My young son said to me a few years ago that The Lord of the Rings seemed more real than reality, and of course it is because it better reflects the truth in reality than what passes for reality in this world now.

IS ALBION AN ANGEL? (WW)

Bruce Charlton's speculation that Albion might be a woman got me thinking. I confess I hadn't been considering the question along those lines. Not just about whether Albion is male or female but about the degree to which he or she is actually a person. I know the personification of Albion in Blake's poems but that's, well, Blake! I also know the mythology of a sleeping giant but I had really been thinking of Albion as the hidden spirit of the land, without making that spirit into a person.

But, of course, all countries do traditionally have a masculine or feminine ruling genius. Germany is the Fatherland, India is Mother India, France is definitely feminine, Italy probably masculine. England seems masculine to me too, and I'm not sure about the U.S.A. Since Russia, as Bruce says, is feminine then maybe America is masculine. California is surely feminine, though.

In the same way, the North and the West are masculine while the South and the East are feminine. Sea is feminine, sky is masculine and, while we're at it, earth and water are feminine while air and fire are masculine. So probably everything does have a masculine or feminine polarity. That would make a lot of sense since this polarity goes right back to the primal duality of spirt and matter.

But is Albion a woman? I don't know. Bruce points out that Britannia is female and also that the two monarchs at the time of England's/Britain's greatest moments of creativity and power were queens. These could certainly be good indicators of a strong female characteristic of the country but personally I'm not convinced. English and British achievements, to do with law, exploration, empire, expansion and so on, do seem masculine to me but maybe that's England/Great Britain, and Albion is a different matter. Albion is certainly strongly associated with the land, and the land as ground or earth is traditionally a feminine thing.

So, I'm reserving judgment on this question. However, one idea I am strongly drawn to is that Albion is an angel. I think all countries have their guardian angels. Indeed, it is likely that all animal species have an angel. Angels are everywhere. They are the means through which God works.

To my mind, the best depiction of angels is that of C.S. Lewis in his space trilogy in which the angels are the guardians, or even spiritual embodiments, of the planets. These angels, like the Christian ones, don't have bodies as such because they are not made of matter. They are pure spirits but they can create an appearance of themselves in a person's mind, and Lewis's description of this is very striking. Here's what he says about an angel's face in Perelandra (The Bodley Head 1943).

> One single changeless expression - so clear that it hurt and dazzled him- was stamped on each and there was nothing else there at all. In that sense their faces were as primitive, as unnatural, if you like, as those of archaic statues from Aegina. Pure, spiritual intellectual love shot from their faces like barbed lightning. It was so unlike the love we experience that its expression could easily be mistaken for ferocity.

If Albion is, as I think, an angel then Albion is not a woman. Angels have no bodies so no biological gender hence they are not male or female. However, angels are not neuter. Nothing is. Lewis's angels are masculine or feminine and, of course, St Michael and St Gabriel are masculine too. Albion could be feminine, as Bruce speculates, but he could also be masculine and that would be my instinctive feeling.

THE LAND OF ALBION

THE OLD COUNTRY (WW)

In February 1985 I returned to England after five years away living in India. In those days of my relative youth five years felt a lot longer than they do today. Now they don't seem much at all. But back then it seemed an age since I had last been in England and, as I travelled west from London to my parents' house, the countryside appeared quite new. It was early morning. The sun had just risen and there was a thickish frost lying on the ground. You can imagine the contrast to the heat and strong colours of the subcontinent. Part of me did feel as though I had come home but, on another level, it was as if I had entered a magical kingdom, one that was familiar yet otherworldly. The dawn sunlight on the frosty fields added to that feeling and so did the fact that since I had left England my parents had moved from the suburbs of London to an 18th century house in Wiltshire so what I was seeing now as we drove through the country really was different to what I had left. It was England but not the one I had known. A rural rather than urban place with very little of the artificiality and dead soul quality of the modern environment. There is a timeless quality to the Wiltshire countryside, and one can quite easily imagine it as it was in prehistoric or Neolithic times.

This was a feeling I was often to have over the next month. I had no immediate plans so, while I was sorting out what to do, I stayed with my parents in their house which was just outside the small town of Calne. This is very close to a number of ancient English sites of which the best known is Avebury around 8 miles away. Avebury is part of a complex that includes Silbury Hill and West Kennet Long Barrow, and I have visited these places many times since then. They are tourist sites now but they still have a strangeness that speaks of a different sort of consciousness to the one possessed by 20th and 21st century man. We struggle to define it but it was probably based on a sense of the immanence of nature. Nature to early human beings was alive. There were spirits in everything and the whole world was perceived as a manifestation of creative energy. Whether they had an idea of a transcendent Creator is another matter. Probably they did, and he was perhaps associated with the sun, but I imagine their principal spiritual focus was on the spirits they could perceive in some way in the natural world. I have the idea that at festivals these spirits would appear more fully to them, drawn by the concentrated group aspiration of the tribe. Avebury was obviously a major centre for this kind of spirit worship, though communion might be a better way of describing what went on, and it is not mere fancy to claim that one can still detect distant echoes of this at the site. The rough and weathered stones perhaps carry within them a memory of the remote past that a sympathetic imagination can respond to.

This all took place a long time ago. Human consciousness has moved on since then as our sense of a personal self has crystallised and we have a more intellectual approach to reality. This is both a loss and a gain. The loss can be keenly felt by the sensitive soul and we are reminded of it when we visit sites like Avebury. We have lost the sense of participation in nature, the felt sense of oneness. But this loss is also a gain as we become more active agents in life. This has been the path followed over the last few thousand years and it has reached something like a peak today which explains, in part, the widespread feelings of alienation. Now we have the task of moving into a new consciousness that combines the best of both worlds, an active rather than a passive union with life in which both individuality and oneness are preserved and, in fact, made stronger. We cannot retreat to the past though many try to. We cannot rest in the present though most of us appear to want to do so. We must forge ahead into the future which requires fully embracing a spiritual world view, preferably focused on Christ who is the best exemplar of the higher state, while retaining the fruits of our developed individuality and mind. This will eventually make us full participants in life and even co-creators with God.

In Wiltshire, and no doubt elsewhere but it is powerfully felt here, there remains a strong sense of the old country and the old ways. We can be inspired by this, refreshed by it in the godless world of today, but we should not try to recapture it as it was then. Life moves on and the law of life is growth. It would be just as mistaken to try to go back to the early days of human consciousness as it would be for a grown up to try to return to childhood. And yet we should also remember that "unless you change, and become as little children, you shall not enter into the kingdom of heaven". The future consciousness of man should build on the past but not imitate it. It must include but go beyond oneness with nature to reach a conscious sense of true spiritual understanding which is as different from the passive awareness of the past as the mind of Christ is to that of Adam. For Adam represents primeval man when he was one with creation, or part of it, but Christ demonstrates a true and fully self-conscious oneness with the Creator, an individual union with the Father in which the keynote is love.

BEACHY HEAD AND ALBION (WW)

The picture above shows the cover of a book but it's not the book I want to draw attention to. The picture is of Beachy Head lighthouse standing at the foot of the chalk cliffs on the Sussex coast of England near Eastbourne. I used to live in the nearby village of Meads and would regularly walk along the downs between Meads and Beachy Head, attracted by the calm and peaceful atmosphere of the place which was rather at odds with the cliff's sinister reputation. The springy grasslands and flinty chalk spoke of an England of the distant past, while the view of the sea from high up on the downs had something timeless about it. I would look across the waters, occasionally blue but more often tending to grey, and feel connected to a period long before history. For me, this was definitely a place where the veil between Albion and England was thin. But that's only one reason for drawing attention to this photograph.

Sometimes it's best not to try to interpret a symbol but just let it speak to the intuition without undue analysis. That way it feeds the imagination rather than the outer mind and this gives it greater meaning. However, on this occasion I would like to say a few words about why I consider this to be a suitable cover for a book about spiritual matters.

When you begin to wake up out of your materialistic slumber, if I can put it like that, you see that there are three basic levels to reality which are the physical, the psychic and the spiritual. You only start to understand the true nature of the world when you acknowledge this and learn to discriminate correctly between the various levels, seeing each in its proper place and not confusing one for the other as, in their different ways, the materialist and the New Age psychic both do. These three levels are shown in this picture by the land, the sea and the sky, otherwise earth, water and air. When we come to the limits of the physical world we find a new world, a world of imagination where thought can appear to take external form and form itself is malleable to the mind, but that is not the spiritual world though it may initially seem so to the unwary. The psychic plane, like the sea, teems with life of all descriptions. There is beauty and mystery. There are warm waters to bathe in and depths to explore but there are also sharks and even monsters. Like the sea, the psychic world is constantly moving, changing, reflecting images from above that disappear when you touch them, and, as with the sea, you have to learn to swim.

To find a more stable truth you need to go beyond the sea to the sky, beyond the psychic to the spiritual, but that requires an immense change in behaviour and attitude. It's relatively easy to go from land to sea and most of us can swim, to some degree at least. It's not so easy to get up into the sky, and even when we do learn to spread our wings and fly we still have to penetrate an intermediate zone, that of the clouds, clouds of darkness and clouds of illusion, which can only be dissipated by the heat of the sun. That is to say, by the divine fire of truth.

So, there are these three worlds of existence that are shown in this picture. There is also a lighthouse which we can say stands for guidance and illumination. It is a little bit of the sun come down to Earth. Normally a lighthouse warns ships to beware of rocks but this lighthouse, which we are seeing from the land rather than the sea, is fulfilling a different function. It is pointing up out of the sea into the sky and lighting the way clear to heaven. It is the beacon of spiritual tradition which is there to provide clear and reliable guidance. Nowadays, most of us completely ignore it but it is always there, available to anyone who wants to find the path that leads to the sky.

The one thing you can't see in this picture is the sun, though without it you wouldn't be able to see anything. That also has a meaning.

For me this picture is a true image of Albion. Albion is the white island and here we have both chalk cliffs and sea as well as a hint of the spiritual vastness to be encountered when one opens one's eyes to the vision of Albion and what lies beyond even that.

THE BRITISH MYTH (WW)

The notion of Albion Awakening is tied up with the so-called British myth as described by Geoffrey Ashe in his book Camelot and the Vision of Albion. This includes such ideas as the discovery of the Holy Grail and the return of King Arthur. Taking the second first, the well-known story is that Arthur did not die after his final battle against a treacherous usurper, a kind of Judas figure, but was spirited away to a realm somewhere between heaven and earth to be healed of his wounds prior to one day returning and leading his country to a new Golden Age. I suppose the parallels with Christ can't be helped but Arthur is also believed to have absorbed some characteristics from pagan and classical sources, notably the story of a deposed giant, sometimes associated with the Greek Titans, the gods before the gods, sometimes with Albion himself, who lies slumbering on an island in the far West.

The Holy Grail is more mysterious. Was it the cup used at the Last Supper and therefore symbolically or even literally the container of Christ's blood? This is how it is usually presented but it has antecedents in a Celtic cauldron which had the power to bring dead men back to life. It is a feminine symbol and therefore associated with new birth, in this case spiritual. It is also a receiver of the spiritual life force which is why most of the stories that surround it insist on the purity demanded of anyone who would see it and benefit from its virtue. Its loss has led to the desolation of the natural and spiritual worlds as experienced by human beings ever since. Its rediscovery by the worthy leads to spiritual transformation.

Nowadays King Arthur is seen as a legendary figure built up from a composite of real and imagined sources. In his origins he's not even a king, just a war leader who may have won an important battle against the Saxons and perhaps held them at bay long enough for them to have become more Christianised when they eventually did conquer the country. Clearly a real dark age Arthur would have been something like this. But the Arthur of the imagination is not like this at all. He is a far grander and more noble figure. The trouble is that by reducing Arthur to history we lose contact with the imaginative version and with the power of that version to inspire. But the historical version is the true one, you might say. Is it? True in one sense, of course. However, the Arthur of the imagination is also true and perhaps it is true in a more profound way just as, for example, The Lord of the Rings is truer than practically any 20th century novel set in the real world you might care to name.

It's the same with the Holy Grail. The more you reduce this to an actual cup or physical object the more you diminish its ability to kindle the imagination and open it up to new ways of being though the association with Jesus would always have a magical effect of some sort. But what we require so badly now is something that connects us to a higher level of reality, something that shows us that our everyday mode of consciousness actually restricts the amount of truth we can receive. We don't need change. We need transformation. This means we need something which shows us that our current way of life is so false and so wrong on every conceivable level that it must be rejected utterly. It just cannot fit into a new way of being. It must be left behind.

The mystery of the Holy Grail is that only the worthy can see it. To be worthy is to be pure and very few are sufficiently pure. But all are called to this purity because it is our true state. We really are holy beings in potential. All men and women are manifestations of the divine but we are so in seed form only and often that seed fails to grow as it should.

Transformation is tough to put it mildly. At the same time, it is the path we are called to take and what we need to do is essentially quite simple. We just have to take up the cross which means renounce our worldly self and be prepared to accept the suffering that will inevitably incur and follow Christ. The rewards will almost certainly not be discernible in this life but the spiritual path is about the life in the world to come and that is what our eyes should be fixed on.

Perhaps when the symbolism behind the story is opened up this is what the British myth is all about. The transformation of natural man through spiritual rebirth.

ALBION SET APART (WW)

For those who believe in God everything in the world is a sign pointing to him and the way he works. It's a fallen world so not everything is a perfect sign but still we can read symbolic significance into nature and its parts. The four elements obviously have symbolic value and are a clue to something beyond themselves, and the same is true for the sun and the moon, the wind, the sea, the eagle, the lion and so much else. Creation is a book which when you learn how to read it points straight at its Creator and gives you an insight into his mind.

With that thought might we consider that the physical position of countries has some bearing on the role they are intended to play? Before I try to answer that let me say that I do believe many countries have divine destinies. Perhaps all countries do to a certain extent but some do to a large extent. Their role is to bring something new into the world, an attitude to life, a mode of relating to the world, focus on a particular divine characteristic, even a quality of consciousness. We can think of Indian metaphysics, Egyptian religion, Greek philosophy, Italian art and those are just some of the more obvious examples which don't exclude the contribution of other countries and cultures in those fields. Seemingly at certain historic periods a group of souls in a particular place acts as a kind of conduit between this world and the higher ones and grounds qualities of truth that take humanity as a whole forwards.

So, does the fact that Great Britain is detached from Europe (you could say in it but not of it) and at the far west of the continent mean anything? Was it meant to be a land set apart, in some sense a country not quite of this world? It has not been much like that for the last 2,000 years since the Roman conquest brought it into the wider world but there are grounds for thinking it was perceived along those lines in classical times. It was supposed to be where the druids had their most important sanctuaries and a mysterious island hidden behind gleaming white cliffs. It was just beyond the known world and had the aura of somewhere rather strange and enigmatic.

You might point out that Albion may have been perceived as otherworldly from the outside but life for its inhabitants would presumably have been more or less the same as life anywhere else. Perhaps, but I remember as a boy reading a book called Guardians of the Forest by J.E. Hood, an author of whom I've not heard elsewhere.

The book was about the first Roman invasion of Britain by Julius Caesar and the country it depicted was slightly magical, almost as if there was still a connection to non-physical realms that had been lost in more civilized parts of the world. The otherworld could sometimes be glimpsed just behind this one. Some spiritual teachings describe a gradual hardening of the environment over time as the world becomes more material and primitive contact with higher dimensions is lost. The Guardians of the book's title are people who still have something of that contact which gives them, amongst other things, a benign power over animals. They protect the country and succeed in driving the Romans out though, of course, it is only a temporary victory. The Guardians know they are the last of their kind and that they will soon disappear. Their role as custodians of the land is nearly over. The modern world is arriving.

What I am saying is that it is possible that Britain's physical location has some significance. The country has a purpose that requires it to be in some degree isolated. This would explain the fact that many people who want Britain to leave the EU can't really define their reasons in a straightforward pragmatic/rationalistic way. A lot of them know that economically Great Britain might be worse off but still there is this sense of needing to separate the country from something that is antithetical to its destiny. It is intuition that tells us this. The people who favour Britain remaining in the EU often lack this imaginative connection to something deeper than the material world. They cannot understand it and when they suspect its presence they may dislike it and try to tar it with the brush of stupidity, ignorance or prejudice. On occasion they might be right but underneath all that there is something else which is the knowledge that Albion has a mission and that mission requires it to be true to itself.

Sometimes when I have travelled in certain parts of Britain I have felt this connection to the otherworld. This is particularly the case in the West Country and the Highlands of Scotland though I am not saying it is restricted to those places. That is just my experience. Nor am I saying it is restricted to Great Britain. Of course it's not. Everywhere has places like that. But when we talk of Albion this is what we mean. A connection to higher dimensions of being within the country. And it is by aligning ourselves with the spirit behind these places that we can help to bring Albion back into the outer world. Reawaken the sleeping Arthur you might say.

Countries are real. Albion is real and it has a part to play. Some of the nature of its role is indicated by its geographical location and it is up to its inhabitants to look within themselves and also within their land for a way in which they can help Albion come into expression and give the world the gift it has to offer. This is no call to a shallow nationalism, other countries have their own tasks, possibly the supreme example being ancient Israel, but there is a reason for the fact that Albion has been slightly set apart. It is the trustee of something precious which it has a duty to protect and uphold and then bring out into the world for the benefit of all.

(This essay previously appeared in The Spiritual Crisis of Modern Man.)

PILGRIMAGE (WW)

Nowadays most people in the Western world expect to have at least one holiday a year but wouldn't it be a good thing if we thought about making a pilgrimage sometimes too? After all, if the mind and body need to be refreshed perhaps the spirit does as well. This needn't be a dramatic affair but it should require a little effort and sacrifice on our part, and it ought to be made with the right attitude which is reverence mixed with aspiration.

In the past people went on pilgrimages to renew a connection to God which, even when it exists, is often weakened during the rough and tumble of everyday existence in the material world. They went to absorb holy influences from a recognised sacred site, sacred either by association with a saint or just in itself because of the spiritual power to be sensed there, and they also went as an act of penance or contrition. They went too to give thanks to their Maker. All these motives help to revive the sagging spiritual impulse. A pilgrimage can also be thought of as an externalisation of the inner spiritual journey and so aid and strengthen one for that task since, by being something anyone can do physically, it is rather easier to accomplish. It should not be taken as a substitute for the need to make that inner journey but it can be used as a support and inspiration for it.

The effort involved in reaching a place is an important part of any pilgrimage. If you simply turn up at a holy site having driven there in comfort you are not going to reap the same spiritual benefit as you might if your journey had been more arduous and required real effort, even a degree of hardship. This is why some people made all or part of their journey barefoot or even on their knees. When I lived in India I noticed that many people would shave their heads when going on a pilgrimage. Some would fast as well or take a temporary vow of celibacy. Of course, this can be taken to excess and the actual pain or deprivation involved be seen as a virtue in itself which is a mistake. But if it is seen symbolically and as a gesture of penitence and humility then there is a point to it and it can be spiritually constructive. We recognise that we must approach God emptied of self and without any preconditions on our part, and although the ideal is to do this on a mental level, that is hard and to do it physically is a step in the right direction. It's a reasonable substitute that sets the mind on the right course. Physical privation or hardship is not on its own going to make you a more spiritual person, any more than poverty can, but the acceptance of it can assist in turning around the worldly self and helping it submit to true spiritual values.

It is well known that Christianity didn't just set up its own brand new holy places but adapted them from former pagan sites, effectively baptising an already holy place. Now this could have been for two reasons. One, the people accepted that site as holy so it was easier just to put it under new management. The already existing sacred aura of the place could simply be converted to Christian usage. It merely required rededicating to Christ or the Virgin Mary or a saint and cleansed of any lingering potential defilement by the appropriate rites. But I think there is another reason too. Some places really are more sacred than others. If we think of the Earth as a body with lines of what, for want of a better phrase, we can call psychic energy running all over it we can understand that there are certain nexus points where that energy is concentrated and where it may take on a particular quality. These are also places where, given the right conditions and receptivity on the part of the visitor, the veil between this world and the next can be thinner than elsewhere. Such localities are well suited to adaptation for worship and pilgrimage.

Britain has several pilgrimage sites, some very well known. Canterbury, Glastonbury and Walsingham come to mind as sacred places where a strong Christian influence has persisted for centuries. Lindisfarne and Iona are holy islands which are probably nexus points as described above but have also benefitted from the presence of saints, Cuthbert and Columba respectively, and from the veneration afforded these saints by their followers. This is actually an interesting point. The presence of true spiritual aspirants can add to the sanctity of a place or at least enable it to come out. If people come in a spirit of devotion and reverence they can both receive and give. They can receive the spiritual virtue of the site but they can also contribute to building that up by the quality of the feelings and motives they bring with them. If their hearts are pure and properly directed to goodness and truth they can, as it were, feed the atmosphere. But the reverse is also true and present day Glastonbury is an unfortunate example of this. If people come to take and with unworthy motives then they can suck all the good atmosphere out of a place, driving its virtue underground.

Glastonbury is certainly a holy place which means it has a powerful energy. Regrettably this attracts all sorts of types including those who just wish to feed off that energy, and these people corrupt the atmosphere through their desire to appropriate the energy without being worthy of it or able to live up to its quality. That is why, ideally, all holy places should be guarded or protected from the profane by a dedicated priesthood or something of that nature. If you wish to enter a sacred place or space you must make yourself worthy of that. Everybody, both pagan and Christian, understood that very well until recently.

In a sense, then, pilgrimage might be considered as a symbol of the return to God. That is a long journey, though, and, as one of the outer supports to treading the inner path, a physical pilgrimage can be of great value for it not only brings that inner journey into focus but it can also inspire and revitalise us for the road ahead.

DOORWAYS TO ALBION (WW)

I suggested to John Fitzgerald in a comment on the Albion Besieged post (see below) that it might be a good idea to do a little series on places where the spirit of Albion seems particularly strong. I believe it is through landscape that we can best enter into Albion though poetry and myth are also good avenues of approach. There are many and varied aspects to Albion and the different landscapes show different sides to the archetype, some wild, some mysterious, some peaceful and so on. There is no single description which can encompass the whole of what this idea is. And while some of these places are completely natural, some are part-shaped by man.

Anyway, with that in mind, here are a few pictures of places I associate with Albion. Meditation on these images or, better, a visit to them can bring one into contact with a spiritual quality that we associate with the idea of Albion. One should add that traditionally guardian angels exist in many places, both national and regional. As we have suggested, Albion is the guardian angel of England and perhaps the whole of Britain, but other places have their own angels. Though under the overall rulership of Albion, there will be many more local angels with their own special qualities.

Let's start with the Seven Sisters, the white cliffs of Sussex.

Image from Wikimedia Commons

The origin of the name Albion is not known for certain but one suggestion is that it is linked to the Proto-Indo-European word for white (albho-) and so could refer to the chalk cliffs on the south of the island. These cliffs date back to the late Cretaceous period which was between 60 and 100 million years ago and were formed when microscopic skeletons of plankton that had drifted down to the seabed were transformed into rock by the dual processes of heat and pressure. But another more esoteric interpretation could be that Britain was the White Island in a spiritual sense, a haven set apart where the gods walked in a kind of dream time of the archaic past. Pure speculation, perhaps, but carrying a poetic resonance that seems not out of place when you walk along these cliffs which lead eastwards to the equally powerful site at Beachy Head. Is this a major entry point to the island of Albion? When you consider that Pevensey Bay, where William the Conqueror landed in 1066 and where, around 600 hundred years before him, invading Saxons attacked these shores, is just down the road, the idea is not so fanciful.

Tintagel (Wikimedia Commons)

More sea and cliffs but of a very different, much wilder sort. This is Tintagel on the Cornish Atlantic coast, now inevitably a big tourist destination but at one time sufficiently out of the way to attract few visitors and therefore retain much of its mystery, though that could be said of many sites around the coasts of Cornwall. But the association of Tintagel with King Arthur can't be ignored in any overview of places significant to Albion. Even setting aside the doubts over his actual existence, Arthur was never really a king of England. He was, and perhaps still is, the king in Albion. He inhabits the land of imagination that lies between this world and the next and, as such, he carries in his mythic personality a link to Albion that all places associated with him pick up on. Tintagel's physical connection to Arthur may be tenuous but in the magical world of imagination and vision, that is not so important. If the stories are believed in, they become real in a mythical sense and the association is then valid.

Avebury Stones (Wikimedia Commons)

A Stone at Avebury

Silbury Hill (Wikimedia Commons)

Here are pictures of some of the stones at Avebury including a close-up showing their wonderful weathered antiquity, and of Silbury Hill. They are near each other in the county of Wiltshire, and are presumably part of the same religious complex or sacred landscape.

Avebury consists of an outer henge (a henge being a circular embankment of earth with an internal ditch which you can see in the photo on page 146) which contains a large stone circle of about 100 stones (not all of which have survived) within which are two smaller stone circles. Its construction and expansion spanned the 600 years between 2,800 BC and 2,200 BC, a long period of time which tells us that this site was once of great spiritual significance. I think it also tells us of a community that was highly developed in a way that may not make much sense to 21st century materialists but should not be dismissed on that account. To walk around Avebury with one's imagination sympathetically engaged can open the inner mind up to feelings and ideas that have slipped far below the threshold of consciousness in modern man. An awareness of the sacred quality of the land and an insight into the oneness of earth, sky and human soul can be felt if one suspends the strictly rationalist attitude. This largely passive awareness is not one we should seek to fall back into completely, but we can be inspired by it to move beyond our limited form of self-consciousness to something higher and more in keeping with our divine origins.

Silbury Hill, which was built around 2,400 BC, is the largest prehistoric man-made mound in Europe but its purpose is not known. There doesn't seem to be a burial inside so one is free to speculate. Is it a crude pyramid, an astronomical site, a temple that brings one closer to the gods as one ascends to the top? You can't climb the hill now because of the damage hundreds of pounding feet would cause but years ago you were allowed to and I remember walking up and feeling quite elated on reaching the summit even though it's not that high. The land around is fairly flat so the views are extensive but the most dramatic sensation at the top comes from experiencing the vastness of the sky which comes into greater prominence when one is part removed from the earth. For early man, unused to any great heights, it must have been awe-inspiring in the true meaning of that over-used phrase.

The entrance to West Kennet Long Barrow (Wikimedia Commons)

Just over the way from Silbury Hill is West Kennet Long Barrow which is a burial site. It dates back to 3,600 BC and there were up to 50 people buried here though the inner chambers must have been used, presumably as a place of ritual, over a very long period of time since the tomb was not sealed until around 2,500 BC. If Silbury Hill opens one up to the sense of the infinite then this place, which is effectively a cave, takes one in the other direction, deep inside oneself. These are the two principal religious experiences that our forefathers would have known and their constructions were probably aimed at stimulating them. They can be related to height and depth, and associated with Father and Mother, the two parents of Creation.

Wiltshire is a county that still seems to speak of the Neolithic period in many ways. Not only does it contain a host of structures from that time, Stonehenge being the best known, but the landscape itself, while clearly very changed, retains a strong connection to the past. Many walks have convinced me that the communities that lived here thousands of years ago have left a mark on the land that has endured down through the ages. Were they in touch with Albion in a way we cannot comprehend now? Did they actually live in Albion?

Cherhill White Horse (photo by MacFodder)

The Cherhill White Horse near Calne was only cut out of the chalk in the 18th century but it harks back to something considerably older. The hill itself is like a natural amphitheatre. For our ancestors, aspects of the landscape would have spoken of spiritual realities, actual beings associated with the place. They would have sought their good will and protection and attempted to avail themselves of their powers, sometimes through offerings and sometimes through adapting the landscape to bring out and focus more fully its inherent qualities. Until relatively recently the link between a land and the people who lived on it was almost familial.

CHRISTIAN ALBION (WW)

The last chapter contained a lot of pagan Albion and there's a lot more, enough to fill a large book or even several. But I want to move on to Christian sites because I think that Christianity in England was a little different to elsewhere and some of that is down to the Albion influence which I shall leave mostly undefined. The impression I get, though, is that medieval English Christianity, or some aspects of it, owed a good deal to an affinity with Nature especially as manifested by some of the early Celtic saints who, in turn, may have got this as a legacy from prehistoric native religions such as the one that would have been practised at Avebury. These earlier traditions were purified and baptised by Christ but the good in them survived as a strain in the new Christianity.

The story of Christ's visit to these shores as a young man is usually dismissed as legend. But I find it much more convincing than the other stories that he travelled to the East and received some kind of mystical training in India. That makes no sense whatsoever. There is nothing of Eastern religion in Christ's teaching. He was a Jew, speaking squarely from within the Jewish tradition. But the idea that he came to England with his uncle, Joseph of Arimathea, is not beyond the bounds of possibility. Which doesn't make it true, of course, but it would fit in with our sense of there being something of deep spiritual significance locked up in the heart of this island. Perhaps this story is best left as a legend which has its own power and ability to inspire on the level of the imagination. But maybe.....

How can one write of Albion without mentioning Glastonbury? It's a sad fact that anything pure and holy will inevitably come under attack from demonic powers, and this is surely true of Glastonbury from the destruction of the abbey during the dissolution of the monasteries in the 16th century to New Age tourism and the present-day association of the name with a music festival that celebrates the complete separation of the instinctual from the spiritual thus facilitating falling below the rational self instead of rising above it. But, despite all these depredations, the ruined abbey still retains something of its ancient peace and sanctity. Whenever I have visited it there has seemed to be a kind of clarity in the air as though some light from higher worlds was filtering through into this one. I don't doubt that where men and women have lived lives dedicated to prayer and holiness that affects the quality of the location, and when that location is one of the Earth's sacred spots in its own right, the effect is magnified.

Glastonbury Abbey (Wikimedia Commons)

Just down the road from Glastonbury is the city of Wells. Wells is not very big but it is a city because it has a cathedral. This is the seat of the bishop of Bath and Wells, and it was built between 1175 and 1490, though there had been a church there since the 8th century. As Gothic cathedrals go, it is not that large but its most striking feature certainly is. This is the West Front which is 100 feet high and 147 feet wide. It is a stupendous sight now but would have been even more dramatic in the Middle Ages when the many beautifully carved life-size figures illustrating the Christian story were all painted in bright colours. For people at the time this would have been like a trip to the cinema, telling stories from the Bible with many different characters represented, Old and New Testaments both included.

The West Front (courtesy of Wells Cathedral)

Forgive me for including another ruin. But ruins have long been recognised as something deeply evocative. They are not just broken buildings but seem, by the fact of their physical destruction, to allow something of the spiritual essence behind the outer form to be made manifest. This is especially true of religious buildings. There is also the sense of how time consumes everything, even the most durable of substances. A ruin, through its reminder of the transient nature of things, speaks of eternity on a higher level.

Fountains Abbey (Wikimedia Commons)

This is Fountains Abbey in Yorkshire, a Cistercian monastery founded in 1132 by monks seeking a remote site to practise a more devout way of life than had been possible for them in the city of York. That's part of a common pattern in which those wishing to lead a contemplative life remove themselves from centres of worldly distraction. A criticism is that they can escape from the world outside but not the world within which will be with them wherever they go. While admitting the truth of this, it is equally true that there are helpful and unhelpful atmospheres in which to pursue the spiritual life and you are much better off seeking an environment which best reflects the inner state you wish to cultivate or, at any rate, does not actively work against it. That is also why those who would take the spiritual path seriously are advised to seek the company of like-minded souls and avoid worldly associations. This is not always possible and sometimes the opposite is required. After all, Jesus was criticised for mixing with sinners but then he was Jesus.

Fountains is Britain's largest monastic ruin. The abbey was rich at one time, mainly from trading in wool, a major source of medieval England's wealth. But, like Glastonbury, it fell to that act of national vandalism which was the dissolution of the monasteries, surely a time when the anti-Albion forces were let loose and given their head. Whatever the abuses that may have existed in the religious world, for a nation to overturn and smash its spiritual heritage so completely is quite simply an act of self-destruction. There is a big difference between moving on from a tradition having fully absorbed all its lessons to demolishing it with nothing comparable to take its place. Some people might think we are engaged on a similar path now.

St Martin’s, Bremhill

From the grand and nationally important to the small and local. This is St Martin's church in the Wiltshire village of Bremhill. It's of personal significance to me as my parents are buried here but I don't include it for that reason. It earns its place because it seems to capture a quintessential Englishness. The construction of the church goes back to around 1200 AD and the tower comes from the later 13th century with 15th century additions. Inside, the worn flagstones speak of generations of local people being christened, married, buried and, of course, worshipping here. The priest when I used to go had formerly been a tax inspector which has a noteworthy antecedent, and the local pub, as is proper, is only a short walk away. All this represents Albion in its domestic and familial mode which may not be the most romantic or mythically enticing of its aspects but might just be the one that is the basis of everything honest and human.

When Christianity came to Albion it was recognised by the wise as the fulfilment of pre-existing spiritual traditions. These pagan religions, originally based on psychic and intuitive responses to natural cycles and supernatural powers, were superseded by the Christian revelation but left their mark in many ways. Where they were absorbed and transformed by Christianity you had the best of both worlds, and Christian Albion is the fruit of that.

IONA (WW)

I've only been to the island of Iona once and that was over 20 years ago. My maternal grandfather was Scottish and in the 1960s I spent several summer holidays in Findhorn and Banff in Morayshire near to where he grew up, but we never went as far as the west coast of Scotland even though his grandfather had come from the island of Benbecula in the Outer Hebrides so there was some kind of link.

But in 1998 I had the opportunity to visit Mull and from there it is a short ferry ride over to Iona so I went and spent a few days on the island. There were no cars allowed (good!) but it's not very big and you can walk all over it quite easily which I did, and I have to say its reputation as a holy island did not seem unmerited. The connection with St Columba is its main claim to fame, and for me he personifies Celtic Christianity which combines a deep awareness of the immanence of nature with dedication to the reality of Christ as Saviour. In this approach, Christ did not simply replace the old religions but through him the good in them was transformed and baptised in a new light. Demons were chased away and wind and water, sun and earth were recast as angels serving Christ rather than being seen as gods in their own right. This sanctified creation as holy instead of either revering it for its own sake (paganism) or dismissing it something existing in opposition to God which later Christianity sometimes had the tendency to do.

I did not find the abbey on Iona especially interesting. It's of fairly recent construction and didn't seem to me to have much of a sense of spiritual vitality, no more than similar places anyway. However, the island itself possessed a kind of glittering quality which showed it to be one of those places where the veil between this world and the next is less opaque than elsewhere. Now, I realise that some of this can be explained away physically as due to the weather conditions of sun coming out after rain which always leaves the air with a sparkle, but that is not all there is to it. Walking over Iona one often had the feeling of being taken through the outer form of nature to what lies behind nature. The ongoing work of the Creator and those non-physical beings who carry out his will can be intuited if one is open to such things. Those who believe in nature spirits can find something to support them here.

Bay at the back of the ocean. Next stop, America! (southernhebrides.com)

Machair, the dune grassland typical of West Scotland coastal areas

Port Ban with its white sand and turquoise water is the equal of any beach anywhere - when the sun is out

During and after Columba's time in the 6th and 7th centuries, Iona was one of the most important monastic communities in Great Britain, responsible for many conversions on the Scottish mainland and in Anglo-Saxon Northumbria. Its scriptorium may even have been the place where the world-famous Book of Kells first began to be put together, and the stone Celtic Crosses with their solar circles that surround the intersection of the vertical and horizontal arms might also have originated on Iona. An additional point of interest is the actual rock of which much of Iona, like the Western Isles as a whole, is formed. This is known as Lewisian Gneiss and at around 3 billion years old is the oldest rock in Britain and among the oldest in the world. It's a metamorphic rock, originally igneous but changed many times as the earth's crust became molten and then hardened. So the feeling one gets in Iona of a deep ancient past is geologically justified.

A Celtic Cross on Iona

Bruce Charlton wondered whether Ireland formed part of Albion and concluded that yes, it did. I would ask the same question about Scotland and come to the same conclusion. After all, Alba is the Gaelic name for Scotland. It may be that Albion has different parts to it but it is a unified whole too. The fact that there was a roughly similar Neolithic culture spread over the whole of Great Britain and Ireland, best exemplified by the standing stones such as the ones at Callanish on the Isle of Lewis not far from Iona, corroborates this. Albion is the spiritual backdrop to these two large and several small islands. It manifests itself variously, according to local conditions, but there is an overarching identity as well that needs to be discovered in order to resolve the quarrels between these family members, quarrels that really only exist at the political level not the spiritual one.

MAUMBURY RINGS (WW)

Between 1985 and 1988 I lived in Bridport in the county of Dorset during which time I worked 15 miles down the road in Dorchester at the Dorset County Museum. Dorchester and the area around it are interesting in that this is a region which has been continuously populated since at least Neolithic times, and by cultures that have left their mark. There are not many parts of the country you could say that about.

My job at the museum was to sort through the enormous amount of material that existed in the museum's archives, mostly the result of archaeological digs over the previous decades. This included Stone Age axes, pounders and arrowheads, Bronze Age jars and pottery, Roman glass and ceramics, mosaic tesserae and medieval monastery tiles, often beautifully decorated. There were even around thirty large boxes of oyster shells going back to Roman times, all diligently catalogued and kept on shelves in the deconsecrated All Saints Church on the High Street just down the road from the main museum. Experts could tell weather patterns of the time by examining the shells, of which there were so many because oysters had been a staple food back then. I learnt on the job and it was fascinating to handle all these artifacts and find out their history, together with the ancient history of the area in which they had originated.

There are several earthworks in the area, of which Maiden Castle is the most famous. This is an Iron Age Hill fort though archaeological digs have shown that the site has seen human activity going back almost 6,000 years when there was a Neolithic causewayed enclosure there consisting of an oval area surrounded by two ditches. We will come back to that in a minute.

During this period it is probable that the site would have been of religious significance since for human beings at this time life was essentially religious. They lived in much deeper communion with nature and their gods than we can imagine. I believe that faith as we envisage it would not have been a major part of their spiritual life. It did not need to be since their consciousness was open to spiritual reality, though largely in a passive sense. They experienced a kind of primeval identification with their environment, both physical and psychic.

Maiden Castle (dorsetlife.co.uk)

Later on in Iron Age times, this form of interaction with the landscape and the spirit world had begun to fade away. The site, perfectly positioned for defensive purposes, became a hill fort, one of over 100 built at that time in the West Country. But this one was expanded over the years until it became the biggest in Britain and one of the biggest in Europe. Walking on the soft turf up there still has the power to take one back in imagination to a distant past when human beings lived lives tied to the land and the cycles of nature, and had not fully separated themselves from their environment. At least, it does if you can respond to that sort of thing and have not, like so many people have, spiritually "dumbed yourself down".

There is another earthwork actually in the town and I would occasionally go there during my lunch break just to sit in a peaceful atmosphere. This is Maumbury Rings, a Neolithic henge. Here's an aerial photograph.

Maumbury Rings (visit-dorset.com)

We have returned to the oval area enclosed by a ditch. That is to say, there would originally have been a ditch, formed by the construction of the outer banks, but that has long since been filled in. But still the basic layout of an oval demarcated by a border remains. Now, forgive me, but what does this remind you of? All I can say is that I have to assume it was constructed as a sacred space dedicated to the Mother Goddess. In its time it's been a Roman amphitheatre, a fort in the Civil War and even an execution ground in the 18th century during the Monmouth Rebellion, not to mention farmland and a place of assembly. But it is over 4,000 years old and its original purpose would have been religious. Archaeologists frequently say of ancient things when they are not sure what they are for, "used for ritual purposes" and I expect they are often right in that, but this clearly was a sacred space used by the local tribe for their most profound encounters with the numinous. When I used to go there 30 years ago it still had a feeling of peace and stillness, and there was also a sense of being safe and secure. Is it too fanciful to think of it as a kind of spiritual womb? Rites of death and rebirth are among the oldest and most widespread forms of human spiritual activity, and I think that is what Maumbury Rings would originally have been associated with.

England has one of the highest proportions of prehistoric sites in the world, and many of them retain an atmosphere that links to their past. If you approach them with an open imagination you can, to an extent, 'tune in' to the consciousness of our ancestors, and if you manage to do that you will find that our modern view of the world is really very limited. Obviously, no one is suggesting that we should, even if we could which we can't, return to that mode of being but we can certainly learn from it and seek to incorporate it in our own modern consciousness insofar as that is possible. What we have lost in the sense of identification with the natural and spiritual environments can be recovered but in a higher form in which we are no longer simply passive experiencers but can become creative participators in a spiritual world that extends beyond this one yet is fully enmeshed with it. But the world is a creation and we can only really achieve the kind of spiritually conscious interaction with it I am talking about when we acknowledge that which means acknowledge the Creator. For creation, and that includes ourselves, is only properly understood when we see it in the light of God of whom it is the expression.

THE LONG MAN OF WILMINGTON (WW)

When I was about 10 years old I went on a school trip which remained in my memory long afterwards as a very enjoyable time even though I couldn't remember much specific about it. I knew it was somewhere on the south coast of England but had forgotten where though I did remember the highlight of the trip being an excursion in which we had walked across grassy downs on a bright sunny day, blue sky above, birds singing in an English morning, suddenly to discover at our feet a massive chalk figure carved into the hillside. The teacher had wanted to surprise us and he did. I knew the figure was of a man holding what appeared to be sticks in each hand, but it was one of those indistinct childhood memories that have receded so far into the past that they have become almost dreamlike. Nonetheless, the impression of having encountered something otherworldly stuck with me and the sight of this enigmatic figure awoke my imagination to the deep, ancient past of this island.

Fast forward thirty years and I was living in the Sussex town of Eastbourne. One day I was talking to someone who asked me if I'd seen the nearby Long Man of Wilmington yet. I'd heard of it but not realised it was in the vicinity. It turned out to be about 6 miles away so off I went to have a look. There was the figure of my childhood.

(photo courtesy visitsoutheasternengland.com)

This is how he appears when seen more or less from the road. He is standing facing forwards though his feet are set sideways. He is depicted in outline with no features which makes him appear more archetypal than individual. It also gives him the air of mystery I noted when I first saw him as a child, an air that his companion in Dorset, the Cerne Abbas giant, does not have though that is for other reasons too. He conveys an impression of watchfulness and seems almost like a guardian so it is no wonder some people have speculated that he stands at the door of the underworld (not hell but a spiritual realm beyond this earthly one), guarding the threshold from unworthy intruders. The fact that he is positioned on the side of a hill emphasises this even though that was undoubtedly more for reasons of display since, as far as I am aware, all English chalk figures are on hillsides, making them visible to more than the birds. But still, this gives the impression of a gateway into somewhere beyond this mortal world.

What are those things in his hands? Are they sticks or staves, symbols of his office perhaps or the remains of what were once agricultural tools, or are they the sides of a doorway, the gate he guards as he blocks the entrance to the next world with power and authority for he does indeed embody those qualities, his muscular frame and bold stance telling us that, if we are not entitled to pass, we shall not pass.

The Long Man is 235 feet tall which makes him the largest representation of the human figure in Europe. It was once assumed that he came from the Neolithic or Iron Age (there is a long barrow nearby), probably representing a pagan deity, but it turns out that there is no documentary evidence for him from before the 18th century, and the general consensus now is that he goes back no further than the 16th or 17th centuries. But if he does who or what is he supposed to be? He used to be known as the Green Man because that was how he appeared before a 19th century restoration embedded chalk into his outline, for though he is carved into a chalk hill, the soil on top of the chalk is relatively deep. This name, of course, also links him with the old pagan religion.

Maybe he is no more than a few hundred years old but he surely reaches back to something much earlier. For me, the idea of him as some kind of guardian of the land makes the most intuitive sense since even if this was not his original role, it is what he has become. I am tempted to speculate that he might even be a representation of Albion himself, a giant carved in the white earth on the southern shores of England protecting the land from invaders but also welcoming people as he stands at the entrance to England. My feeling when I first saw him as a child was he did have something sacred about him, something that is linked to the land of which he is a part. Could it be that he was always there on the ground but sleeping until the 16th or 17th century when he was not created so much as woken up? This time period does, after all, coincide with the rise of British power, albeit material not spiritual power. Perhaps this means he is still only half awake (the lack of facial features supporting this idea) and we await his true rising.

If you are looking for a visual depiction of Albion, here is one as good as any.

LONDON (WW)

I was born and brought up in London and lived there for the first 23 years of my life before leaving, vowing never to go back. However, 21 years later I did go back and here I have been ever since.

The reason I left was that I had become aware of the spiritual path and London epitomised worldliness to me at that time. The people and the place, their goals and its atmosphere, were materialistic through and through or so it seemed to me in the light of my new approach to the world.

I spent the next 21 years leading a largely contemplative kind of life though that description does seem a little grand. But it was a quiet life centred around prayer and meditation and the attempt to lead an existence dedicated to the spiritual quest. I was a vegetarian and had no social life to speak of. I lived on not much and was without a proper job though I was not idle doing occasional part time work in museums and teaching English, depending on where I was. I read, wrote a bit, walked a lot, gardened when I had a garden and so on. But I allowed nothing to interfere with my main purpose. Sometimes I felt a little concerned that I should be doing more but when I asked my spiritual instructors about that was told that for now this was my task.

As implied by that statement this period came to end and many years after I had left London I found myself back there again, living and, for the first time in a while, working full time. It was quite a change. If London had seemed worldly before it was a veritable Babylon now. It hardly even felt part of England, such had been the enormous demographic changes over the past couple of decades but the cultural and political changes had eaten away at it too. Babylon was presumably a city without a heart. London has surely become that now.

Let me come to the point. Actually, I have two points. Point one is that sometimes God puts us in a decidedly unspiritual environment either to test us or perhaps to see what we can put back, in however small a way it might be.

Point two concerns London itself. In many ways I had been very attached to the city in the way that anyone is attached to where they are born and bred, but also because certain parts of it did seem rather magical to me when young. Most particularly, the parks and gardens but there were also little areas full of character all over the city. These seemed far fewer to me on my return, partly no doubt because I was older but also because modernism and modernization had done their best to destroy much that was individual.

When I was at school I had the good fortune to attend a service at Westminster Abbey several days every week in the term time for four years, making my way there by walking through the East Cloister as people have done for centuries. For one year I even sat in the Choir, and probably the most terrifying moment of my life was when, aged 13, I had to read a lesson to about 400 people from a lectern up by the High Altar. Inevitably, as a schoolboy I took all this for granted but now, looking back, I am very grateful for the experience and feel that Westminster Abbey is the spiritual heart of London and has deep national significance. I went back recently for the first time in over 40 years, and though the place is now almost completely given over to tourism and the heritage industry, I would say the spiritual power there is not dead but sleeping.

Westminster Abbey

And here I come to my reason for writing this piece. I believe there are important places, spiritual power points if you like, all over the planet and London is one of them. It is for this reason that the demons who seek dominion over this world have done their best to destroy it. They have done the same with England as a whole and they are currently hell-bent on doing the same to the United States. Of course, they do this everywhere but their primary focus is always on undermining those places where there is most potential for good. It is just so obvious that certain places have been marked for attention and that they are being brought low and corrupted so that their spiritually leavening effect is diminished. It is not chauvinism to recognise this but plain common sense. There's not much we as individuals can do about it other than to point it out and try, as best we can, to stand against the spiritual degradation of those places in the Western world that have the potential to awaken humanity to higher ways of being. Both Great Britain and America have, however imperfectly, played that role in the past, and the fact that so much energy is expended on trying to destroy them rather indicates that they have the potential to do so again in the future.

I have no idea what the future holds but one thing I do feel sure about is that both Britain and America stand for real freedom and it would be to humanity's great loss if that were allowed to be overwhelmed by a kind of globalized, liberalised internationalism that pretends freedom but is really about conforming to a secular uniformity in which control, though disguised, is everywhere.

According to some esotericists Lord Nelson still stands guard over England.

THE STRANGE SHIP (JF)

'The Angel came to me on Pentecost morn, while it was still dark. "Dindrane," he called, and I woke and saw him at the foot of my bed - flashes and flickers of gold all about and a Presence and Shining in the air. And in my mind a hope and excitement that I too might be overshadowed by the power and grace of the Holy Spirit as was our blessed mother, Saint Mary.

'But no. Not that way for me. "Dindrane," he said. "The Most High God requests you to cut off your hair and place it in the gold and silver casket which I shall leave with you."

'It seemed such a little thing this request, such an odd and purposeless thing, and I was struck with sadness that this was all Heaven should ask of me. But the Angel said more ... about my brother, Percival, who I have seen not for ten years, and of Galahad and Bors, his companions on the Quest. He told me the high end my long brown hair - which I love very much and shall greatly miss - will now help bring about. And he also spoke of my own passing from this world, but no sooner had I felt the weight of his words than he left me and I heard the bells of the holy convent, over the mountains and by the sea, ringing out as they do every dawn. And it was the morning of Pentecost. And the bells were ringing and the task was at hand ... '

... Galahad rode fast and far through the late-summer night and all the next day. Forest, field, river, stream, valley, hill and dale sped by. Though nature rang and shone, he had an inner sense that the Wasteland and Carbonek Castle were close at hand. But he felt no desire to force the issue. He had had enough of forcing things. That approach had led him nowhere and had brought too many of his companions either to death or an ignominious abandonment of the Quest.

He came upon a round stone tower with a white cross painted on its door. As if he had seen him coming, a tall hermit with a long beard and a red robe opened the door and stood outside. 'God be with you, Sir,' he said, and Galahad brought his horse to a halt before him. 'I will stay here for a night or two,' he decided, 'and reflect and pray on how the Grail may best be found.'

So the hermit took him inside and Galahad had a bath and a supper of rice and bread. Then the hermit spoke certain secret words and took him to the chapel where he said Mass. Then Galahad fell asleep on a bed piled high with straw and would have slept long past dawn but for a hammering on the door in the middle of the night.

Something inside him knew that the hammering was for him. He got up, sped down the stairs, unbarred the door and found himself face to face with a young woman on a white horse, dressed in blue and gold. A brightness shone around her and at first Galahad thought she was holding a lantern in her right hand. But then he saw that it was a casket of some kind, but so golden and bright that it lit both horse and rider up as if it was a miniature sun. In the glow cast by the casket Galahad could see that the rider's hair was brown and short.

'Galahad,' she said. 'It is time to leave. Take your horse and ride with me to the coast that looks out onto Ireland. There you will find your companions again and the ship that will bring you to your heart's desire.'

Then Galahad took up his horse and the hermit came out and gave him his blessing. He saluted the rider, and Galahad had the sense that they knew each other already. Then they were on their way, riding side by side through the dawn and the morning and the afternoon and the evening and all through the night until they came to the sea.

They turned their horses loose and picked their way through the boulders down to the shore, where a ship with a single white sail stood waiting for them. Two figures stood on deck waving, and Galahad's heart leapt for joy when he saw that it was Percival and Bors.

They climbed aboard and greeted each other heartily. Galahad noted the affection with which Percival and the brown haired girl embraced each other. Big round tears rolled down Percival's cheeks. 'This is my sister, Dindrane,' he said, and Galahad could tell by the emotion they showed that they had not seen each other for a long time.

The sun rose, the breeze blew, the sail billowed, and the little ship moved off around the shore as if propelled by invisible hands. Galahad, Percival and Bors talked happily of times gone by and the high adventure yet ahead of them. Dindrane stood on the other side of the deck, still holding her luminous casket, watching the waves and the rocky shore go by. Galahad found it hard to take his eyes off her. There was something compelling about her - a presence, stillness and strength that he had seldom if ever encountered in man or woman before. At length they came to a little inlet and the ship ground to a halt between two banks of sand. 'Come,' said Dindrane. 'Follow me.'

They walked up a pebbly hill and down the other side. There, where the waves met the beach, was another, bigger ship, with four white sails. A rope ladder reached down from the deck to the beach. Dindrane climbed up and the others followed. Once on deck, she led them down a flight of steps to a chamber underneath. Galahad saw a bed with a white pillow and silver coverings. In the middle of the bed was a shining sword partially removed from its jewelled blue and green scabbard. Its blade glowed white and fierce and the pommel was set with a wondrous green gemstone. 'Look,' said Bors. 'There is writing on the blade.' And they turned to look and saw words written in a flowing purple script:

'The man who draws me will be the noblest and purest of Arthur's Companions. His destiny it shall be to succeed the hermit Nasciens as High Priest of the Grail.'

'That can only be you,' said Percival to Galahad..

But Galahad shook his head. 'Not yet,' he said. He felt in his heart that there was something else that needed to happen first. Then Bors said to Dindrane. 'Why has the blade been left so exposed? It might only be a hands-breadth, but the sea air will still weaken it.' Dindrane stepped forth. 'I will tell you the tale,' she said ...

' ... Three decades ago, King Pelles, the Lord and Master of what is now the Wasteland, was out hunting with a retinue of followers. They were hunting the great boar, Tryn Twrch, which had crossed the sea from Ireland and was laying Wales waste as it had already laid Ireland waste.

'The hunt was a successful one. A great splashing was heard and a number of hill men came to King Pelles to report that they had seen the boar scrambling into the water and wading back to Ireland. But by the time the news came in the day had grown late and the King found himself separated from his men and the forest quite impenetrable. With one hill man to guide him, he came out upon this beach where this ship is now moored. And it was moored here that evening too. 'Rest you here for this night, Sire,' said the hill man, 'and when morning comes we shall be better able to pick our way through the forest.'

'So Pelles climbed on board, then down the staircase to this chamber. When he saw the sword he desired it greatly and strode forward to take it. But a voice rent the air and cried out, 'Do not touch the sword, O King, for you are not worthy.' But the King carried on and pulled it out by the hands-length you see here. And a spear swooped down at him, wounded him in the thigh and sent him spinning to the floor. And all his lands were laid waste. Blasted and charred.

'Pelles took the spear from his thigh, hobbled off the ship and crawled back to Carbonek on his hands and knees, his wound bleeding profusely. He lies there still with one blessing left, the presence of the Grail and the Grail's High Priest, Nasciens. That and the prophecy given hundreds of years ago by Joseph of Arimathea - that the King of Carbonek will one day suffer from an unstaunchable wound and will have to wait in penitence and faith for the Great Restorer to come - he who will heal the King, let loose the waters over the land, and become High Priest after Nasciens.

'But know this. If Pelles had not lusted after the sword, the Restorer would still have come, though not so soon as this. He will come again at the end of time and he will have enemies to fight, both now and then. He will need a sword. Here it is.'

They stood in silence for a long time. Then Galahad observed something. 'Sister,' he said to Dindrane. 'The sword belt is not in keeping with the beauty of the sword and scabbard. Let us find or make a new one.' It was true. The leather belt attached to the scabbard was worn and frayed and looked as if one touch was all it needed for it to fall apart.

Dindrane nodded, took up her casket and opened it. They looked in and saw a belt of brown, lustrous hair, fastened with clips and brooches of the purest gold and silver. She handed the belt to Galahad, while she unclasped the old one and laid it in the casket. 'Fasten the belt,' she whispered, and Galahad leant forward and tied it to the scabbard. 'Now draw your sword,' she said. 'See, it responds to your touch. The writing has faded.'

So Galahad pulled out the sword, and his heart and mind and the whole way he thought and felt about the world were changed. For the first time, everything felt right and in its proper place. All the uncertainty and indecision were gone. He had a dim sense that people were kneeling down around him - more than three people too - but the sword was so bright and the air so dazzling that it was hard to see anything clearly. But he did notice that Dindrane was missing. And that was a shame as there was much he wanted to say. But no need to hurry. She would be up on deck looking out at the waves as usual. Plenty of time, plenty of time ...

'No, not for me the fulfilment of the Quest. Not for me the high and holy things, the voyage over the sea and the mystic city of Sarras. I have just one more task left now - to give my life as a ransom for many as soon as we touch land. For this is what the Angel told me. First my hair, then my life. It is a harsh schooling, but in my heart - the deepest, most secret, most sacred part of me - I welcome it. For I have been granted my dearest wish - to follow after our blessed mother, Saint Mary. So I can say too, "Behold the handmaid of the Lord, be it done to me according to your word." The Grail itself, and everything good and true that pours from it, cannot outshine the simple, holy grace of those fifteen words of trust, faith, patience, longing, love and hope.'

THE LAST OF LOGRES (JF)

There is one particular aspect of the Arthurian mythos which, as far as I am aware, has not been reflected on as much as it should. After the Last Battle and Arthur's voyage to Avalon, a number of surviving knights join a monastic community which, in Rosemary Sutcliff's retelling, *The Road to Camlann* (The Bodley Head, 1981), later develops into Glastonbury Abbey:

> Within half a year came Sir Blamore and Sir Bleoberis, and little by little certain others of the old lost brotherhood of the Round Table. And when in due time the ancient Archbishop died, Sir Lancelot, whom he had made a priest while he yet lived, stepped into his place and celebrated Mass for the rest as he had done and for all who chanced to pass that way.
>
> So they continued for seven years, living in prayer and poverty and giving their help and comfort to all who sought it; and keeping the last light of Logres alive as they kept the honey-wax candles burning on the rough altar, while the darkness flowed in over the rest of the land. For though Constantine, Duke of Cornwall and a young kinsman of Arthur, had taken the High Kingship and led his troops to battle under the dragon banner, he was not Arthur, and there was little that he could do against the Sea Wolves and the Old People from the mountains and the North.

What is notable here is that the knights seem to intuit that the time for action is past and the time for contemplation has begun. Martha cedes place to Mary, you might say. The knights could, of course, have carried on the fight, pledging their allegiance to Constantine or forming a resistance movement in the hills. But no, they understand that fighting is behind them now and that the Round Table has served its purpose, leaving behind a glorious legend that will inspire the men and women of Albion for centuries to come. They recognise that something different is required from them, a prayerful, inner-directed counterpoint to the years of struggle and striving in the outer world. And this new orientation bears fruit in unexpected ways. After Sir Lancelot's death:

> Sir Bedivere and several of the brotherhood remained at the little church and its hermitage all the rest of their days, gathering others to them, so that at last the place became an abbey again; and later still, mighty and beautiful stone buildings arose where the little wattle church and its surrounding bothies had been. And men began to call it Glastonbury.

The Sea Wolves sweep a across the land, but the little church keeps the flame of faith alive, becoming a 'mighty and beautiful' abbey, a foretaste of the Christendom that gave us the great cathedrals which stud the land like jewels, from Carlisle to Salisbury and Canterbury to Durham. These mighty edifices - these 'sermons in stone' - are storehouses of spiritual energy, worthy successors to the stone circles of the Celtic and Neolithic eras and becoming increasingly popular. Visitor figures have been up for a while now, with Choral Evensong especially well-attended. Their finest hour may still be yet to come.

It is good to reflect upon these themes on Good Friday and Holy Saturday, two days of apparent defeat and despair. As Saturday evening in Jerusalem shades into Saturday night, nothing seems to be happening at all. There is nothing more to happen in any case. All is over, finished, consummated. Or so it appears.

But how deceptive appearances can be. Transformation is a mysterious, unquantifiable thing. Its ways are not our ways. Think of the tiny seed in Jesus's parable which grows without fanfare or headlines into the mightiest tree in the forest. This should give us hope on the micro-level too - all those occasions when we feel stuck, frustrated and shorn of inspiration. 'I've nothing to show for my life', we sometimes say, but we don't know that yet. We don't know it at all, in fact. For Jesus's followers on Holy Saturday, everything looked done and dusted, yet all the while He was setting the spirits of the dead free in Hades and breaking the power of death. The real work - Christ's Harrowing of Hell being the great archetypal example - goes on in secret and in silence.

THE ADVENT OF ARTHUR (JF)

When the Emperor Honorius withdrew the Roman legions from Britain in the year 410, there were many who thought the country's collapse was close at hand. The land was plagued by pirates - Saxons to the South and East, Picts to the North and Irish from the West. How could the Britons survive without the might of Rome to protect them?

Later that year, Rome fell for the first time, while in Britain, Constantine the Strong - half-Roman, half-Briton - was crowned High King at Winchester. He made a new flag for the country - a red dragon on a gold background - and unfurled it for friend and foe to see from the highest tower in the city. He rallied the people, and for thirty years held all enemies at bay. But Vortigern, Prince of Gwynedd, was jealous. He put poison in the High King's cup and killed him at the royal table. Vortigern was crafty. He had already won the support of a large number of nobles, promising them money and land and an easier life than they had ever had under Constantine.

As soon as the High King slumped face-forward, Vortigern's men drew their swords and ran through the castle, searching for Constantine's two teenage sons, Ambrosius and Uther. But they were nowhere to be seen. It was only on the eve of his coronation that Vortigern learnt the truth. The boys had been spirited away on the night of the murder by a mysterious stranger, a tall young man in a red and blue cloak. They were in Brittany now, already plotting their return. Many leading Britons had joined them there.

Vortigern, his reign barely begin, was consumed with anxiety. Sensing weakness, the Saxons thrust further inland than ever before, harrying Lincoln and the market towns of the East Midlands. The Picts stormed Hadrian's Wall again, while the Irish seized captives galore from the Welsh coast. Vortigern didn't know what to do. He wasn't the kind of leader who could inspire men to fight and die for him. His usual ploy was to offer them gold, but now he had no gold to give as he was spending it all fighting the barbarians and protecting his throne from Constantine's sons.

He withdrew to the mountains, gathered his druids and asked their advice. 'Stay here, O King,' they replied, 'and build a high tower. Call the master builders, pay them well with what little remains, and you will see a tower rise that neither force of arms nor guile can ever overthrow.'

Vortigen followed their guidance. The foundations were dug and the stones laid up. At the end of the first day the tower was halfway built, but the very next morning the builders arrived and found their work in ruins. Blocks and shards of stone lay scattered and strewn all over the hillside. And it was like that every morning for fourteen mornings. The tower was built by day and cast down by night. Vortigern called back his druids and demanded an explanation.

They studied their lore for three days and nights. Then the Chief Druid stood before the High King and said, 'My Lord, the gods require a sacrifice. You must find a man with no mortal father and slay him here in your throne room. Any man will do. The only thing needed is that his father must be immortal. Only then will they permit your tower to be built.'

Vortigern groaned. He didn't believe a word of it, but felt he had no choice in the matter. So he sent his messengers far and wide and was surprised the next evening when two of them returned with a tall young man in tow. He had a thatch of black hair; dark, deep-set eyes; and a hawk-like nose. He stood before Vortigern in the throne room, carrying himself with dignity and pride, as if he were the king and Vortigern the subject. The setting sun slanted in through the high, narrow windows, lighting up the stranger's haughty face.

'Who are you?' growled Vortigern.

'My name is Myrddin Emrys. In my home town, Carmarthen, I am known as Merlin.'

'Why are you here?'

'It is said in Carmarthen that my mother, Rheged of the Red Hair, was visited by an angel nine months before I was born. Some say an angel of God, others an angel of Lucifer. My mother died shortly after my birth so I never had chance to ask.'

'Kill him at once, Sire,' hissed the Chief Druid in Vortigern's ear. 'The gods grow impatient. He is dangerous too. I smell a threat to your throne.' But Vortigern waved him away. He was curious, and greatly struck by Merlin's nobility of bearing and speech.

'Tell me more,' he said. 'Who raised you after your mother died?'

'I was adopted by Blaise the Bald, the Hermit of the Northern Marches, he who lived to be a hundred and twenty and was reputed the wisest man in the Empire. He taught me many things, some of which will be of interest to your person.'

Vortigen leaned forward. 'What things?' he whispered.

'Blaise taught me wisdom,' said Merlin. 'He showed me how to look deeply: how to see beneath the surface of things. I have studied your tower and can tell you that sacrifice will be no use whatsoever. I say this not to save my life but because it is the truth. Come outside with me, order your men to dig down beneath the foundations, and you will see.'

So Vortigern ordered everyone outside. The tower, which was made of white stone, loomed above them in the sunset, half-finished as it always was at the end of each day. The builders grumbled when they were told to keep working, but it wasn't long before they had dug down past the foundations and not long after that when suddenly there was no more earth to dig. A vast, round cavern opened up below them, with bare brown earth in the middle and grey rocks around the sides. Two mighty dragons lay sleeping on the rocks, a white dragon to the left and a red dragon to the right. 'Light your braziers,' said Merlin to Vortigern's servants. The sun sank, the torches were lit, and straightaway the dragons awoke, rushed together in the centre of the cave and started to fight. They flailed, clawed and belched out fire all night long. The ground shook and the tower trembled. At first the white dragon had the advantage. He pushed the red dragon back to the rocks until, around the third watch of the night, the red dragon turned the tide and thrust the white dragon back in turn. As dawn approached it seemed certain that the white dragon would be killed but somehow he recovered his strength and charged the red dragon until they were locked together furiously in the middle again. The tower fell at last with a mighty crash, and then, once the sound of tumbling masonry had ceased, a bell began to ring, far-away but clear as crystal in the pre-dawn air.

Vortigern knew the sound. It was the bell for Matins at Saint Martin's Monastery in Deganwy, over the mountains and by the sea. At the third chime the dragons turned away from each other, went back to their rocks and fell asleep at once. Vortigern ordered everyone back inside. Merlin stood before him in the throne room once again.

'What does all this mean?' asked the King.

'The fight,' replied Merlin, 'is a picture of Britain under your rule. The land is paralysed. There can be no peace - no victory for either side - as long as you sit on this throne.'

'No peace?' Vortigern interrupted, but Merlin raised his right hand imperiously and carried on talking.

'No peace,' he repeated. 'The white dragon stands for the Saxons, and the red for the Britons. The white dragon cannot kill the red. If it was your destiny, despite your present difficulties, you would find a way to turn the tables and drive the invader back, as far as the Saxon Shore and beyond. But he would only recover his strength, as the white dragon did, and come at you again, waging war for ever in the middle of your kingdom. But this is not your destiny, nor is it Britain's.'

'Destiny?' yelled Vortigern, standing up and towering over Merlin. 'What do *you* know about destiny - mine or my country's? Who gave you the authority to pontificate like this? Did Blaise teach you to see into the future as well?'

Merlin neither blinked nor flinched. 'Blaise,' he said, 'gave me wisdom, as I have said, but my father, the angel, gave me the gift of prophecy, and this is what I see. Very soon, Ambrosius and Uther will return to avenge their father. You will not escape. They will crush the Saxons, Picts and Irish, and one of them shall father a son who shall be the greatest king this land will ever know. He will never die and will come again in glory at the end of time to save this realm from its gravest peril and prepare the way for the second coming of Our Lord and Saviour, Jesus Christ.'

Vortigern sat back down, shaking his head, a broken reed all of a sudden. He knew, in his heart, that Merlin was speaking the truth. His words and manner had the ring of authenticity. 'But what about me?' he pleaded. 'What must I do?'

'Repent and pray,' said Merlin softly, and he would have said more but one of Vortigern's men who had been watching Merlin closely stood before the High King and shouted, 'Sire, do not believe his weasel words. He is a traitor and a spy. For I have seen him before. On the night we slew Constantine. For it was this man and no other who shepherded his sons to safety.'

There was an almighty commotion and the King's men rushed forward to lay hands on Merlin, but right at that moment the sun rose outside, arrowing in through the high windows and blinding their eyes. When they could see again, Merlin had vanished - gone entirely - as if he had never been in the room at all, as if his presence and prophecies had all been as insubstantial as a dream.

That was exactly what Vortigern's druids told him. That it had all been a dream. But he had no more faith in them. He went to Deganwy instead and confessed his sins to the monks, repenting of the jealousy that had led him to kill Constantine. But everything fell out just as Merlin had predicted. Ambrosius and Uther landed at Falmouth three days later at the head of a great force. Three days after that and they were in Snowdonia, taking Vortigern's stronghold by storm. The fighting was brief but bloody. Vortigern was killed along with most of his men. Some of his druids escaped to the isle of Ynys Môn but Ambrosius, who was the elder brother, decided that too many lives had been lost already and chose not to pursue them. He was crowned High King at Stonehenge four weeks after, and it was Merlin himself who presented him with the royal and ancient British crown, first worn by Brutus the Trojan in the dim and distant days at the very beginning of our island's long, unfolding story.

From that day forth, Merlin was always by the side of one or both of the brothers, inspiring, guiding and illuminating. But Ambrosius, in truth, did not need too much advising. He knew his own mind very well. He had a silence and stillness about him as well that commanded respect - this lithe, slim figure, with his oval-shaped face and cap of dark hair. He had green eyes that the wise women said were twice as deep as the Irish Sea. He was a far-sighted man, a visionary leader, who meditated deeply on the rumours coming from Rome that the city had fallen for the second time. One more fall, he thought, and that will be the end of the Empire forever. 'If only,' he told Merlin, 'we can make Britain strong enough so that when Rome falls again we can pick up the torch and restore the Empire here in this land, carrying the light of civilisation forward for generations yet unborn.'

Ambrosius, many believed, was well on the way to fulfilling his vision, but he met his death too soon - on a stag's antlers one crisp January morning while hunting in the Royal Forest. Merlin and Uther were far away, marching through the Wirral peninsula to head off a detachment of Irish. That night, a blazing comet scorched across the sky from East to West, bursting apart into two smaller comets, one of which broke up quite quickly in a spectacular display of fire and light. But the other kept going and going and growing and growing until it passed out of sight at the Western rim of the world, three times bigger, brighter and longer than the original comet. Merlin and Uther gazed up at the sky. Merlin sighed and put his hand on the young man's shoulder. 'Your brother, the High King, is dead. See, the first comet burns in his honour. But good shall come from his passing. The second comet is for yourself. You shall fight like a lion and go down in a blaze of glory. And the third comet is for your son, he whose advent I foresaw five summers ago in Vortigern's throne room, the great monarch who will restore all things for Christ, not once but twice.'

So Uther was crowned High King. But his coronation was a rushed and hurried affair, and he struggled for a while to set his lands in order, for the Saxons, Picts and Irish swooped down once more, hoping that Ambrosius' death had left the country rudderless and adrift.

Uther was as strong as an ox and as brave as any man who ever lived, before or since. But he wasn't as mentally sharp as Ambrosius and he relied on Merlin a lot to help him make the big strategic decisions. But after a few months he was happy enough with his progress to declare a week-long coronation party at Caerleon. He invited all of his nobles together and their wives, and that was the first time he set eyes on Ygraine, the wife of Gorlois, Duke of Cornwall. Uther was impulsive and hot-headed, and he fell in love at first sight, showering Ygraine with attention and gifts. She complained to her husband, and Gorlois took her back to Cornwall and his ancestral seat at Tintagel Castle.

Uther was furious and laid siege to the castle. Merlin counselled against it, as Gorlois was one of the King's best and most loyal generals. His castle was impregnable as well, perched high on the rocks, far above the waves. The only way in was to climb up a long, narrow causeway that only let one man pass at a time. Uther had brought ten thousand men with him but he might as well have come on his own for all the help such strength in numbers gave him.

The siege dragged on for fourteen days and nights. Many lives were lost. Merlin decided to visit the King's tent and urge him, as strongly as possible, to make peace. But as he stepped into the March night he beheld a star shining above the castle which hadn't been there before. It was green and translucent and throbbed and glowed like a ruby or sapphire. Merlin ran his hand through his hair and wondered what it might mean. Perhaps it was a sign? He returned to his tent. Better wait a night or two and see if the star remained. And it was there the next night, and the one after that, and the one after that. Merlin knew then that it was indeed a sign and that the great king to come was destined to be conceived at Tintagel. But how was he to get Uther over the causeway and into Ygraine's chamber?

He pondered the matter deeply. He had been to the castle as a boy with Blaise once, so he knew his way around a bit. He made up his mind and appeared in the King's tent exactly an hour before midnight. 'My Lord,' he began. 'It is time to speak plainly. You cannot win the Lady Ygraine by force. You must try another way.'

'What way might that be?' Uther asked wearily.

'Follow my instructions and I will give you two hours with Ygraine in her chamber.'

'Two hours!' snorted the King. 'I haven't come all this way and lost all these men for a measly two hours.'

Merlin nodded. 'Yet a measly two hours, O King, could lead to many more. Once you make a start and set the ball rolling, none of us - not even myself - can predict how destiny will work itself out.'

Uther threw up his hands. 'Very well. I give up. I can't go on bleeding my army dry, can I? What must I do?'

'Nothing. I will cast a spell and transform you into the very image of Gorlois. I will become the likeness of his right hand man, Briastus, and together, this very night if you wish, we will cross the causeway. No-one will think anything of it, only that Gorlois has left his camp to visit his wife.'

Two hours later, Merlin and Uther were on their way. 'Promise me this,' whispered Merlin as they approached the causeway. 'If by any chance Gorlois should be killed and you marry Ygraine, and if by any chance a child is born nine months after this night, then you will give that child to me and let me raise him.'

'I don't understand,' muttered Uther.

'Surely you have not forgotten what I told you on the night your brother died?'

'No, I have not forgotten. But a child, to be honest, is the last thing on my mind right now. I will do it if I can, but I doubt I will be able to. Gorlois is too shrewd a soldier to get himself killed.'

'Well, we'll see,' said Merlin.

The guards waved them through, and Merlin showed Uther the door to Ygraine's chamber. He withdrew to the courtyard, watching and waiting as the scudding clouds raced across the sky. The star, he observed, was shining brighter than ever, sparkling and twinkling in the raw spring air.

It was a long way back to the camp. When they got there, all the lanterns were lit and everyone was astir. Gorlois, inexplicably, had launched a night raid and had been killed in the subsequent skirmish.

Uther was astonished. Gorlois was normally such a cautious general. But there it was, and one hour later Uther was back in the castle, not in disguise this time, but as himself - a conqueror.

He stayed for a year and a day. Ygraine sorrowed grievously for her husband, but over the following weeks and months she grew very fond of Uther and they were married on Mid-Summer's Eve. He was aware from an early stage, of course, that Ygraine was pregnant. 'It is a mysterious thing,' she told him, 'that at the hour Gorlois was said to have been killed, he himself, or one exactly like him, visited me here in my chamber.' So Uther told her the truth - about the comet in the sky, Merlin's prophecy, and his own promise to hand the child over. Then Ygraine wept again. She had already lost a husband and now she was to lose a son. Yet she marvelled at the same time and wondered greatly at the extraordinary destiny predicted for the boy.

Uther kept his word and handed the babe to Merlin on a frost-flecked late-December night. Ygraine had wrapped him carefully and tenderly in white swaddling clothes to keep him warm. Merlin held him in the folds of his cloak and headed down the sands via a path through the rocks he had made himself and that no-one else knew existed. At the bottom was a cave, which he had carved out of the rock, and in the cave was a pool, and on the pool a wooden boat, which Merlin had spent the last two months building. He stepped aboard, unfurled the sail and pushed out the oar. He was voyaging to a secret place that Blaise had told him of years before, where the wise women who came often to Ambrosius would bring the boy up until the time was ripe for him to appear in the world.

Merlin rowed steadily for five minutes then turned around to look at the castle. It had disappeared into the night. Only the lanterns in the windows and the green star hovering above told him where it was. And as he looked he heard a noise - not with his ears but with his heart - far-away but crystal clear - the sound of falling towers and tumbling masonry. And he knew it was a sign and that Rome had fallen for the third and final time.

He kept looking and the star seemed to grow and expand and change colour, so that it was as big as the sun and not just green any more but green, red, gold, blue and white, all together and all at the same time. It whirled and spun like a wheel of rainbow fire, faster and faster, fizzing and crackling, until it burst asunder into ten thousand shafts of light, a legion of shooting stars, filling the firmament and bathing the world in warm, rejuvenating light. And then, one by one, the spears of wondrous light dipped and fell into the sea - splash after splash after splash after splash, leaving silence and peace in their wake as an almighty hush descended. The silence of the Holy Spirit, thought Merlin - the richest, deepest silence, stillness and peace that he had ever known.

He held the child tight in the crook of his arm, turned back to the sea and pushed out the oar again. And all he could hear was the beating of his heart, the lapping of the waves and the soft, rhythmic breathing of a new-born babe.

THIS CHARGED LAND: ALAN GARNER'S *ELIDOR* (JF)

The prophet breathes the air of freedom. He smothers in the hardened world about him, but in his own spiritual world he breathes freely. He always visions a free spiritual world and awaits its penetration into this stifling world.

Nicholas Berdyaev, *Freedom and the Spirit.*

Every word in *Elidor* is freighted with gold. Published in 1965, Alan Garner's third novel does for Manchester (and all cities by extension) what *The Weirdstone of Brisingamen* (1960) and *Moon of Gomrath* (1963) did for the valleys, woods and hills of Cheshire. He imbues the cityscape with a numinous depth charge. The stuff of everyday urban life - lamp posts, railway bridges, terraced houses - take on an almost sacramental glow, pointing to a level of understanding beyond the reach of materialist models of reality. One world segues into another. Take this passage, for instance:

> Roland ran along the wider streets until his eyes were used to the dark. The moon had risen, and the glow of the city lightened the sky. He twisted down alleyways, running blindly, through crossroads, over bombed sites, and along the streets again. Roland stopped and listened. There was only the noise of the city, a low, constant rumble that was like silence.
>
> He was in the demolition area. Roof skeletons made broken patterns against the sky. Roland searched for a place that would be safe to climb, and found a staircase on the exposed inner wall of a house. He sat on the top in the moonlight. It was freezing hard. Roofs and cobbles sparkled. The cold began to ache into him. He wondered if the others had decided to stay in one place and wait until he came.
>
> This thought bothered him, and he was still trying to make up his mind when the unicorn appeared at the end of the street. His mane flowed like a river in the moon: the point of the horn drew fire from the stars. Roland shivered with the effort of

> looking. He wanted to fix every detail in his mind for ever, so that no matter what else happened there would always be this. (pp.188-192)

Who can forget writing like this? No-one in my experience. I've never known a book, at least among my circle of friends, which retains its impact for so long in the reader's imagination. People can recall whole scenes. Either that or specific images, such as the fiddler in the slum clearance area, leap into their minds as soon as the book is mentioned. Garner's story, in this respect, has much in common with Andrei Tarkovsky's 1979 film *Stalker*, another quest for meaning through a magical but treacherous landscape. Tarkovsky calls his liminal space the 'Zone', and *Elidor* has two such 'Zones' - both wastelands - sites of blight and dereliction - the parallel world of Elidor itself and a mid-1960s Manchester which bears absolutely no resemblance to the 'swinging sixties' of popular imagination.

Malebron, Elidor's 'king in exile', disguises himself as a fiddler to lure the Watson children into his world through the portal of a North Manchester church on the brink of demolition. Once there, the children encounter a pre-industrial mirror image of their home city - the bitter legacy of moral and spiritual decline:

> "The darkness grew," said Malebron. "It is always there. We did not watch, and the power of night closed on Elidor. We had so much of ease that we did not mark the signs - a crop blighted, a spring failed, a man killed. Then it was too late - war and siege, and betrayal, and the dying of the light." (p.44)

The children are charged with rescuing the four Treasures of Elidor - a spear, a sword, a stone and a bowl - from within the sinister Mound of Vandwy. Their next task is to take the Treasures back to Manchester and guard them until Malebron sends word. The difficulty is that there are clearly other powers at work in Elidor than Malebron, determined to seize the Treasures for their own ends. Their attempts to break into the genteel suburban *milieu* created by the Watsons' parents form the substance of the second half of the book.

For Roland, the youngest and most sensitive of the children, this is a particularly heavy burden. He is greatly impressed by Elidor and more in sympathy with Malebron than any of his siblings. Malebron's goodness and Elidor's physical reality mean everything to him. When his brothers, Nicholas and David, attempt to rationalise what happened in the church, Roland is uncompromising in his defence of Elidor's veracity:

> "But you're pretending it doesn't matter," said Roland. "Didn't it mean anything to you - Malebron and the Treasures, and that golden castle, and - everything."
> "Listen," said David, "Nick's not all that dim, although you think he is. A lot of what he says makes sense, even if I don't agree with everything myself."
> "What does he say, then? That there's no such place as Elidor, and we dreamed it?"
> "In a way," said David.
> "He's off his head."
> "No, he's gone into it more than any of us," said David. "And he's been reading books. He says it could all have been what he calls 'mass hallucination', perhaps something to do with the shock after the church nearly fell on us. He says it does happen."
> "If you can believe that, you can believe in the Treasures," said Roland. (pp.116-17)

Roland is proved right in the end, but his vindication comes at a price and brings him no joy. Roland is a prophet, and he shares in the eternal lot of prophets - sidelined, patronised, and seen as no more, even by his own mother, than a temperamental, overly-wrought schoolboy:

> "I did see somebody!" said Roland. "I did!"
> "Now come along inside, Roland," said Mrs Watson. "You know you're own worst enemy."
> "But Mum, I did see somebody!"
> "I don't doubt it," said Mrs Watson. "But you mustn't let your imagination run away with you. You're too highly strung, that's your trouble. You'll make yourself ill if you're not careful." (p.122)

The consensus among my friends is that Roland does indeed make himself ill and that, by the end of the book, he is close to 'cracking up' or 'losing it'. I'm not so sure. Roland's only mistake, as far as I can tell is to confuse Elidor - a parallel world to our own and nothing more - with Heaven itself. It is an error which comes from a good place, however, born out of Roland's great capacity for spiritual insight. It is exactly this ability to see what her older siblings cannot see that guides Lucy Pevensie to Aslan before anyone else in *The Lion, The Witch and The Wardrobe* and *Prince Caspian.* It is worth bearing in mind as well that participating in the final two chapters of *Elidor* would be an intense experience for anyone, let alone one so finely tuned as Roland. Nonetheless, I don't find anything in the text to suggest that he can't recover, go on to fulfil his potential and live a life of value and meaning. I take encouragement from Malebron's commendation after Roland has succeeded where his brothers and sister fail in the Mound of Vanwy: "Remember, I have said the worlds are linked ... and what you have done here will be reflected in some way, at some time, in your world."

Roland is a lantern bearer. He unfurls the banner of the Imagination, in both Elidor and Manchester, at the points where disenchantment and desacralisation seem strongest. I also see in him a herald of the coming spiritual resurgence, the Age of the Holy Spirit prophesied by Joachim de Flore in the twelfth century and Nicholas Berdyaev in the twentieth. Roland stands in the High Places, watching and waiting for the signs of this imaginative renaissance. It is a fine and noble calling, and possibly all that can be achieved at this time. Because who can say with certainty if the 'reflection' promised by Malebron has already been revealed, is currently with us, or still to come? The impact made by *Elidor* these last fifty-two years serves as sign and symbol enough, perhaps, that the greening of the wasteland - the recharging and resacralisation of our imaginations - might be nearer than we think.

We will know the day when it comes. Like *Elidor*, it will be freighted with gold:

* The illustrations for *Elidor* were drawn by Charles Keeping (1924-1988), who also illustrated many of Rosemary Sutcliff's children's stories set in late-Roman and early Anglo-Saxon England, such as *The Silver Branch*, *The Lantern Bearers* and *Dawn Wind*. This provides a nice link, I feel, between one era of 'decline' and another.

** The edition of *Elidor* I have used in this essay was published by HarperCollins *Children's Books* in 2008, in the *essential modern classics* imprint.

ALBION AND RUSSIA (JF)

He showed me a little thing, the size of a hazelnut, in the palm of my hand, and it was as round as a ball. I looked at it with my mind's eye and I thought, 'What can this be?' And answer came, 'This is all that is created.'

Julian of Norwich, *Revelations of Divine Love*

I remember how astonished I was as a boy, around 1982, or 1983, when I heard the High Tory statesman Enoch Powell refer to Britain and Russia as 'natural allies'. This, at the time, seemed wrong on every level. It was the height of the Cold War, and Russia (or the USSR or Soviet Union as it was more widely known) was viewed as the great enemy of the West and an existential threat, both to our freedom and physical survival.

I had not read Dostoyevsky then. I did not know about the 'Holy Russia' that existed before the Bolshevik revolution of 1917 and had been so relentlessly persecuted by the Soviet state ever since. My geopolitical thinking, such as it was, ran in conventional East versus West lines. I lacked Powell's imagination, and the historical and political artistry which revealed to him Britain and Russia as kindred spirits. It seems as plain as a pikestaff now - two great powers on the peripheries of Europe, one to the East, one to the West, both with one foot in and one foot out.

It is nothing new. Tension has existed in Russia for centuries between Westernisers in the mould of Peter the Great (1682 - 1721) and Slavophiles (Dostoyevsky being a good example) who regard the West as at best a corrupting influence and at worst a mortal threat to the Russian soul. A similar ambivalence towards Europe has been on view in Britain for much longer than is often supposed. One thinks, for instance, of the Imperial usurper Carausius, who declared himself Caesar in 286 and claimed Britannia for his own, an act which led to the province's recapture by Constantius Chlorus (the father of Constantine the Great) ten years later. The story is superbly told in Rosemary Sutcliff's *The Silver Branch* (1957), with its skilful interweaving of Roman and Celtic motifs - the 'Federal' and the 'National', if you like.

I have been reflecting a great deal of late on Powell's perspective, wondering if there might be a more meaningful affinity between our nations than the geographical accidents which he saw - in classic 'great game' style - as opportunities to wield joint influence to curb the ambitions of any overweening continental power. It is a tempting consideration. Certainly on the religious level. Maybe the political too. Russia, it appears, is leaving her post-Christian era behind, while Britain (and the whole Western world) wilfully races into one of her own. As terror becomes the 'new normal' in Europe, I have increasingly felt that our wisest course of action is to request Russian assistance. We seem incapable of arresting our own decadence and wholly unable to root out the enemy within. Would we do better under Russian auspices? Perhaps, but great discernment and caution is nonetheless called for. It is easy for me to sit here and invite Moscow to start pulling the strings. There are, however, traditionally-minded people a-plenty in the former Warsaw Pact countries who would not add their names to the invitation. I have no experience of Russian hegemony. They have.

It is crucial, therefore, that any partnership between Britain and Russia is built on rock not sand - not on projection, wish-fulfilment, fear or mutual convenience, but on a deep and rich appreciation of each country's spiritual essence and core. To this end, I would recommend that before any talking begins, a long period of silent contemplation is needed, because it is only in silence that space can be cleared for this inner truth to make itself felt. There are innumerable objects, themes and places that both parties could focus on, but for now I will suggest just two, one Russian and one English, one an icon and one a chapel.

First, on the Russian side, the *Descent of the Holy Spirit*, a late fifteenth-century icon of the Novgorod school.

There is a stillness and quiet authority to this icon which I find utterly compelling. This is no pell-mell dash through Jerusalem on Pentecost morning, everyone speaking in tongues with flecks of fire dancing above their heads. What we see instead is pattern, harmony and peace, the Apostles and Evangelists sitting serenely in a semi-circle - a true community of faith - as the Holy Spirit descends discreetly in twelve short rays. Look at how much space there is - space for the Spirit to breathe, blossom and spring forth into the world, symbolised here by the weary-looking king at the bottom. His white garment bears the twelve scrolls of the Apostles, signs of his (and our) approaching liberation from the clutches of Hades.

'Beauty will save the world,' as Dostoyevsky famously wrote. It is on this level, I feel, that Russia can achieve her spiritual destiny - the fraternal, gem-like flame of her religious tradition pointing the way towards a more balanced, harmonious way of being, an alternative point of reference to the destructive mantra of 'individual choice' currently sowing so much chaos and unhappiness in the West and beyond.

As for our own country, well, there is clearly a Divine sensibility native to these lands. The British Isles, since long before the days of Carausius and Constantius, have been deeply receptive to the mystical and metaphysical. The Druids of Britain and Ireland, the stone circles of Avebury and Stonehenge, and the sanctity and courage of the Celtic saints bear potent witness to this. A whirl of commercial activity in recent centuries, allied to a coarsening and narrowing of vision, has served to obscure this underlying predisposition. But it hasn't left us. The Divine sensibility, and what it points to, remain - under the surface for now, but no less powerful and real for that. What it points to is the 'peace which passeth all understanding', and when one experiences that peace, a shift in levels takes place and that peace becomes all there is. All else ebbs and fades. Conflict becomes meaningless; discord and strife unthinkable. Peace is all that there was, will be, and is. It is 'all that has been created,' as Christ, the Prince of Peace, told Mother Julian.

Image – www.theimaginativeconservative.org

When my wife and I stepped out of Julian's cell on a Sunday afternoon early in 2014, it felt like the world had been subtly transfigured, the Holy Spirit sprinkling largesse onto the rooftops, chimneys and turrets of Norwich. What happened in the cell cannot be framed in words, but I regard that sacred space as the architectural equivalent of the Novgorod icon, and it is in standing before this icon and kneeling in this chapel that Albion and Russia can meet, connect and begin carrying out God's work in the world.

The Icon and the cell are both sites of reality; zones of silence, stillness and prayer. Only the real carries weight. Anything else is a sham - self-promoting fantasy or another 'great game'. What is real saves, heals and gives life. No matter how tiny, feeble or insignificant it seems. The real breathes, blossoms, and springs forth into the world to turn the tables on Hades at the appointed hour.

It is the destiny, I am sure, of our two great nations to be present and active at that hour. Let the great bell sound, therefore, the silence commence, and the peace which passeth all understanding - from Vladivostok to Tintagel - come down upon us all.

DWELLERS ON THE THRESHOLD – A FICTIONAL MEDITATION ON THE HOLY GRAIL (JF)

'I suppose you'll want to go to the ruins again?' said Gina.

'It's Friday afternoon,' said Charlie. 'We always go on Friday afternoons. Don't we?'

Gina's black bob glinted gold in the September sun. She shrugged, but turned left all the same, down Dundonald Road, past the terraced houses, towards the 'ruins'.

'I can't be doing with this anymore,' said Jack. 'It's babyish.'

Charlie sighed. The ruined church and school stood tall and skeletal at the bottom of the street – first the school, then, across the old railway, the church. They clumped through the weeds. A wasp attacked Jack's white shirt. He brushed it off, but it shot straight back and settled on his tie, mesmerised, it seemed, by its silver and red diagonal stripes and the sky-blue, upturned sword of the Didsbury High School badge.

Charlie led the way, across the playground – the school's broken towers and cracked, pointed windows to his right. Then came five stone steps and the underground passage – a cigar-shaped air raid shelter – below the thorns and thistles of the disused Manchester to Stockport line.

The floor clanged, as the chipped tin of the walls and ceiling mirrored their passing in a blur of grey and black. How different, Charlie recalled, from that sparkly May morning when the reflections had galloped by like the Horses of the Sun, the dull sheen set aglow by seven sacred candles, as Charlie guided his Company through the tunnel and into the church to find and save the Holy Grail.

He had Jack and Gina with him then, of course, plus Billy, Paul and Christina, as well as Adam, who had been the first to go just after half-term. Soon, bar Jack and Gina, they had all gone, heads turned by music, make-up and clothes. They were the only two left now, and not for much longer by the look of things.

Still, Charlie felt hope. He had a plan. Five steps up brought them to the church forecourt and the twin steeples. He bore left, past the Great Tower and the South Transept's crumbling brick, to the back of the church and an ivy-clad door. He knew what he would do – take them up the Lesser Tower to the roofless chapel, where the sun would shimmer on the faded frescoes, shocking Jack and Gina out of their grown-up play world, bringing them back to themselves and the great myth that Charlie had inspired them (and himself) with ever since the monks of Saint Michael's Church and School had shut their mysterious doors.

Why those doors had closed remained largely unexplained, even now, two years on. The grown-ups huffed and puffed, but no-one seemed sure of anything. Different people said different things. Charlie reckoned that the Holy Grail had been hidden in the church. Dark powers were hunting it down. His dad said that the monks, who were called Constantinians, had simply ran out of money, while Fatty Holloway claimed they had been busted by MI5 for plotting to overthrow the governments of Europe and restore the Roman Empire. But the few ex-St. Mike's kids who had been sent to Didsbury High (most had gone to St. Mark's, the other Catholic school) just smiled and shook their heads at the juicy tale. The monks were strict, but nice, they said, and Charlie could get nothing more out of them. Like everything else about the place, it was all very strange.

Light cascaded in, every ten steps, through thin slits of windows along a spiral stone staircase. The roofless chapel, once they arrived, was the same as ever – a round stone chamber, with a bare altar in the middle, three glassless windows behind, and a gaping, jagged hole at the top. The sun crashed through, as Charlie had hoped, slashing down and around the altar in a halo of arrowed light. The frescoes glittered and throbbed with vitality – numinous, transfigured – poised, it appeared, to spring from the walls and take 3D shape in the room – a ship, a crowned king, a rearing horse, three winged angels, and a burnished, fire-flecked chalice.

The scene was gorgeous – heart-stoppingly so – but Jack and Gina paid no heed, loping listlessly around instead, Jack to Charlie's left and Gina to his right. The wasp flew from Jack's tie and vanished through the middle window. Charlie watched it go. Then Gina said, 'I'm sorry, Charlie. This is the last time. We can't come anymore.' He turned to her, but Gina shook her head and looked away, towards the king on the wall and his sceptre and orb.

'Come on mate,' said Jack, his flaxen hair bleached white by the sun. 'It's kids' stuff, this. There's miles more exciting things to do than playing fairy tales here.'

Charlie turned and faced the door. He didn't want them to see him cry. 'Look Charlie,' he heard Gina say. 'I know it's hard, I know you're an only child, I know how much these legends mean to you, but we can't stay children forever.'

Charlie gasped, stopped listening, blinked, rubbed his eyes, and blinked again. He couldn't believe what he was seeing. A girl was standing in the doorway, right in front of him, tall with long brown hair and dressed in dazzling white. She held a lit candle, with purple letters looping around, forming words in a foreign language – Latin, perhaps – that Charlie couldn't understand. He glanced down, muddled and shy, and when he looked up she was walking straight towards him. He tumbled back, panicked, tripped over and fell, scrambling to his knees to see the girl in white already behind the altar, standing on the right-hand side, holding her candle aloft.

Charlie buried his face in his hands, peeping through his fingers. The girl bowed low, but not to him. He turned around and saw a new girl, smaller than the first, her hair as black as Gina's, but with a rounder, more childlike face. She wore a scarlet robe and carried a big book with a golden cover – a red cross emblazoned on one side and a soaring eagle on the other.

She walked forward, carrying her book before her, and stood behind the altar to the left. Both girls bowed. Charlie turned again, and there, standing on the threshold, was a woman in blue, the tallest woman (or man) he had ever seen – seven foot at least – with a face he couldn't see, because in her hands was the Grail itself, blazing like a thousand suns, filling the chapel, and both Charlie's worlds – the mythic and the real – with healing, hallowed light.

A song began – holy, high and wild. Charlie looked up. It was the girl with the book. The woman in blue was in front of the altar now, a yard or so away. Her hair was black and streaming, flowing half-way down her back. The singing stopped. She lifted the Grail up high. Charlie closed his eyes, and a bell rang three times.

When he came to, Jack and Gina were the only people there, standing by the left-hand window, looking down at the railway and school. 'Did you see? Did you see?' Charlie spluttered, shaking them by the shoulders.

'See what?' said Jack.

'The Grail,' said Charlie.

'The Grail,' Jack snorted. 'Honestly mate, talk about imagination. You've seen a thousand Grails since you've been taking us here.'

'Please Charlie,' said Gina. 'Let it go.' She stretched out her hand, but Charlie wrenched it away and ran off, across the threshold and down the stairs. At the bottom he spotted another staircase – one he'd never seen before – spiralling down to the right of the door.

He raced down the steps, hope restored. An orange glow crept and curled around the corners, closer all the time. Hammer-hammer-hammer went Charlie's heart. 'This is it,' he thought. 'The book, the candle, the girls, the Grail.' But when the stairs ended, none of them were there. He was in a round chamber again, the same size and shape as the roofless chapel. A burning brazier, high to his left, lit the room, evocatively exposing, in red and yellow tongues of fire, the painting hanging on the wall to his right. Charlie walked across, then stumbled two steps back, stunned by an unsuspected force and power. It was a portrait of an old man. He had a red cape, a shock of white hair, and a face that struck Charlie as wise and kindly, yet also forceful and strong.

It was a face of experience and depth – a noble face, a royal face – a face, Charlie felt instantly sure, of one like him, who had searched for the Grail when young, found it, lost it, and set out after it again and again, a man who had suffered and lost but never surrendered, a man who had wrestled with angels and flung back everything the world could hurl at him – highs and lows, ups and downs, twists and turns, all of that – and won through. Charlie saw it in the bright blue steel of his eye – passion, pride, commitment, integrity, service – everything he needed and yearned for to give shape and direction to the mess of his own life.

He wondered who the old man was. A saint? A monk? Or the Emperor himself – Constantine the Great – who, so Fatty claimed, the monks had named their order after? Whoever he was, and despite the years between them, Charlie felt a connection and kinship, a bond and deep affinity – like they were living at the same time, sharing the same journey, and bearing the same load – brothers, comrades and friends.

He sat on the ground, drew his knees up to his chin and reflected on his troubles. No-one understood him. Parents, teachers, mates, no-one. Except old Hanrahan, of course, but that had been years ago and Hanrahan was no longer his teacher. But, then again, Hanrahan had never really been a teacher, not in the way that Edmonds and Handysides and all those bores were. He was an Irishman and a storyteller, who had given Charlie the myths, legends, songs and stories – from Cuchulain to Lancelot, to Heracles, Jason and Odysseus – that electrified his mind and transformed the daily round of home and school from black and white to colour. It wasn't Hanrahan's fault that Charlie had pushed too far, like Icarus floundering in the air or Phaeton tussling vainly with the Horses of the Sun. Roping in his friends, Charlie realised now, and trying to make the legends real had made him all too easy prey for the great wave of change sweeping their childhoods away.

His friends had found it a laugh at the start, so much so that Charlie thought his Company might last forever, but virtually overnight, once everyone turned thirteen, they all lost interest and drifted away. They didn't care like Charlie did. They were cut from a less intense cloth. They didn't have his desire, his hunger, and his mad, undying hope that one day he'd head out for school and burst straight through the screen of surface appearance into a realler, deeper, truer world – through the magic forest to the Grail Castle and out the other side, across the Western Sea with to the Isle of Heroes where the Holy Ones dwelt in the hallowed, healing light of God.

Charlie stood up and stared into the old man's eyes, his folly laid bare and his silly schemes smashed. But in the steady stillness of that gaze, second by second, then minute by minute, a new strength dawned and shone within. This dynamic, kinglike face, he perceived, was offering him so much – the brotherhood he longed for, the guidance he needed in his voyage from boy to man, and, most terrifically of all, a sign and prophecy of what he might one day become if he dug down deep inside and tuned into what was real, in himself and in the world outside.

A buzzing noise distracted Charlie. He looked around, but couldn't see where it was coming from. And in that moment he saw a truth – that there was no division, no clash, no threshold even, between the real and mythic worlds. They were the same. One and indivisible. And that, Charlie recognised, was the old man's parting message – that if he learned to trust and listen, learned to touch, taste, hear, smell and see things as they really were – not as he hoped or feared they were – then this fuzzy world, this world of fumbles and frustration, would flip around in a numinous flash – hallowed and transfigured – as holy, high and heart-stoppingly gorgeous as the frescoes on the wall – the ship, the king, the horse, the angels, and the burnished, fire-flecked chalice.

The buzzing was bugging Charlie now. This time he clocked the culprit. It was the wasp, whizzing around the top of the frame. Charlie stretched out his hand, but the wasp backed off and disappeared into a crack behind the painting.

Charlie smiled. The brazier crackled behind him. It was time he went back upstairs. He bowed low to the old man, said 'thank you', and turned to go. And as he left, high above somewhere, faint and far off – in another world, perhaps – a bell rang three times.

VOYAGE TO THE WEST (JF)

The notion of Albion (or Logres, as Charles Williams and C.S. Lewis called it) as a hidden reality underpinning daily life is one that stirs and stimulates the imagination. Several place-names and sites across Britain have become associated in the popular mind with this 'secret country'. One thinks of Tintagel, for instance, or Glastonbury Tor, or Avebury, or the White Horse of Uffington.

For myself, it is a particular train journey which is most emblematic of Albion - from Newcastle to Liverpool, from East to West, from the courts of the morning to the couch of the setting sun, from the North Sea and the banks of the Tyne to the mouth of the Mersey and the Irish Sea.

We begin on Tyneside. England's north-eastern seaboard looks out towards Scandinavia, calling to mind the successive waves of Viking raids, invasions and settlements that bedevilled Northumbria between 787 and 1066. As we proceed westward, a number of different but inter-linked Englands emerge, starting with the England of Christendom and the Ages of Faith, given such outstanding embodiment in the Medieval splendour of Durham and York Cathedrals. Next come the twin industrial powerhouses of Leeds and Manchester, separated by the Pennines, that stark and spectacular mountain range, the 'backbone of England' and the heartland of the formidable Brigantes tribe in the age of the Roman Conquest and the lost Ninth Legion that set out to subdue the Celts and disappeared without trace in the mists of the North.

At the westernmost edge of our journey, the train clatters through the tunnels on the approach to Liverpool Lime Street. Sunlight flickers on the moss-lined walls from narrow slits of bridges overhead. The world, between the bridges, turns shadowy and dim. My reflection stares back at me, pale and luminous in the darkened window. Then, just like that, it vanishes, rendered invisible by the brightness of the station, spreading out around us like a rough-hewn open air theatre. The city beyond, with its vivid sunsets, artistic flair, and princely (if sometimes shabby) air, has a faintly Otherworldly feel, not fully of a piece, it seems, with the country before the tunnels. Just as Newcastle looks out onto the Norse world, so Liverpool turns towards Wales rather than England, towards Ireland and the Western Ocean; as far as the Isles of the Blessed, those mysterious realms at the rim of the world, where this level of reality ends and the next begins.

The veil between the worlds is thin in Liverpool. It is a numinous place, a Celtic place, an in-between place, yet as vital a piece in Albion's mosaic as all the rest - Manchester, Newcastle, Leeds, the Pennines, and the Cathedrals of Durham and York, which find their echo and reflection in Liverpool's pair of twentieth-century Cathedrals. And it's this symmetry and symbolism which makes the journey what it is for me - this multi-faceted slice of national life and history - following the day from sunrise to sunset, from the sea-road to Asgard to the great white ship that sails every night for Tir-Na-Nog.

Whenever I set out on this this voyage, you see, I sense the existence of the underlying pattern behind these varied aspects of Albion's story. Sensing is one thing, however, piercing the veil another. To perceive the pattern as a whole, to recognise and comprehend the deeper reality - to name it and articulate it - that would be to unveil and usher into the light of day the hidden meaning and purpose of this island Kingdom. The return of the Holy Grail to Logres would be one way of describing it. The maverick English prophet John Michell suggests another:

> The answer, when it comes, takes the form of a revelation. That does not mean a god or a UFO descending, but something that enters minds just when it is needed. Basically it is a pattern or a codification of number, and as you study it you realise that it is the pattern of creation and the human mind. *Confessions of a Radical Traditionalist*, (Dominion Books, 2005, p.285)

Michell's understanding is true, certainly for himself and maybe for others, but not for everyone. Each of us experiences reality in a form and manner unique to ourselves and our own characteristics. As a lover of the word, for example, I suspect that the revelation might appear in the form of a narrative - a story, perhaps, or a speech, song, poem or play. Shakespeare came close to expressing it, I think. As did Blake. So too, in a different key, did Winston Churchill. But the *right* word - or the right combination of words - is yet to come. That will be the 'something' that enters our minds when we most need it.

I feel its approach though, its growing presence and strength, as the train rolls out of Lime Street and the lamps shine like silver moons in the dusk. Two station staff, a man and a woman, stand talking at the end of the platform. The man says something, then points to the sky. They look up, as do I, but it's no good, not for me, because we're back in the tunnels and it's dark again except for my reflection gazing back at me in the window. Then it comes - the revelation - or something like it - on the far side of my face - golden letters in a flowing script, standing out distinctly against the greeny black of the tunnel wall. There isn't much to see. A handful of lines, nothing more. Barely a paragraph. The train gathers speed and I catch a couple of words: 'Wasteland' and 'waters'. There's a 'when' and a 'tree' and a 'King' too. Then it's gone and we're out of the tunnels, rounding the curve of the engine sheds, past the city walls and into the country beyond.

The moment has passed; the vision departed. But I don't feel downhearted; not in the slightest. I smile and sit back. 'Albion is here,' I say to myself, as the train rattles on through the night, towards the eastern coast and the return - nearer with every turn of the wheel - of the renewed, rejuvenated Sun and - I know it in my heart now - the rebirth and restoration of this holy land.

THE DECLINE, FALL & POSSIBLE RISE OF ALBION

THE VACUUM OF LEADERSHIP (JF)

It should be enshrined in UK law that anyone who aspires to become Prime Minister must read and reflect on 'The Hunt' by David Jones, a mid-length poem which features in his collection, *The Sleeping Lord,* (Faber and Faber, 1974).

Jones's Arthur is 'a diademed leader.' But the jewels do not betoken a show-pony or a 'big-time Charlie.' Quite the reverse. They are worn by a man who knows, cherishes and values the worth of his land and the people of his land. He protects and he serves. He does what he does out of love and a sure and certain knowledge of what is noble and pure and has to be defended, to the last breath if need be. He pits himself face to face with the Great Hog who is ravaging his country. In doing so, he incurs the grievous wounds that render him the 'Sleeping Lord' of the next poem in the sequence, that avatar of Albion who the writers and readers of this blog, and many more all around the world, are endeavouring in ways great and small to awaken.

Arthur 'directs the toil.' His face is 'furrowed with the weight of the enterprise,' his 'visage fouled with the hog-spittle whose cheeks are fretted with the grime of the hunt-toil.'

Though his forehead is 'radiant like the smooth hill in the lateral light,' it is also 'corrugated like the defences of the hill ... '

Jones's Arthur goes to the deep places - physically, spiritually and mentally - 'because of his care for the land and the men of the land.'

It's not a game. It really matters to him. 'If his eyes are narrowed for the stress of the hunt and because of the hog they are moist for the ruin and for love of the recumbent bodies that strew the ruin.'

Now, is there any potential Prime Minister today at all capable of such vision, integrity and self-sacrificial love for the land he or she represents and, in a sense, incarnates as leader? I would say no. The last Western leader, as far as I'm aware, who invested his role with this level of high seriousness was Charles de Gaulle. Winston Churchill too. Perhaps it's no coincidence that both were high quality writers who believed in the saving, transformative value of arts and culture. They were men of intelligence and imagination allied to a strong ethic of sacrifice and service.

How rare these attributes are today. How quaint and old-fashioned it all seems. Not at all post-modern. We are too sophisticated and knowing now - too ironic - for characters like this who actually thought that religion, literature and history were real things, not just intellectual webs signifying nothing more than the letters and words on the page.

But it's exactly this level of intensity - this spark of genius - that we're missing. There are too many middle-managers in leadership roles. Too many people-pleasers and company men. As the theologian and poet, John Milbank, wrote on Twitter recently:

> Somehow the brightest people no longer figure at the top and this is part of why we are in a mess. Our elite institutions are not sufficiently shaping people of wisdom or else not many of those go into politics.

Things have to change and quickly. Because where we are at the moment the time is ripe for that 'Man of Lawlessness' spoken of by Saint Paul to rise up and make his mark on the world. And there will be no 'diademed leader' to stand in his way and take the hit for us.

Unless, of course, he awakens and raises his standard in the little time that remains to us.

THE GLORIOUS '50S (JF)

I have been thinking about how so many of the books that have shaped my imagination and formed my appreciation of Albion were published in the 1950s.

The *Chronicles of Narnia* are an obvious example: *The Lion, The Witch and The Wardrobe* (1950), *Prince Caspian* (1951), *The Voyage of the Dawn Treader* (1952), *The Silver Chair* (1953), *The Horse and His Boy* (1954), *The Magician's Nephew* (1955) and *The Last Battle* (1956).

So too the three parts of *The Lord of the Rings: The Fellowship of the Ring* (July 1954), *The Two Towers* (November 1954) and *The Return of the King* (1955).

Roger Lancelyn Green's classic retelling of the Arthurian mythos, *King Arthur and his Knights of the Round Table*, was published in 1953, with his *Adventures of Robin Hood* following three years later.

Rosemary Sutcliff's stories of Roman and post-Roman Britain first appeared in the 1950s, most notably *The Eagle of the Ninth* (1954), *The Silver Branch* (1957) and *The Lantern Bearers* (1959), while Colin Wilson began his prolific career with *The Outsider* (1956), *Religion and the Rebel* (1957) and *The Age of Defeat* (1959).

I would also add that Alan Garner's Alderley Edge novels, *The Weirdstone of Brisingamen* and *Moon of Gomrath*, came out at the start of the next decade, in 1960 and 1963 respectively. In his collection of essays, *The Voice That Thunders* (1997), Garner suggests that the generation of children's writers that emerged in the aftermath of the Second World War, including Susan Cooper (*The Dark is Rising*), Sutcliff and himself, were greatly influenced by the strong sense of good versus evil the war inculcated in people's minds.

This clear delineation between good and evil and right and wrong (or, in Wilson's case, between a life oriented towards meaning and a life immersed in trivia) is highly marked in all the writers listed above. So too is a yearning for stability and peace - the good order established by Aragorn after the War of the Ring or the longing to rebuild Roman Britain that animates Aquila in Sutcliff's *The Lantern Bearers.*

The 1950s are routinely derided today for precisely this quality of uncomplicated simplicity. They are damned as 'boring' and 'grey'. Traditionally-minded types are lambasted for 'wanting to take us back to the 1950s.' Viewed from 2017, however, after five decades of social and economic liberalism and a growing sense of chaos and insecurity, the stability and simplicity of the '50s looks very attractive indeed. It could also be the case that the limited work and entertainment options people had in those days - the lack of choice and the absence of technology - helped forge a slower, more reflective mental climate, more conducive to creative endeavours than the fast and furious 'marketplace' we live in today.

It is a craving for this kind of rootedness, I believe, that lies behind the recent wave of political populism, which has made so many waves across Europe and the US. It seems to me, however, that the 1950s was a decade peculiar to itself in many ways - a period of suspended animation, where the horrors of the war had not yet properly sunk in and where the pyrrhic nature of Britain's victory and Europe's complete loss of power had not yet been consciously acknowledged (though Rosemary Sutcliff's elegiac reflections on the decline of Roman Britain suggest an unconscious awareness on her part at least of the UK's changed status).

We can learn a great deal from the decade though. A Christian renaissance in this country will need to base itself on the two pillars exemplified by the '50s - the stability, security and simplicity we have lost in a bewildering haze of complexity and choice, and the imaginative flair illuminated so well in these great books. 'Keep your feet on the ground but your eyes on the stars', in other words.

A DEEPER REALITY (JF)

I have been reading a short essay by the Eurasianist thinker, Laurent James. The piece is in French and can be read at his site www.parousia-parousia.blogspot.co.uk.

James uses the results of the first round of voting in the recent French Presidential election as a springboard for a meditation on two competing visions of his country - what he calls 'Gaul' and 'France'. Gaul for him represents an imaginative, intuitive, spiritually-attuned worldview inherited from the Celts, while France stands for a quantitative, rationalistic understanding of the nation's role, beginning with the Frankish kings and continuing up to the newly elected President.

A similar dynamic is at work in Britain too, I feel. On the one hand, an ambience of restless activity, financial and emotional insecurity, and growing social and cultural fragmentation; and on the other the 'still centre' of the great cathedrals, the rugged coastline, the lakes and mountains, and the ramparts, hill-forts and 'tors' of pre-Christian antiquity. William Blake called this second aspect 'Albion', and it is his evocation of the primordial spiritual essence of this land that animates both his poetry and his painting and accounts, I believe, for his enduring popularity.

This is the eternal Britain, the true Britain. It has always been here and always will be. Sometimes it is visible, other times not. It is occluded at the moment but will emerge again into the light of day, like the Hidden Imam in Shia Islam, at the appointed time. The current dispensation, in my view, is not as solid as it seems. The contemporary West lacks any kind of religious or philosophical underpinning and therefore, despite all its technological achievements, cannot continue indefinitely. Its fall is assured.

What will replace it then? All kinds of doom-laden scenarios inevitably spring to mind, but I would like to think that the present order, which ignores reality and pretends it isn't there, will cede place to a general awareness and waking up to the things that are fundamentally real and true. This doesn't necessarily need to be articulated in a political programme or a set of beliefs. Truth and reality lie at a deeper, more instinctual level. Type 'Tintagel' into YouTube, for example, and look at some of the clips of the castle and its surroundings. Feel the elemental rawness of it all - the sea, the sky, the stones, the silence, the sun, the wind. As William Wildblood recounts in his book, *Meeting the Masters*:

> When, on a trip to Cornwall with my family, we visited the rocky promontory of Tintagel, I had my first exposure to one of the sites of the Western Mysteries. Naturally I knew nothing of that tradition then nor was I aware that some places truly are places of power but my lack of knowledge did not stop me being deeply affected by the castle and, more especially, its setting. The sea, the stones, the wind and mist all combined to thrust me back into an archaic past when the veil between the spiritual and material worlds dissolved much more readily than it does now.

This is the baseline spiritual orientation our society has lost - a deeper reality existing beyond and before words and concepts and emanating from the heart - our own hearts and the heart of the land. We have slipped our moorings and turned our backs on the deepest part of ourselves and our country. We have forgotten who we are, individually and collectively, losing sight of God in His most basic, primal form. We are left with a spiritual vacuum and this, I feel, is the underlying metaphysical reason for why we are being attacked at the moment.

Reconnection with this sacred core - on both the personal and national levels - is the first and most necessary step towards a religious renaissance in the UK. The specifically Christian elements of this revival will make themselves clear in time. For now, the most important thing is simply to recognise the hand of God at work in both the topography and history of our 'sceptred isle', so that we are at least facing the right way again.

We shouldn't fuss and fret, therefore, about how this reorientation might play out in the political realm. Laurent James, in his piece, has critical words to say about both Marine Le Pen and Emmanuel Macron. A vote for Le Pen, he suggests, is a vote for the aggressive French state that attempted to crush the Gaulish spirit, while a vote for Macron would endorse the Western globalism which is strangling the French nation in its turn and doing to France (and every other country) what France did to Gaul. It is a false choice, in other words, and the hour of the Great Battle and the true, spiritual nationalists -

the sons and daughters of William Blake - is not yet at hand.

We are the lantern bearers, and we should refuse to be drawn. Our vocation is to sit lightly to the revolving door of Presidents and Prime Ministers, take the world's bluster with a pinch of salt and not be intimidated by the darkness thickening around us. Ultimately, it has no reality. Our role is to watch, wait, pray, and tune ourselves in to the Truth, passing on the torch, when and where we can, in thought, word and deed, so that when the great horn sounds and the gold and silver standard of Christ in Glory is unfurled, we may be in every sense ready, prepared and 'on point.'

As the little Welsh priest in Rosemary Sutcliff's *Dawn Wind* (Oxford University Press, 1961) declares on hearing of the Saxon advance:

> 'Brothers, the Light goes out and the Dark flows in. It is for us to keep some Lamp burning until the time that we can give it back to light the world once more; the Lamp, not of our Faith alone, but of all those beauties of the spirit that are kindled from our Faith, the Lamps of the love of wisdom in men's hearts and the freedom of men's minds, of all that we mean when we claim we are civilised men and women and not barbarians.'

6th June 2017

THE OLD PORT (JF)

It was half past four. The rehearsal had finished at four but Genevieve and Fintan were still there, bickering about faith, meaning, and Genevieve's supposed religious vocation.

Fintan went for a wander on the stage. He'd had enough of banging his head against a wall. Genevieve was unmoved - as fixed as the Northern Star - obstinate and obsessed. But then again, he mused, weaving his way between the statues and columns, so was he.

Fintan approached the dais and picked up the crown - a golden, gleaming circlet. He held it in his hand, fondling and caressing it, longing for Ambrose, Archbishop of Canterbury, to appear like a ghost from the stalls and ease it onto his head. Someone would crown him one day, no matter what Shakespeare said in *Julius Caesar.* He was twenty-seven, and consumed with ambition. To be hailed as a legend - a king among princes - the foremost Shakespearean actor of this second Arthurian age. That was the prize. That was what it was all about.

'You'd better be quick if you're coming,' whispered Genevieve from the wings. 'Mass is at five.'

Fintan put back the crown - for now - and followed her out of the theatre.

Sunlight stung his eyes and wind nipped his cheeks, as the raw March air snapped him out of his royal reverie. Down the cobbled hill, to his right, the big ships shimmered in the harbour. Waves bounced and sparkled in the setting sun. But Genevieve turned the other way, uphill through the narrow streets and the Old Port's celebrated mesh of cafés, pubs, galleries and music halls. The breeze whipped her long dark hair across her face. Seagulls cawed and chattered overhead. Down below, the place was buzzing, stuffed to the gills with good time Charlies from all over the Empire - sailors, showgirls, scholars, seminarians, you name it. The town had gone from strength to strength since the Great Restoration, no doubt about that.

There was still some damage showing from the war, of course. It was only five years ago, after all. Where the *Castor and Pollux* hotel once stood, for instance, was now a boarded up plot of empty space. The plywood boards, Fintan saw, as they passed by, were festooned with posters for all manner of books, performances and exhibitions, including one for their own play, *Julius Caesar* - seven-thirty every night at the *Gaumont* from March 10th to March 31st.

Valentina Ivanovna, the Director, had drawn the poster herself - a depiction of Fintan reaching up for a crown - the same circlet he had just been holding - that hovered and hung in the air, eluding his grasp like it was sitting in a pocket of time and space all of its own. He was there again in the top right corner, in a kind of inset, his blood-soaked form lying crumpled at the foot of Pompey's statue, the conspirators looming over him with their reddened knives. Fintan frowned. It was a nice picture - stylishly done - but Valentina had made him look distinctly non-regal. He would have a word tomorrow. They turned right at the *Round Table* café onto Charles Stuart Boulevard. The new British flag - a rearing red dragon on a backdrop of gold - billowed and fluttered from the wrought iron lampposts. It was here, four years previously, that Alfred II had led the first of his Reconciliation Walks, comforting the bereaved and healing the wounded with his touch. His son and successor, Arthur, had processed through the town just last year. Alfred and Arthur had visited Fintan's home town, Leicester, too, but he had missed them on both occasions. Four years ago he had still been a Prisoner of War in Minsk, and when Arthur came he had been preoccupied in looking after his parents. He had never seen a king. He felt it acutely - almost as great a loss - more in many ways - than the left hand he had lost in the war.

They walked past the Art School. Its Doric columns reminded Fintan of Valentina's stage set. That was another reason, he realised, why he felt so intensely at home in the Old Port. It had high culture and low culture but nothing middlebrow - no mediocrity, no bourgeoisie, no middle class. Genevieve felt it too, he knew. She had an integrity, a passion for quality and a spark of nobility, that set her apart in his eyes. He had lost so much in his life - his Mum and Dad last year, his hand, his comrades and friends - that he couldn't bear to lose Vivi now - not when he was just getting to know her; not with the chance of a few days together in the Old Port after the play's run. Somehow or other he had to divest her of this tomfool idea of becoming a nun.

Fintan could hear the great bell from Our Lady's Church now, calling the faithful to Mass. They turned right, down St. Joan Street. Smaller premises surrounded them - humble convenience stores and artisan's dwellings. 'It's funny,' said Fintan. 'In the play, you're my wife. 'You try and stop me going to the Senate. Going to my doom.'

Genevieve nodded but kept her eyes fixed straight ahead. Fintan pressed on. 'It's the other way round now, isn't it? I'm not your husband but I'm doing the same thing - trying to save you from yourself.'

He was being provocative. Fishing for a reaction. But none came. Not even a shrug. Then it was too late. They were at the church. Fintan rested his hand against the grey, almost silvery stone, unaccountably out of breath, tears welling his eyes, people thronging all about. All or nothing now, he thought. One last chance. He leapt across the doorway, blocking Genevieve's path. 'Vivi,' he gasped. 'This is insane. Think of what you're throwing away. You're an actress. You're a historian. You're a playwright. You've written a play about Charles I for God's sake. That's all the rage these days. The world's not like it used to be. There's a home here for you. Don't shut yourself away. Don't throw it all away.' A bizarre sight in the *Throne and Altar* pub opposite distracted Fintan. A wiry, bald little fellow, surrounded by a clapping, cheering crowd, was balancing a pint pot (it looked like Guinness) on his head. Then Genevieve jinked past him and was gone. 'Come and see' was all he heard her say.

Fintan was at a loss, swamped by a sea of Mass-goers, streaming past him on either side. He wanted to bolt - cross the road for a pint and a smoke and cheer the wee chap on. But someone had taken his arm, he didn't see who, and spun him around. Into the church. 'Just sit down for a while, son,' a gruff Northern voice growled in his ear. 'It'll be alright.' Rough hands shoved him into a pew - the back one on the right hand side. By the time he got his bearings, Fintan had lost all sense of who it might have been who had manhandled him. He drew a deep breath and drank in his surroundings.

Fintan was surprised by the size of the church. It had a wide, spacious feel that worked like a tonic on his nerves and gently settled the chaotic beating of his heart. He looked down the nave, his eyes drawn to the six tall candles on the Altar, then up to the curve and swell of the dome. A remarkably life-like mosaic - Christ washing the disciples' feet - swept across the ceiling in gold, white and blue.

Our Lady's appeared to Fintan as if ablaze in candlelight - from top to bottom - on the Altar, in the two side chapels and in front of the countless statues. Incense permeated the air. A profound silence - penetrated only by the tolling of the bell - restored rhythm and depth to his breathing.

The church was about two thirds full - a good mix, so far as he could see, of young and old, male and female. Some of the women and girls wore white, lacy veils. Genevieve, he noted, remained bareheaded. He could see the back of her head, on the left hand side, about four rows from the front. She was kneeling down, her attention absorbed in a pocket-sized, gold-leafed book.

The great bell fell silent. Fintan heard a faint tinkle, then everyone stood up. Male voices, high above, struck up a slow, meditative chant. Far away in the front left corner, a silver crucifix followed by four flickering candle flames edged steadily forward, bobbing up and down over the worshippers heads. Fintan lost sight of the procession momentarily, only for it to reappear beside him, sweeping past him on his left as the Servers, with the Priest behind them, approached the Altar for the start of Mass.

Fintan counted five Servers - one very old, one very young, two about his own age, and one (the cross-holder) whose face he didn't quite catch. They wore black, overlaid by a white, tunic-type garment. The Priest was a burly, tough-looking individual, with close-cropped hair and stubble to match. If it hadn't been for his long purple vestment, Fintan might have had him down as a bouncer rather than a cleric.

The Priest and his Servers genuflected in unison before the Altar. The cross-holder slotted his crucifix into a small square plinth to the Altar's right. The candle-bearers peeled off, two to each side, while the Priest and the cross-holder stood motionless in the centre. They turned around together, as the chant rose, fell and rose again like the waves in the harbour. They marched down the aisle, the Priest sprinkling the people with water from the cross-holder's brown jar.

Fintan saw the Server's face now. He had a cruel-looking scar - curved like a scimitar - across his left cheek. Fintan felt oddly certain that he had come by that scar in the war, just as he had lost his hand and - worse than that - Jan, Marco, Adam, Brendan, and so many more. Schoolfriends and comrades. The best (and only) brothers he ever had.

He felt a deep and sudden affinity with the Server. The Priest too. They were men - just as he was - and in that instant he wanted nothing more than to be part of their fraternity, to feel again that bond of brotherhood he had known at school, at the front, and in the camp at Minsk. Holy water splashed him in the eye as Priest and Server passed him by, and Fintan saw that he had been searching for this brotherhood - this sense of meaning, this intensity of feeling - ever since his release but in totally the wrong place - in in a vain and futile quest for individual glory and renown. Worse, he had projected his deepest spiritual and emotional desires onto Genevieve, a woman whose destiny clearly - and rightly, Fintan saw now - lay in a completely different sphere.

The Priest and Server returned to the Altar, and the Mass began. The congregation knelt down, and Fintan knelt with them. He couldn't understand, and in any case could hardly hear, the Latin prayers going on at the front. The Priest had his back to the crowd anyway. But Fintan didn't mind. No-one, least of all himself, had come here to be entertained. There was the whole of the Old Port for that. It was a relief as well, to be honest, not to be looked at by the Priest. Fintan didn't want the Mass to be about him or the people beside him. He wanted the Priest and Server to keep their focus on the Altar. It took some of the pressure off that he used to feel in church (on the few occasions that he went) before the war.

A new chant started up - female voices too now - *Kyrie Eleison, Christe Eleison, Kyrie Eleison.* Even Fintan knew what that meant - *Lord have mercy, Christ have mercy, Lord have mercy.* The words felt right and fitting. The follies, sins and errors of his life flashed before his inner eye. He hid his face in his hand and prayed to God for mercy and forgiveness for the first time since his capture and blindfolding.

The longer the Mass went on, the more it felt to Fintan like he was waking up from a long period of madness. There was something in the way the Priest and Servers moved together - the Servers standing so close to the Priest as he incensed the Altar - left side, right side, centre - that gave Fintan the sense of being present at something real - something sacred and substantial - a genuine, living mystery. He was astonished. It was all such a far cry from what Mass had been like before the Great Restoration, when it was still said in English and the Priest faced the people. Those Masses, Fintan recalled, were well-meaning, but banal. They didn't compel him - didn't captivate him - and he had gone elsewhere to find meaning and value. But now he felt like he was coming home - home to himself and home to the truth. A new world - surprising and strange, yet deeply familiar as well - was opening out like a flower before him.

Everyone stood up. The Priest ascended the carved pulpit, candle-bearers beside him, and chanted the Gospel. Everyone sat down, and the Priest gave his sermon - short, sharp and clear. He had a Liverpool accent, not quite as strong as Genevieve's, but similar in tone and intonation. Fintan wondered if they knew each other. The sermon was on the temptations of Christ and the seductiveness of worldly power and prestige. Staying true to ourselves and staying true to God are one and the same thing, the Priest said. Our deepest desire - what we long for more than anything else in the secret recesses of our heart - that's the key to who we are, and that's God's deepest desire for us too. We need to take steps, therefore, wherever and whenever we can, to build a culture and society that's congruent with this true self. 'We become what we contemplate,' he concluded.

The Mass continued. Fintan knelt down. The Priest blessed the Host, then the chalice, turned around to the people, turned back to the Altar, said a prayer and fell silent as the choir sang again - a haunting, plaintive tune, full of yearning, that stirred him to his depths:

Sanctus, sanctus, sanctus,
Dominus Deus Sabaoth.
Pleni sunt caeli et terra, gloria tua.
Hosanna in excelsis.
Benedictus qui venit in nomine Domini.
Hosanna in excelsis.

Silence descended. The Priest bent low over the Altar. Fintan had the impression that something momentous - something earth-shattering - was about to happen. The Priest lifted the Host high into the air. The man with the scar struck a great silver gong - once, twice, three times. The Priest genuflected, bent over the Altar again, and lifted up the chalice. Its golden gleam caught and held Fintan's eye, as the gong rang out again. And Fintan felt a presence - something (or someone) totally outside himself - wholly other - existing beyond the confines of his mind - his projections, plans and schemes - beyond everything he knew about himself, yet intimately linked somehow with that deepest, realest, truest self the Priest had spoken of in his sermon.

The gong sounded for the fifth time. The chalice hung in the air still, cradled in the Priest's hands, hovering, it seemed, between this world and the next. It drew Fintan's eyes up to the dome and the white-robed, kneeling Christ, washing a reluctant St. Peter's feet with His towel and bowl. Fintan gasped and shuddered. The mosaic, with the clarity of a thunderbolt, showed him in a flash what true Kingship really means - not being hailed as a legend, the foremost man of the age, and so forth - but sacrifice, service, and love - acting, in other words, as a brother to your people.

King Arthur II knew this well. His father, good King Alfred - the Restorer - knew it too. Fintan saw now that he had actually been involved in a lot of this throughout his life - a sacrifice, service and love that he had both given and received in great measure - at school, in the Army, and most of all, perhaps, in his parents care for him as a boy and his care for them when they were ill. Something softened, then snapped inside him. Ice broke and melted. The memory of his school-friends, his comrades, and his Mum and Dad was too much for him. Fintan buried his face in his hand again and wept for the first time since Jan, Adam, Marco and Brendan fell at the Siege of Tallinn. The gong resounded for the sixth and final time - booming, echoing, resonating, then fading. Fintan beat his breast three times. 'Kyrie Eleison,' he whispered. 'Christe Eleison, Kyrie Eleison.' The Priest genuflected, stood up again, and carried on with the Mass. Silence enveloped the church once more.

A triangle of light - brightening, dimming, then brightening again - steadily lit up the stage. Fintan let go of the dial. Three-quarter light was fine. He didn't want it too bright. He jumped up onto the stage, striding purposefully between the statues and columns.

Valentina - in that earnest, Eastern European way of hers - had given each of the actors what she called a 'secret key', so that, as she told them, 'you can come to this place - this *sanctum*, this sacred space - at any time of day or night to better connect with the play, the characters, and yourselves - as actors, human beings, and children of God.' Fintan, in his arrogance, had chuckled to himself at the Director's flamboyant speech. He'd thought he had all the answers in those days; both for himself and for others. He knew better now. The Mass had taught him that.

Fintan took up the crown - Julius Caesar's deepest desire - and held it in his hand. He heard a click behind him and turned around. There, in the wings, illuminated in a halo of light, stood the tall figure of Genevieve. They looked at each other for a long time in what should have been total silence but wasn't quite. Genevieve must have left the door open. The sounds of the Old Port at night - seagulls, cheers, and clinking glasses - stole through into Valentina's sacred space. It was right and fitting, Fintan felt. He remembered the little chap with the pint pot on his head and smiled.

'Remind me, Vivi,' he said. 'What's the last line of your play again? Charles' final words on the scaffold?'

Genevieve smiled. 'I go from a corruptible to an incorruptible crown,' she replied. 'Where no disturbance can be, no disturbance in the world.'

They laughed together, and Fintan threw her the crown in a looping, swooping arc. For a moment, mid-way between them, it seemed to pause and hover in the air, hanging there - a spinning band of golden fire - sitting in a pocket of time and space all of its own. Fintan looked closer, rubbed his eyes, and looked again. The crown appeared different to him - no longer a circle, but a curving bridge of molten light - a bridge between levels - between Heaven and Earth, the human and the Divine, the ego and the Self - a bridge of healing, unity and reconciliation - a bridge between Fintan's splintered post-war consciousness and what he longed for more than anything else in the secret recesses of his heart - quality, nobility, purpose, fellowship, and peace.

A great restoration.

COME AND SEE (JF)

Then Jesus turned and saw them following, and saith unto them, What seek ye? They said unto him, Rabbi (which is to say, being interpreted, Master,) where dwellest thou? He saith unto them, Come and see.

John 1: 38-39

We followed him up the coffee-stained stairs as what they used to call Great Britain disintegrated into rubble outside. it was dark, but not late - half-four, five o'clock - something like that. There were a good few hours left in the call centre day, but the heart (if that's not too strong a word) had long quit the place.

We walked the length of the corridor, passing Rooms B1, B2 and B3 on our way. People were still working, or pretending to work. Red-faced supervisors - yesterday's big guns - huffed and puffed, pointing to graphs and charts on whiteboards that mattered less and less with each explosion, each random alarm and each plane screaming overhead. Management and staff alike glanced nervously out of the windows. Rain sheeted down in slanting Manchester stair-rods. The lights went out in the insurance place opposite. We arrived at Room B5.

We stood together, James and I, on one side of the desk, while he addressed us from the other. He spoke with clarity and authority, not the sham authority of the 'management team', but a deep, rich, golden lordliness - serious and jovial at once - welling up, it seemed, from the centre of his being.

'That's the bloke you need,' Jock the security guard had told us not five minutes before. We'd watched him as he passed us by, coming back from the broken tea machine. It was hard to credit, looking at him, that this was the one we had been seeking - the one to give pattern, purpose, shape and direction to our lives. But there it was. Jock knew his stuff. He radiated inner authority himself.

There was nothing special about the new guy, you see. Not at first sight. It's only been later, since we've had a bit of time and space, that we've started to get a sense of what he's about.

I found it hard in the call centre to tell how old he was. Some days he'd look young; others old. He was tall and slim, with brown spiky hair and a long, stubbly face. His accent was local; more the north side of town than the south, I thought. Salford, perhaps. But it was what he said that counted. He promised us nothing ... yet everything.

'Andrew, James,' he began. 'You have come. Now you see. Here I am. Here's where I live - here at the heart of things when the world splits apart. This is my home. These are my people - broken, weak and fallible - people like you; people like me. You'll always find me here, in the chaos and collapse, when the glass towers fall and the shattered limbs of analysts and executives lie scattered on the boardroom floor.'

'Abide with me,' he went on. 'Work with me. I offer you nothing in terms of medals, praise, renown and worldly security. Quite the reverse. I can, however, guarantee you everything that burns most fiercely in your hearts and has done since you were boys - your desire for fellowship and nobility, for dignified, meaningful work, and for lives dedicated to the service of the sacred.'

He paused, then fixed us with those wide, brown eyes. 'Gentlemen, are you with me?' I glanced to my left. James was fiddling surreptitiously with his phone. I smiled. I knew what he was doing. Texting his brother, John. That's what gave me the idea. I put my hand in my pocket. It was time I contacted my own brother.

'We've not got time to be messing around with phones,' he said. But there was light in his eyes and a smile playing around the corners of his mouth. 'Especially not in a call centre.'

Outside, another powerful explosion rent the air. Then the lights went out with a little *phutt*, and we were left with the glow of our phones. Mine vibrated in my hand. I held it up and looked at the screen. 'On my way,' said the text. Then the alarms went off.

ANOTHER CHANCE? (WW)

I believe that England was intended to be or it was hoped that she might be a pioneer for a revived form of spirituality in the late 20th century but this failed. It failed through a combination of social and political actions that came about in the 1980s but had their roots earlier, sometimes much earlier. We are still living with the consequences of that today.

At any one time there is always a jostling mass of thoughts and ideas lying beneath the surface seeking concrete form in the future. Most of these can take a good or bad turn. They can manifest themselves in human consciousness positively or not as the case may be, sometimes both together. It all depends on the receptivity and ability to translate the sensed concept both of individual human beings and of groups. Ideas of love and freedom are obvious examples but there are many others. These ideas can be encouraged in a positive form by spiritual forces but they can also be manipulated and perverted by demonic ones and sadly humanity at the moment is often more prone to respond to the latter since this will usually be more in line with its desires and weaknesses, and require less effort on its part to bring into expression.

Many ideas pertaining to a fresh spiritual understanding rose to the surface in the 1960s though pinning a time to these things is always problematic since nothing comes from nothing. These ideas had been around for decades, if not centuries in some cases. But in the '60s they broke through to a greater extent and became more embedded in general consciousness. And what was the central idea around which all the other ones revolved? It was that God was not just the transcendent law maker out there but that he was within us as our very being and that we could individually realise that. In essence, the idea was that we were divine beings with divine potential. Naturally enough, this idea wasn't usually understood in quite those terms. People responded according to their own capacity and within the limits of their own understanding or pre-existing ideologies. Nevertheless, realised as such or not, this was the fundamental root idea behind all other ideas to do with freedom, increased democracy, exploration of consciousness, artistic innovation, living in harmony with nature etc, etc. Man can become a god. It has to be said that there was nothing intrinsically new in this. But it was at that time brought out more than before and potentially available to everyone. It was in the air. The possibility of spiritual renaissance existed.

Unfortunately, however, whenever there is something new that promises to expand our horizons, the corruption of that thing follows closely behind. This is the consequence of us being fallen beings living in a fallen world. The potential for rebirth that was there in the '60s ran aground. It was diverted away from spiritual ends into social and political ones on a much lower level of consciousness. Even when expressed spiritually, as it should have been, it fizzled out into the often narcissistic banalities and trite platitudes of the New Age movement. England, which had the chance to be a pioneer in new understanding, failed to take up that opportunity. She was not alone in this. Other countries, most notably America, were jointly involved in this destiny but they all failed and were sidetracked into lesser preoccupations by their own shortcomings and by listening once again to the voice of the tempter, always seeking to lead astray.

But from failure can come success at a later time if the lesson is learnt. Might it be that we have another chance to awaken to the realities of the spiritual world? Could the current turmoil in the world lead to something like that as people react against all the absurdities of the modern world? Politics has failed us, science has failed us, art has failed us, pretty much everything has failed us. Spirituality might seem the only option now. However, if this does happen and significant numbers of people turn to God then every effort has to be made to ensure that this revival is not poisoned at source as happened last time, and that any nascent spirituality is not contaminated by a human-centric perspective as it was in the '60s but instead submits itself to the wisdom of tradition. True spiritual tradition is never outmoded. Christ came to fulfil the law and the prophets not to replace them. It's worth repeating.

Any new spirituality cannot really be new. It can only be a restatement of what has always been. Spiritual truth does not change though it may grow, or our perception of it may grow, but if it does grow, it does so organically. And we must not forget, as previously we have forgotten, that although we do have the potential to be gods ourselves this must always be on God's terms and never our own. Satan always offers the same temptation as he did in the garden of Eden and all too often we succumb to that temptation.

ENGLAND LED THE WORLD INTO MATERIALISM (WW)

England was the first country to adopt the mindset that led to the current materialisation of consciousness and present-day attitudes in which God has no place. The nation was a pioneer in many areas that formed the contemporary world. You can't trace this back to any single formational event or time but Protestantism was certainly one step towards the separation of the natural and supernatural worlds, and then the English Civil War was another. One religious, the other political. The fact that both of these things may have had positive elements to them is beside the point. The basic truth is that they opened up a gap between the spiritual and the material which, once opened, could be expanded exponentially until the point was reached at which the spiritual was so far removed it no longer existed in any real sense and could just be denied reality. That is now. Consciousness has effectively contracted to the material which is not just perceived as primary but as all there is. This has affected even religion which is largely earthbound and moribund these days. That contraction may have been beneficial in some areas, such as the development of certain qualities of selfhood and the exploration and dominance of the physical world, but these cannot be said to compensate for the spiritual loss that has accompanied them even if they have their own short-term validity.

It might be pointed out that these external events were just the manifestation of inner changes in consciousness which brought them about and therefore they were secondary. That is perfectly true. Nevertheless, they also hastened the process of materialisation and grounded it in a way that enabled it to proceed and spread much more rapidly. And it was in and through England that this largely (though clearly not exclusively) came about.

The development of the physical sciences really started to take off in England in the 17th century with the founding of the Royal Society a seminal moment, and thereafter there are too many English scientists at the leading edge of their disciplines to count. Newton and Darwin are obvious examples of people whose work changed the world but there are many more. Again, this was not something that was limited to England but if anywhere was the centre of this work then it was England which was also where the industrial revolution first took hold. The same is true with regard to the new socialist political movements. When I lived in France I used to enjoy teasing the French, still viewing their Revolution through rose tinted spectacles, that the English had killed their king long before they had killed theirs.

So, blame England for the modern world!

But there is another side to this story. Alongside the prosaic, mercenary, matter of fact qualities of Englishmen of the 18th and 19th centuries there existed the romantic Englishman, best exemplified by the poets whose names are too well known to require mentioning, but also appearing in other forms of literature and perhaps too in a special concern with landscape and natural beauty. And I would say that it was chiefly in England in the 19th and 20th centuries that new approaches to spirituality began to be explored, often in clumsy ways, it is true, but the intentions were generally good and the aspiration to higher things real. The reaction against materialism first took place in the country that was principally responsible for it.

At present, any opening to spiritual awakening that seemed possible at various times over the last 150 years appears to have gone away. We are currently more locked into materialistic attitudes than ever. Even the revivals of the New Age, self-indulgent and foolish as they were, seem to have faded away. Perhaps the damp squib that was 2012 was responsible for that. Some people look to Brexit as indicating a stirring of some sort but that seems optimistic to me. Brexit is a patriotic reaction to the destruction of this country's individuality but in the vast majority of cases the people who voted for it were not considering spiritual factors.

Nevertheless, I do consider that Britain still has a part to play in the spiritual awakening of the world. As does America which is one reason why these two countries are relentlessly attacked and their inner integrity constantly undermined by the powers dedicated to the destruction of spiritual truth. Sometimes great light and darkness are to be found in the same place which makes sense when you consider that the devil would naturally focus his guns on the areas of greatest threat to him. Thus, although there is much darkness in this country there is also light but that is less easy to see because it is a spiritual thing and works mostly behind the scenes. But it is there and we have to do our best to foster it, both in ourselves and in the world around us. Even if a few little candles of light remain that will eventually be enough to light others and eventually banish the darkness.

England led the world into materialism. That had a purpose at the time but its time is past. It is now time for England to remedy the situation and try to lead the world back out of the materialistic despond. She must rediscover the spiritual light at her heart and set it up on top of a hill so that it can be seen by and inspire all. She will not be alone in this but it is possible that, just as Rome was first the centre of an empire and then became a spiritual centre, so the pattern might be repeated in England or the United States, the destinies of both countries being intertwined to a degree as I believe.

EMPIRE AND ALBION (WW)

The British Empire gets a bad press these days. It was, so the story goes, greedy, rapacious, exploitative, racist, snobbish, well, you know the rest. And no one can deny that all those elements did exist within the totality of what it was. It certainly started off as an exercise in plunder and, while it probably wasn't so at first, it did end up being what we now call racist, though more or less the whole world was that then and not just Europeans. The colonised were no different to the colonisers especially in India, the jewel of the empire.

But I submit there was considerably more to it than that. In fact, I would even go so far as to say that the British Empire had a divine mission, an opinion which would probably get me escorted to the exits in most civilised places nowadays. So be it. We have become far too over-sensitive to truths that don't coincide with our modern prejudices, but those who look for truth above all have to be prepared to look for it in places where it may not currently be thought to exist.

There can be little doubt that when what became the British Empire began in the 17th century and right through the 18th, the impetus behind it was enrichment of the mother country with little to no thought of the countries colonised. But the motives in the 19th and early 20th century gradually changed and so did the actual purpose of Empire viewed from above. It became a vehicle to spread civilisation throughout many parts of the world that had either fallen into a kind of stagnation or else needed bringing up to speed because they lagged behind in terms of development, both intellectual and technological and even, dare one say it, moral. It had, or so I would maintain, a spiritual purpose which was linked to the evolution of consciousness, a new phase of which began in the West and needed to be spread worldwide. This was how it was done. It's no good saying it could have been done in ways which did not involve one country taking over another. At the time that was simply not possible in many places.

The British in the late 19th and early 20th centuries may have been insular by the standards of the present day, they may have been snobbish and they may have been rather limited as regards imagination. But they were mostly fair and they were mostly honest and they had a strong sense of duty. I don't think it is understood how many people genuinely thought they were serving a cause for the betterment of humanity. Of course, all the usual human sins and foibles were present.

How could they not be? But I would say they were considerably less present than in previous and other contemporary exploits along similar lines. When I lived in India in the 1980s practically everybody I met who had been alive before Independence in 1947 recognised the qualities of the people who had governed them, and they admired them. There was appreciation of what had been accomplished in their country even if they all knew that what may have been beneficial at one time had certainly run its course by the mid-20th century.

It's very easy to condemn the British Empire from the vantage point of present-day morals and ideals. It's also completely absurd and, to use a popular sniffy word of our time, inappropriate. The British Empire accomplished mighty things in that it spread certain standards and values around the world. It had its faults, sometimes grave ones, but show me something that does not. On balance, it did a lot more good than harm, and I believe most of the people who lived under it appreciated what it did for them, how in many respects it liberated them. My particular knowledge of it extends only to India but, as I have said, when I met people there who had been alive during the time of the Empire hardly any had a bad word to say about it. You might say that was just politeness but I think there was more to it than that. There was a genuine recognition that the country had been well governed by largely honourable people who were far from perfect but also sensed and tried to carry out a real mission.

The question then arises as to whether this has any relevance at all now or is it just a period consigned to history along with Henry VIII who probably seems no more alien to young people today than members of the British Raj. Here's a conjecture. A groundwork was laid both culturally and linguistically which might be able to be exploited further on down the line. I see a parallel with the Roman Empire which, after it was no more politically, rose again in a certain manner in Catholicism and the Latin language which were two of the most important ingredients of the religious Medieval civilization. Might something similar occur with the old British Empire? Patterns in history tend to repeat themselves though not in the same way so we should not look to an exact repeat of what happened in the past. Nevertheless, the seeds of something might be there. If a spiritual Albion has any role to play in the future that might be built from the ashes of the old Empire even if the two things seem very different in their basic orientation.

ALBION STILL ASLEEP (WW)

This book and the blog from which it derived are called Albion Awakening. If we identify this idea with the notion of the majority of the inhabitants of the United Kingdom waking up to spiritual truth it's clear that Albion is not going to awaken at any time soon. We are too drugged by entertainment and the media, too brainwashed by atheist/materialist propaganda, too in thrall to technology and machines and too comfortably established in our artificial environments to wake up without being forced to by pain and suffering. That may come if we really show no sign of stirring but, generally speaking, the powers that be only use pain as a last resort.

But if the spirit of Albion is awakened in the country on a lower but still significant level, that might be a different matter. I am not talking about Brexit. The EU is obviously an organisation that pursues an anti-spiritual agenda wrapped up in a liberal, humanist package. That is why it is so popular with the educated elite who can pursue their materially comfortable way of life without disturbance. But Brexit on its own will lead to a situation that is little different spiritually and may be worse economically. It is not irrelevant but by no means enough. However, it might be a background in which Albion, England's spiritual alter ego, could waken from slumber as it has done occasionally in the past when roused by threat or great need or some other circumstance which calls to the depths of the national soul.

If this does happen it will be on a psychological level. What form could it take? Perhaps there might be an increasing disgust with the shallow superficiality of modern entertainment and a search for deeper meaning. Perhaps there might be a rediscovery of history not viewed through the distorting, self-hating lens of political correctness. Perhaps there might be a sudden realisation that we are destroying our country in both its physical and natural form and in terms of its people. Or perhaps there might be a revival of interest in the stories surrounding King Arthur and other luminaries of the British past, one that responds to the true meaning of these kings, saints, poets and heroes without distortion by modernist prejudices. But, however it comes, any awakening will be sensed by us through the imagination. This is why it is the imagination that it most under attack by demonic powers through the perversion of art and culture inter alia.

One thing I can guarantee is that any incipient awakening would immediately be attacked by those powers. What I mean by this is that the demons who are currently trying to manipulate our reality to their advantage and our great loss would try to co-opt and derail any awakening as they have done in the past. As they did in the 1960s, for instance, when they corrupted the nascent spiritual revival with the agenda of the sexual revolution, and as they did in the 1980s when New Age ideas were channeled into psychic rather than spiritual channels. Even the green movement, which had a lot of potential at one time, was hijacked and turned aside from any true spiritual direction by a left-wing ideology which effectively neutralised it.

Whenever truth appears the attempt to corrupt that truth follows. That is why we must remain vigilant whatever happens and never rest on our spiritual laurels. The dark powers always try to drag spiritual revivals down to a lower level so that the essence of the revival is lost though the form may remain. That is why purity of mind and heart is so important. Any weak spot will be sought out and exploited, whether that be lust or pride or greed or hate or fear, whatever. It is up to us to guard against these vices within ourselves. We can protect ourselves through prayer and visualisation of Jesus or other spiritual ideal but it is also important to be completely honest with ourselves. The devil is a liar and he works through lies and deception. For example, he will try to get us to lie to ourselves about our motivations. But if we try to walk at all times in the path of love and humility while at the same time aspiring to truth at its highest then we are well protected.

God needs his foot soldiers in this world and if you are called to that position, as most people reading this book probably are, then you are fortunate indeed even if you suffer in your worldly life as it is more than likely you will. We have been assured that any hardship here and now will be more than compensated for later on.

September 2017

ALBION BESIEGED (WW)

A point made in this book is that England had a spiritual task to accomplish but is failing to do it. Occasionally the country has started on that work as with the poets of the Romantic era, the moral concerns of the Empire (and, yes, the British Empire certainly did have those as expressed in ideas of decency, integrity, fair play, emotional restraint and the like), the groundbreaking work in the field of imagination of the Inklings, the mystical/spiritual revival of the 20th century which may have disintegrated into the self-indulgences of the New Age but which had a lot of potential at one time, and so on. But none of these things developed as might have been hoped even if most have had an impact on the national consciousness at one time. The forces ranged against them have been too many and too powerful for the ideas they put forward to have gained real traction in the minds of more than a few.

So where do we go from here? The vote to leave the EU can be seen as a cry for help and attempt to stop the corruption of the soul of the country and its absorption into a Europe which is itself being taken over by an atheistic, materialistic bureaucracy that recognises nothing of a transcendent nature; indeed, by its policies and ideals actively seeks to suppress anything of that nature, for example by refusing to acknowledge Europe's Christian roots as fundamental. Not that most people thought of things in quite those terms, but they had a sense of loss even if they weren't quite sure what was being lost. They can be mocked by the elites who have bartered their souls for material advantage and whose sophisticated worldliness masks a spiritual emptiness but, while motives are certainly mixed, there are still enough people who realise at some level that something important is being left out of the reckoning and that man cannot live by bread alone. Even though bombarded by materialistic propaganda, seduced by consumerism and cheap entertainment, led astray by the sexual revolution and deprived of any real spiritual education, there remains a core of truth in many people that will not just lie down and die.

Everything comes down to motivation. Do people really want truth and goodness and beauty or will they rest content with fake imitations of these things as long as they are comfortable, well-fed and entertained? There is the theory that greater wealth and leisure give people more time to explore deeper aspects of reality but that does not appear to have been the case at all. Perhaps a degree of economic hardship is what we need if we are to return in any numbers to religion. I don't suppose God ever wants his children to suffer unnecessarily but if we continue to refuse to acknowledge reality, that must eventually have consequences in this world as well as the next.

In the popular imagination England saved Europe from Napoleon and she saved Europe from Hitler, and there is a good deal of truth in that though obviously she did not do this on her own. Without her allies she would have failed and there is a lesson in that. What she needs to do now, though, is save Europe from itself. But if she is to succeed in that she must rediscover a national identity and that must be based on her past, even on an inner mythology that embodies the best of the national spirit, the spirit of Albion. At the moment, Albion is under siege with few to defend its reality but if we can throw off our shallow interest in unserious trivia and start to make contact with the visionary imagination we will find Albion waiting for us there, serving as a gateway to deeper truths. We need to reconnect with the roots of our being for only thus can we be saved from a kind of spiritual wasting away in which our quality of consciousness becomes ever thinner and more monochrome, perhaps to the point of requiring constantly greater external stimulation just to be maintained at a tolerable level.

We are surrounded by lies. Lies pervade every aspect of our life from the moment we become conscious. There are now no institutions that are free from them and most are dominated by them. Education, the media, politics, science, the arts, even the churches, all have been corrupted. If we are not strong enough to find truth within our self then we must look back into the past to find ideas about our country and its role in the world that are honest and true. Albion may have been chased almost completely out of modern life but it is preserved in history and the encounter with it there will help us make a connection to this archetype of the imagination.

WHAT ARE THE SIGNS OF A CIVILISATION IN DECLINE? (WW)

Before we can answer that question, we have to ask another one. What is civilisation? For only when we know what something is, can we begin to understand if and how a supposed version of it is not living up to its purpose.

Therefore, to know if a particular civilisation is in decline we must determine how it stands in relation to the root principle behind all human culture and activity worthy of the name of civilisation.

What, then, is civilisation? I would say it must start with an openness to the transcendent and then proceed with the attempt to organise a group of human beings according to that. Essentially, a civilisation seeks to reflect the pattern of the heavens on Earth, and so it manifests in the world primarily in the form of a religion from which there then develops a culture. But the former must derive from the latter which is the inspiring impulse. You might accuse me of loading the dice here. By defining civilisation as necessarily founded on the spiritual, I may be giving it my own preferred spin and excluding other valid forms of human organisation not founded like that. But, in actual fact, are there any? Any civilisations, I mean, that have started from a non-spiritual beginning, not ones that exist like that now but were not originally so. It seems obligatory that all civilisations grow out of an awareness, however dim, of a higher archetypal truth to which human society should try to conform. And the higher the civilisation, the deeper the awareness is of this truth. There can be no civilisation without religion.

I therefore maintain that any civilisation which merits that description must be spiritual in that it is founded on spiritual principles, even if these are not particularly developed. But openness to the transcendent is essential. Without this there is nothing to act as a magnet to pull a human society out of its concern with physical appetites and self-centred desires. There must be an awareness of a higher reality to give any group of humans an organising principle that is coherent and brings out their creative potential.

Now we have established that, it should be easy to mark traces of decline in any given civilisation. First and foremost, it would start with an increasing loss of the sense of the transcendent. A closing to higher realities, as a consequence of which many other things would arise.

These would include:

- A greater focus on things of this world because that is now seen as all there is.
- The deterioration and disappearance of religion. This results in the rise of vulgarity and barbarism in culture and behaviour. You might question whether these would be inevitable but it is surely obvious that once you reject a higher reality lower forms of being assume greater prominence. There is a hierarchy of truth, goodness and beauty. When the top is destroyed the whole thing starts to collapse.
- The rise of false forms of spirituality to fill the hole left by the disappearance of serious religion. But these would often revolve around the search for emotional experience or therapy (focus on feelings) rather than orientation towards the good because the idea of the transcendent good has been lost or obscured, and the individual is now what matters so it is his personal fulfilment that counts.
- Cultural relativism, there being no acknowledged absolute which would create a hierarchical scale of values with things that correspond to it more being better and things that correspond to it less being worse. A culture worthy of the name arises because it seeks to manifest the higher. It separates the higher from the lower. It sinks when it refuses to distinguish between the two.
- This would also produce egalitarianism. No hierarchy, no better or worse, all is the same. Man as he is seen to be in this world is man as he is in toto. This prompts the interesting thought that democracy only comes about as the religious impulse declines. History seems to confirm this.

These are the main signifiers but from them come other things, some of which in the new despiritualised culture appear to be advances.

- Differences between men and women denied or minimised and an increasing influence of women in society as the masculine pole of spirit is undermined by the feminine pole of matter.
- Worship of celebrity, athletes, singers and actors as human

achievement becomes focused on success in this world and appeal to the desires of the lower man, that being all there is of man.

- Welfare and altruism increase as egalitarianism assumes greater importance and this world is all that matters.

- Mass immigration caused by a wealthy host nation attracting outsiders who wish to benefit from its bounty while it wishes to attract cheap workers. This is also another consequence of egalitarianism but indicative too of a loss of confidence as a successful culture starts to question itself and its legitimacy. Once it does that, history shows it's on the downward path, even if it does so for seemingly benign reasons.

I'm cheating bit here. As the reader will have observed I am listing what is happening today. However, I still maintain that these are indeed among the classic signs of a civilisation in decline and they are listed as such by Sir John Grubb in his interesting research into the fate of empires. The question is, can anything be done about it?

And the answer is, probably not. We may lament the passing of Western civilisation but nothing lasts in this world, and the fact is this civilisation contained the seeds of its own destruction in liberalism which inevitably levels everything down to a flat plane. Civilisations come and go, and while the period of their decline is depressing for those caught up in it, it does help such people transfer their attention from earthly things to eternal verities and transcendent realities. As your world crumbles into dust, you may find it easier to set your sights on higher things. That is the great advantage of living at a time of spiritual loss and cultural decline, a time, moreover, predicted in Christian eschatology which also promises a happy outcome for those who remain true to the inner values of which any civilisation here on Earth, even the best, is only an imperfect representation.

DEVIATIONS OF MODERNITY (WW)

At one time, I thought of writing a book on the deviations of modernity but lost interest as the whole thing would just have been one long round of negativity. The more I thought about it, the more I realised I would have ended up including practically everything about the world today in my analysis of what was wrong with it. Its art, its politics, its science, its philosophy, its culture, its education and even its religion. For nowadays each one of these serves to sidetrack man from his true mission of self-knowledge. None of them really helps to align him with it. Each one is, to some degree, destructive of truth. Most of them are based on lies and reduce humanity to a spiritually shrunken version of itself. The prospect was too unpleasant to contemplate. I didn't want to appear, even to myself, a miserable moaner with nothing good to say about anything.

That having been said, the negativity is not in me but in the world as it is today and, though a book is too much for me to do, an essay here will make the point well enough. After all, there isn't that much to say when you get down to it. All these deviations tie up together and come from the same place. They are all a denial of the fullness of what a human being is. They restrict humanity to how it appears to be in this world. They don't all do this in the same way and to the same degree, but each does it to some extent.

For instance, science has long mistaken the part for the whole and simply denied those aspects of being it cannot access by its frankly fairly limited methods. It hobbles itself by its obsession with what can be measured. The contemporary artist is too fixated on himself as the artist and his response to the world. He fails to see further than himself. And that's not even mentioning the striving for originality. To be original really means to go back to the origin of things and that is clearly God. What artist of the last hundred years does that? Some, certainly, but very few and hardly any whose work is acclaimed.

When philosophy is severed from the intellect, meaning the intuitive faculty of the mind not the rational, it becomes sterile. It concerns itself with concepts that have no bearing on reality as it is but simply with things as they are thought. It is reduced to theory, mind games and empty abstractions. For if philosophy is not rooted in the good, the beautiful and the true, it is useless.

Politics now is what people resort to when they have no spiritual understanding. It is based on the denial of man as a spiritual being. It treats him as existing only in and for this world, and either attacks his individuality or over-asserts it. Consequently, it is practically always the vehicle for some form of oppression. In the modern world, politics has become a means of separating human beings from truth and is at the forefront of the attempt to reconstruct them in a new form that has no connection to what they really are or should be. In this it takes direction from the materialism of science, the spiritual aridity of philosophy and the misconceived misrepresentations of art.

Unfortunately religion and spirituality are also weakened forces. The former usually lacks an inner dimension that would give it spiritual power, and its adherents may be well-intentioned but do not sufficiently appreciate the reality of which they speak, tending, paradoxically enough, to emphasise the horizontal dimension of being over the vertical. The latter is too often vague and self-centred, either seeing reality as a pantheistic mush which aligns all too easily with contemporary atheistic attitudes, or else diminishing the spiritual quest to a search for the true self thereby denying proper transcendence. I generalize but, while there may be many individuals who do not fall into these categories, present-day forms of religion and spirituality largely do, particularly in their more public aspects.

Where then is one to turn? The fact that there is no outer support nowadays tells us that we have to go within. God now wants each person to find the truth inside themselves and to be their own spiritual support. This is both a test of their integrity and also a way for them to develop the insight required to become truly spiritual and not just passively so. This path is not without problems. The possibility of illusion and self-deception is always there but if we work to purify our minds of attachments and selfish desires and wrong thinking, and open our hearts to truth then we can make headway in modern times despite its anti-spiritual bias. In fact, it may be that by seeing through the modern deviations and benefitting from their plus points, because they do have them as anything must, we can make more headway than might otherwise have been the case if we lived in more spiritually understanding times. What are these plus points? Chiefly, I would say, the focus on the individual and the desire to understand not just follow. These have led to the many deviations referred to but they also have their positive side if they are harnessed to correct spiritual understanding. That is, if they are seen as servants rather than masters.

You cannot understand the contemporary world if you do not see it as the closing phase of a long cycle in which openness to spirit is gradually shut off and human beings become trapped in matter. At the same time, you will not understand it if you do not grasp how forces antithetical to God, supernatural forces taking advantage of the spirit of the times, are trying to reframe human beings without reference to their higher nature. This is all presented as a good with resistance to it an evil, the reverse of the truth. It may be a pseudo-good when defined by its own terms and unfortunately many people nowadays, without any knowledge of real religion and lacking insight, are seduced by it and go along with it. Many even line up to promote it thereby fighting for the devil while imagining they fight against him. Of course, those who do this do not have truth in them which is why they can be exploited but they are convinced they serve the good. The devil uses much subtler tactics these days or perhaps it just seems so in the context of the times. But to present good as evil and evil as good is one of his favoured methods of corruption and it deceives many especially when the full force of public discourse is behind it as is usually the case these days.

Let's end on a positive note. It seems to me that as the official line on what reality is becomes more absurd and more untenable, as it must because once something has started going downhill it will carry on until it reaches the bottom unless something powerful stops it, people will start to wake up. Maybe not a majority but the truth that is within us all will surely reassert itself amongst many when they are faced with ever more flagrant challenges to goodness, truth and common sense. At any rate, the increasing divergences from truth will bring us all to the point at which real choices have to be made. Will we then meekly conform to the outer indoctrinations of society and the world or will we listen to the voice of our Creator within us? This will be both an opportunity and a test. Let us pray that we will be equal to it.

BREXIT (WW)

I thought I might give a personal response to the post Bruce Charlton recently put up on Andy Thomas and his Brexit talk because I don't believe I've written on this subject before which might seem strange given the fact that no one seems to talk about anything else nowadays.

I didn't vote in the referendum. That was partly because I don't vote at all, regarding the whole process as flawed, particularly in the modern world when all parties are corrupt and all political ideologies completely separated from any kind of spiritual truth. People say you should at least participate and vote for the least bad option but I've tried that in the past and always feel as though I've betrayed my principles in some way, pompous and self-regarding as that might sound. But I believe the only honest option for me, as things stand today anyway, is to remove myself from the whole process. I am not recommending this for everyone. We all have to follow our conscience in these matters, and I am not saying that anyone who feels they should participate in the democratic process is wrong. But I know what I personally feel about the matter and that is paramount as far as I am concerned. It's not the same thing as not voting because you can't be bothered to or don't care. I just don't want to join in something I regard as corrupt and probably deceitful. The system is broken but that's because we human beings are broken. I know of no solution to this other than the old-fashioned one of spiritual repentance.

I said I didn't vote partly because I don't vote anyway. So that was not the whole reason. The thing is, even if I had been willing to join in the referendum, I would have been torn. Not because I don't believe that Britain should leave the European Union. I do. I think the EU is one of those things, whited sepulchres, that have been designed to look fair on the outside but inside are spiritually rotten. It stands for liberal humanitarianism, social equality and all the sorts of things that sound pleasant to the modern mind, but is really an organisation that is gearing up for a totalitarian control of the whole of Europe, no doubt with the eventual aim of joining a world body dedicated to global control. Typical conspiracy theory nonsense, you might say. Maybe, but I believe that the demonic forces, whose manipulating behind the scene activities should surely be ever more obvious in this world, used it after World War Two, trading on the naive idealism of politicians of the time and their earnest hopes that such a war would never be repeated, and instigated a body that would override national identity, supposedly for progressive reasons but actually for totalitarian ones.

So, from that point of view, Britain should clearly leave. However, our economic and cultural lives, particularly the former, have been so closely woven into the fabric of the EU that leaving is probably going to cause hardship. In the short to medium term, people, especially perhaps poorer people, are going to suffer. Thus, there are two aspects of the matter to take into account. There is the economic side, together with a certain sort of sophisticated cultural side, liberal, outward looking, progressive in the sense that word is usually understood today. But then there is the matter of principles. What is the right thing to do, regardless of how we will be affected?

Britain is part of Europe. It always has been and it always will be. Leaving the EU does not mean leaving Europe even if that were possible. Our whole life has been bound up with the continent for our entire history. Our culture is a European one, unthinkable without huge influences from mainland Europe which have enriched us enormously. And yet we are an island. Materialists will consider this completely irrelevant. But people who believe in God and think that he has a reason for things being as they are will pause for thought. We have been set apart. Yes, that can lead to an attitude of arrogant self-satisfaction but then beauty can lead to vanity. It doesn't mean that beauty is a bad thing. We have been set apart and many of us sense that we do indeed have a special mission, hinted at in our traditions and legends. What that mission may be, no one is completely sure but it has risen to the surface occasionally. It did so at the time of the Spanish Armada. If Phillip II had succeeded in the invasion of England, Spain would have dominated Europe and I don't think that English notions of freedom and individuality would have spread as they did. Perhaps the scientific revolution would not have taken off as it did. Furthermore, it is unlikely that the British would have colonised America to the extent they did and the whole history of the United States would have been completely different. Speculation, of course, but not without some basis to it.

Then Britain freed Europe from Napoleon. Napoleon was a great man but he was also a tyrant and imposed his regime throughout the continent. Britain defended freedom. Not alone but she was the principal agent. Britain's contribution to the defeat of Hitler is clearly another time when her mission manifested itself.

It seems that one of the things Britain can do is save Europe from itself. The British always used to have the particular virtue of mistrusting ideologies and preferring common sense to clever theories. That can lead to the nation of shopkeepers jibe (which is not always an unfair one) but it can also mean that we are not seduced by fancy words and cleverly spun lies. We favour lived experience over ideology. That used to be the case anyway. How much it is now, I'm not so sure but perhaps the Brexit vote shows that the attribute still exists. We may still prefer real life to abstract theory.

If Britain was a nation of shopkeepers, it was also home to some of the greatest poets the world has known and many of these made a mighty contribution to the expansion of consciousness that became known as the Romantic Movement. This might be another side of its mission. Here on this island are supposed to be some of the most sacred sites in the world. These act like spiritual power sources that can inspire and regenerate, even today when their power is low. But they are there and the energy can be tapped. They feed into the national psyche and give those in the nation who can respond, which may not be the majority but is a reasonable minority, a connection to deeper realities. The revival of esoteric spirituality in the 20th century, which admittedly often took strange forms, was frequently led by people from these isles.

Britain has been set apart physically and it has been spiritually too, for better or worse. This is not a cause for an inflated egotism but it means that we in this country have a responsibility. I would say that we have not been true to it for at least 75 years. We have not kept the faith just as Israel, in a different context, did not always keep the faith in Old Testament times. According to Wellesley Tudor Pole, a prominent English mystic of the last century, it was a mistake to join the Common Market, as the EU was known then, and would delay our mission. I would say he has been proved correct. Whether the mission, whatever it might be, has been delayed or thwarted completely remains to be seen.

Most people who voted to remain in the EU did so for what they felt to be intellectual reasons, regarding themselves as responding rationally to the question. Whether they really were is another matter, but they were persuaded that economically and culturally our future lay within a wider body, and they saw the partial sacrifice of national identity and integrity as a trivial thing. On the other hand, it seems clear that many leave voters voted with their hearts and that is why it is easy to caricature them as ignorant. There will possibly be some economic hardship if we do ever succeed in leaving, though, goodness knows, the powers that be seem hell-bent on preventing it. But leave voters may have been reacting at an intuitive level to the knowledge that Great Britain has a destiny that cannot be fulfilled within the EU. This is a spiritual reason that can't be justified in a book of accounts or fitted into a globalist, progressive narrative. But if you want to caricature leave voters as ignorant then you can equally well accuse remainers of having no feeling for the mystique of this country, and of being spiritually rootless people who see a country as only somewhere they happen to live with no deeper involvement, loyalty or connection. You might even say they belong to a world that is passing, a post-World War Two world from which we should be moving on. Perhaps they are the backward-looking people.

The fact that the establishment was so determined to stop Britain leaving tells us two things. One, they were responding to demonic impulse. In this respect that is the cause they are serving whether they know it or not (and the vast majority of them don't know it and would laugh themselves silly if presented with such an idea). The second thing is that Britain does have a spiritual mission and it is important. It is apparently worth a lot of effort to hinder or even stop it.

The spiritual way is often the apparently less attractive way. That is because it demands sacrifice and strips us of the falsehoods we cover ourselves up with. The fair path often leads to a foul end. This is something we should remember in the coming months.

(This was written in January 2019 before the general election of December that year which has changed things in some ways though whether seriously or not remains to be seen.)

BREXIT AND RELIGION (WW)

Apparently the farce or tragedy (take your pick) that is Brexit has seen a great increase in sales of self-help books. Is this to people so shaken by the event that they require psychological assistance? Or is it to those who think the future will be disastrous and they need to prepare themselves as best they can? Either way, what a pity that people turn to such feeble nostrums for sustenance rather than to the genuine medicine of real religion.

But then where can the ordinary person find real religion now? If you have been brought up with no particular spiritual education, and therefore have a very poor and biased idea of what religion is, you may reject it without serious investigation. Alternatively, those who are exposed to what passes for Christianity today will not find much to inspire them there if they are searching for something that really speaks to the imagination and the soul. For modern Christianity is often little more than secular humanism dressed up in religious clothing. Its supernatural element, without which it is meaningless, has been reduced as much as it possibly can be without being jettisoned altogether. Partly this is because Christianity has not responded well to the changes in consciousness that have come about over the last few hundred years as humanity begins to awaken intellectually and become more individual (as was meant to happen albeit not in the way it has happened), but partly it is because of the generally low quality of Christian leaders who for the most part, certain honourable exceptions excluded, have lacked any real vision.

Why do most of the intelligentsia wish this country to remain in the EU? Is it because they are believers in the ideology that unity is always good and separatism always bad? Consequently, they see those who wish to separate from a body that seeks to unite as ignorant and selfish. It rather depends what it wants to unite for, doesn't it? You may think I am reducing something complicated to a simple basic idea but this is more or less how things are. Intellectuals tend to think in terms of abstractions rather than concrete realities and this means they may reject ties of blood and earth which is why they can be perceived as disliking their own country and culture, even to the extent of trying to undermine them. They are, or want to be, men and women of the world which is regarded as being far more sophisticated than those simpletons attached to their native soil. But they are victims of the leftist dogma that humanity is one and the more united it is, the better it is. I call this a dogma because although it may sound very worthy, it is only half the story since ideas of unity should never be used as an excuse to deny or diminish individuality. We may be all one in God in a higher sense but God created us as individuals and it is as individuals that we realise our destiny. You are not required to sink your individuality into a group identity but to enrich the group with your individuality. This is why a Europe of strong individual nation states is a better thing than one in which these nation states have reduced autonomy. Anyone who knows the history and underlying ambition of the EU knows that it has always been determined to follow the latter course, the one that leads to ever closer union with its component parts increasingly weakened and power concentrated more and more in the centre.

The spiritual fact of the sanctity of the individual is the reason that those who have a deeper understanding of what religion actually means are in favour of Britain leaving the EU. A superficial religious understanding, such as most of our church leaders possess, will think that love your neighbour means there is no difference between you and your neighbour. But then he wouldn't be a neighbour, would he? He would be you. The truth is we need love and we need wisdom, and we need both together to make sure we actually do have real love and real wisdom and not simply an ersatz copy of them. For love and wisdom are spiritual qualities but human beings who lack these qualities as spiritual things interpret them on the lower level of feelings and thought and as a result they misconceive them. What they call love is not love but a reflection of it in their emotional nature or even something they just have as an idea or ideal. But if they don't truly feel it as living spiritual reality then they don't know it.

Most people who want Britain to leave the EU are not religious but they have natural instincts which the intelligentsia, including many of those considering themselves to be the spiritual intelligentsia, having separated themselves from reality, have lost. They do not have minds clouded by ideology, always the weakness of those who have intellect but lack intuition. But religion is actually all about intuition. You might even say that the development of intuition is the primary religious task. Intuition tells us that the EU is a corrupt body that ultimately seeks its own good not the good of the countries that comprise it. For that reason, not only should Great Britain leave it but so should every other member state.

If you are one of those people who have turned to a self-help book in this time of crisis let me point out that self-help can only address the earthly human being not the soul. Indeed, it often strengthens the earthly human being *against* the soul by focusing attention on it so that it becomes even more the centre of consciousness than it already is. Forget self-help, however it is packaged, and seek the transcendent truth in God.

March 2019

THOSE WHOM THE GODS WOULD DESTROY (WW)

They First Drive Mad.

This phrase came to my mind recently as a perfect summing up of our present time. We have gone mad. There really can be no other description of what is going on today. In the Western world particularly but everywhere else is not far behind. We started off by denying God and now we are denying Nature. The deconstruction of sexual differences is just the latest step on this path of insanity. And everywhere we are rejecting the idea of some things being qualitatively better than others in the name of an all-purpose egalitarianism, of people, of cultures, of more or less everything. We no longer aspire to truth or real goodness or beauty or to a higher reality that gives meaning to this one.

I looked up the origin of this saying. I thought it came from the ancient Greek world and it seems it does but with various modifications along the way to the present. Here is what Wikipedia has to say about it.

> "The phrase "Whom the gods would destroy they first make mad" is spoken by Prometheus in Henry Wadsworth Longfellow's poem "The Masque of Pandora" (1875).
>
> But the first version of this phrase appears in Antigone by Sophocles as "evil appears as good in the minds of those whom gods lead to destruction". Even this appears to be a borrowing from an earlier, lost play.
>
> Subsequently the phrase was used in Latin, "Quem Iuppiter vult perdere, dementat prius" (Whom Jupiter would ruin, he first makes mad).
>
> Another version ("Those whom the gods wish to destroy they first make mad") is quoted as a "heathen proverb" in Daniel, a Model for Young Men (1854) by William Anderson Scott (1813–1885).

> A Latin version is "Quos Deus vult perdere, prius dementat" (Life of Samuel Johnson 1791) in which the gods become God."

What struck me from this is how the first known version, that of Sophocles, describes precisely the contemporary inversion of true values. This is obviously a phenomenon that has happened before, though I would doubt on such a massive scale, and something well-known to the wise. But one of the signs of our present madness is that we have dismissed the wisdom of the past as ignorance. In fact, not only do we dismiss it, we no longer seriously study it. For many children today, history is primarily the 20th century with only a relatively small amount of time devoted to the several millennia before that. It's as though we are being separated from our past in order to be remade according to the dominating ideology of recent times. If people no longer know the past they will think that it was just a time of ignorance and they will be unable to compare current attitudes with anything else.

The phrase prompts the question, are the gods trying to destroy us and, if so, why? However, I actually think it puts things the wrong way around. When humanity starts to deny the gods, it is then that it becomes mad and that leads to destruction. So, it's not that the gods want to destroy us but when we turn our backs on them we start to evict ourselves from reality and from then on, it's a downward path. There is not some implacable fate driving us to destruction for obscure reasons of its own but it is all the result of decisions we have taken by ourselves.

Madness means losing touch with reality. This is what we are doing. We have replaced our natural contact with reality with twisted ideas of how reality should be according to our materialistic ideology. But when the very ground of truth is rejected then everything else falls out of place. And then, as it has been said, from the one who has not, even what he does have will be taken away from him. This is the path we have set ourselves on. It is why our madness will lead to our destruction unless we repent. The gods are not destroying us. We are destroying ourselves.

AWAKENING ALBION

AWAKENING FROM ILLUSION (WW)

When we talk about awakening we are obviously talking about awakening from something and to something else. But what exactly are we supposed to be awakening from and what to? In the context of this book you would say it is awakening to the reality of Albion which is the spiritual counterpart of Britain but, in a broader context, this means awakening from the sleep of materialism. However, there are many kinds and degrees of awakening and some are just staging posts on the way to other more complete ones. And you can wake up in the night but it is still dark. You have to wake up to the day to be properly awake.

Fundamentally, awakening is spiritual awakening. But we know that what is called spirituality can take many forms and we also know that it can be associated with different, even contradictory, outlooks. For example, most non-traditional spirituality has no difficulty in getting along with the results of materialism in the form of the left/liberal ideology, regarding these as progressive but forgetting that progress along a path that leads in the wrong direction is not actually progress at all. Some spiritual approaches deny the reality of the person. Others think it is all-important.

I mentioned kinds and degrees of awakening. Some people awaken from the illusions of the propaganda with which we are constantly bombarded by the media, political parties of all stripes, educational and scientific authorities etc, but still fail to awaken spiritually. Others might awaken spiritually or, at least, begin to realise that materialism is a false philosophy, but still be asleep when it comes to the nature of what spirituality actually is, what it entails and what it demands. See above. Some people might think they have awoken spiritually but fail to appreciate the significance of Christ. Others might become Christians but only in a superficial sense, neglecting the deeper implications of what Christ means for us and not applying their religion to every single aspect of life as should be the case. There are many partial awakenings but often a partial awakening is little different to being still asleep. One remains under the spell of illusion of some kind.

And so we come to what awakening really demands. We are awakening not from sleep but from illusion. This illusion may manifest itself in different ways and some of them may actually be spiritual, but what they all have in common is a lack of true vision. Sometimes this comes from an inability to shake off the ways of the world. We turn to spirituality without turning away from the world (or the flesh or the devil, for that matter). Sometimes it is an intellectual failure and sometimes it is a moral one. To have real spiritual vision or insight, something that is more than just head knowledge, does require a certain purity of heart and soul that does not normally come without struggle and sacrifice. We are told by the wisest and best person who ever lived that it also requires the love of God. Without that love to keep you on the spiritual straight and narrow, you are likely to stray.

Bruce Charlton has written of seeing through the falseness of the sexual revolution as a pre-requisite for spiritual awakening. This is exactly right, especially in our day and age. It is not a question of old-fashioned puritanical attitudes that deny, suppress or react out of fear, but of seeing the creative power as something sacred which is not to be treated irreverently or as a mere means of personal pleasure. For if you do respond like that, you cut yourself off from the higher manifestations of sexual love and that means you effectively cut yourself off from all higher manifestations of anything. That is because proper spiritual understanding can only come to the pure of heart. The higher consciousness can only arise when the lower (self-centred) consciousness, focused on the physical, emotional and mental levels, has been purified and raised above itself. Purity is not much valued in today's world but it is essential for spiritual awakening.

Illusion is the result of mental error but it can also be the result of a moral choice. I mean it can be freely embraced by an act of will. People can believe what they want to believe as a justification for some sin to which they are attached, be it pride, fear, envy, anger, lust and so on. If you want to free yourself from illusion, it's a good idea to look at yourself honestly and see what you might be thinking or believing because it suits you to do so. Atheists accuse believers of doing precisely this but true believers do not take to religion because of an inability to face a meaningless universe. They do so because they perceive its truth, and they do not then use it to support their failings but to reveal where they fall short and how they might bridge the gap between what they are and what they should be.

The world is deeply sunk in illusion. Human beings have denied reality and turned away from truth. This is usually dressed up as an act of intellectual honesty but often it is a deliberate choice and a justification for self-centred desires and rebellion against the idea of a

Creator because we want complete personal autonomy. If we are not careful that is what we will be given. Unless we awaken from illusion we shall reap the results of its consequences, and our freedom won't be what we were hoping for. Freedom from God is not a good idea.

TRUE AWAKENING DEMANDS DEEP PENITENCE (WW)

It seems to me that, given the way things currently stand, any spiritual awakening is unlikely unless people are brought low by suffering. We are just too comfortable and set in our materialistic ways to change course unless something dramatic which forces us to change takes place. I have spoken earlier of how the spiritual powers that oversee our world have sought to avoid a scenario of suffering for some time but, spiritually considered, humanity has just gone from bad to worse and is currently as far away from God as it has been for a long, long time. Our culture and our politics are all corrupt, our religion, such as it is, is ineffective and when we do turn to some idea of spirituality in the modern spiritual but not religious way, it is usually on our own terms and with no real sense of the Creator. Hence, any spirituality of this sort is directed towards personal growth and does not include the metanoia that is essential for genuine awakening.

We need to change and we need to do so at the roots of our being. Change in the spiritual sense cannot simply be an external thing. It is not just swapping one set of beliefs for another, supposedly more enlightened. Even if the new beliefs are truer and more spiritually correct, that is nowhere near good enough. Real change requires substantially more than just changing one's thoughts or even one's behaviour or way of life. It requires deep penitence, something that goes right down to the very core of what we feel ourselves to be and leaves our old self lying shattered and in pieces on the ground. Do you remember how Eustace in The Voyage of the Dawn Treader turned into a dragon? That dragon was just the materialised form of what he really was like inside. He became in body what he already was in soul, and it was only when he experienced a radical restructuring of the soul that he was able to be liberated by Aslan from that terrible dragon exterior. What if we too appeared outwardly as we are in our souls? Is that a challenge you would wish to take up?

We have to remind ourselves that before Jesus could carry out his mission, the way had to be prepared by someone of a much rougher disposition. Someone who denounced evil for what it was and who actually ended up paying with his life for this. He did not accommodate himself to the world or to the authority of the day. When he condemned sin, he did not pull his punches. He simply spoke the truth. John the Baptist had the mission of calling the people to repentance. Jesus could not have spoken to these people unless they had first been awoken to their sinful state by John. Once they had started to see themselves as they were then Jesus could direct them towards understanding how they should be. But there could be no spirituality without prior repentance. The ground of the soul had to be ploughed and tilled before the seed could be sown. A hard ground could not have taken the seed.

At the moment, the ground of the human soul is very hard. What can soften it up so that the seeds of renewal can be sown? Heavy rainfall is probably what is needed. Nobody can look forward to suffering but we have brought this upon ourselves by our arrogance and vanity, by our rebelliousness and cold-heartedness. Sentimentality is not love. If we will not turn to the truth of our own accord that will create a reaction in the fabric of being. We are not being punished. We will just experience the consequences of our anti-life behavior.

There is no moving forward without repentance, and this is a matter of the will for real spirituality is not so much about overcoming ignorance, as in many Eastern approaches to spiritual truth (even though that is important), as about reorientation of the will. It is in our wills that we are bent and it is that we must address if we are to awaken from our spiritual sleep. Maybe it will not require suffering, let us hope so, but realistically, how long can we continue as we are now?

INCONSISTENCY AND CONFUSION (WW)

Today we live a very contradictory existence. On the one hand, our beliefs are formed by materialism and our lives are largely lived as though that idea were true. This effectively requires that our sense of self be an illusion and any morals we might have arbitrary since one set cannot be better than another in any ultimate sense according to this doctrine. All morals are merely functional, for utilitarian purposes only, which means they rest on nothing substantial and the only requirement is to appear to obey them not to actually do so.

But, on the other hand, we still live as if our self were real as well as those of others. The very idea of love, which we can't quite bring ourselves to renounce, insists that this be so. Surely, we can't have it both ways? Either materialism is true in which case we, as real individual selves with some actual substance, aren't true, or our individuality is real in which case there must be a non-material basis to life. And, if that is so, there has to be a God since something cannot come from nothing nor can things give rise to themselves or the lesser to the greater. Consequently, our consciousness and sense of self must come from something that has these to give.

Moreover, we live as though free will were real but the philosophical basis of our culture, materialism, if true, would mean it could not be. We would just be passive objects formed and impelled to action by mechanical or chemical but certainly external forces. Even the erudite philosophers who deny free will don't actually live as though they had none. Contradictions all over the place. No wonder we live in confused and chaotic times.

But there is a solution. It is to rediscover the feeling of gratitude. Know that we have someone to be grateful to. We have closed our minds off to the reality of God, partly because of the relatively recent full discovery of our own selves and partly because technology has given us such control over our environment. So we are like adolescents who have found the keys to the drinks cabinet and embarked on a binge. At the moment we are flush with alcoholic stimulation but the hangover will surely follow. Perhaps that will teach us wisdom in future.

It is good that humanity has begun to live with the idea that it has some control over its destiny and does not just react passively to the world. That was intended as part of our spiritual development which, let us remind ourselves, involves a descent from unindividualized spirit into matter and then a reascent back to spirit with full individual consciousness. But we have forgotten where we come from. We are resisting the reascendance and that is not good. Our future course must be to seek to engage our minds with the mind of God and become aware of the greater consciousness that lies beyond that centred on our own little selves. We are true individuals but we are also sparks struck from the central fire. We can illuminate these sparks from renewed contact with that fire so they become brighter and brighter or we can grow ever more distant from the fire so that our little sparks eventually fade and darken and perhaps even go out. The problem is that as we initially separate ourselves from the fire our sparks appear to glow more brightly because of the surrounding darkness into which we have passed. That is just an illusion, the false nature of which will soon be revealed and then we will find that we are alone.

For consider this. If there is no God, you are totally alone. You can pretend that is not so, cover it up in various ways, but it is a fact. And if you reject God then one day you will have to face that fact full on. But God is merciful. Anyone can turn to him at any time, and if you do you will find that you are never alone. Of course, you can still be on your own if you wish. That is not what I mean. But alone in the sense of pure existential isolation, naked in a barren universe with the only release to be snuffed out completely, which is what materialism means. That you will never be. This is not in itself a reason to believe. If it were true it would have to be accepted, but we don't really accept it because we don't think through to the logical conclusions of our materialism for if we did it would lead to despair. That very despair would be the soul crying out in protest at the lie it has been induced to believe, at the violence done to its nature.

To reject God which is what most of humanity has done at the present time, certainly the ruling culture in the West, means death. Choose life and, once you have chosen, realise what life means and what it requires of you. You cannot continue in the same old way, just swapping one set of beliefs for another. You must reset your entire being, pointing it away from the things of earth and towards the things of God.

FANTASY AND REALITY (WW)

On more than one occasion in my life I have been informed that because of my spiritual interests I live in a fantasy world. Even well-meaning people have told me that I should forget all that sort of thing and restrict my concerns to everyday reality. My response (unspoken usually, but not always) has been that it is they who live in a fantasy world. By rejecting the spiritual what you are doing is rejecting the real because the spiritual *is* the real, and it is the material without the spiritual that is the actual world of fantasy.

Naturally, this attitude does not entail turning your back on the material in favour of the spiritual alone. Reality is made up of the material and the spiritual, and each should be given its due. Moreover, we live in the material world at the moment and that must receive our attention. Here is where we are born and here is where we are meant to be. We should not try to escape from it but nor should we take it on its own terms, and we have to see which comes first in the order of reality.

Fantasy has to do with replacing the real by the unreal. At least, it means that when the word is used in a derogatory way. It implies that the person to whom the word is directed is unable to come to grips with reality and so seeks to retreat to a land of make-believe where all is safe and secure. A place where his weaknesses and inadequacies can be ignored or even turned into strengths. But when this word is used to describe the attitude of people who take the fact of the spiritual seriously to the extent that they make it the defining principle of their lives, the user is making a rather big assumption. He is assuming the truth of materialism. He is taking for granted that what you see is what you get and there is nothing more. This might be all well and good if there were any rational reason for assuming it to be the case but there just isn't. Because, for all our advances in the scientific understanding of the world, we have not come any closer to knowing what life is or how it arises or explaining anything about consciousness, love, beauty or any of the other qualitative facts of our existence. Materialism only makes sense to someone who wants to believe it and who therefore blithely ignores everything that it cannot explain either by refusing to acknowledge it or else by trying to reduce it to a mere by-product of material processes. It is an example of what Coleridge called the "despotism of the eye", which phrase he used to describe the affliction suffered by those who deny any reality that cannot be empirically perceived or represented by a concrete mental image.

Fantasy is connected to imagination. Now, there certainly are false fantasies but these are the creation of human imagining as opposed to imagination, the difference being that the former is just the everyday mind concocting things out of its storehouse of memories and experiences while the latter is the mind opening up to what is beyond itself. When the mind starts to do this, its connection to inner truths is substantially increased and this is a mode of the intuition which is the faculty beyond intellect, considered as reason, and which, as an organ of cognition, is as far beyond intellect as that is beyond instinct.

Nonetheless, it must be admitted that contemporary human understanding of the spiritual world, even where that understanding exists, is in a fairly rudimentary state. As a result there will be many people who mix in bits of human imagining, or fantasy in the derogatory sense, with their spiritual sensibility, and this inevitably encourages those who dismiss the whole of spirituality as fantasy. But an imperfect grasp of something doesn't make the thing in itself wrong. It's like a poorly tuned radio which receives interference from other sources as well as static. The poor tuning of the instrument does not negate the reality of the transmitted broadcast.

This book is dedicated to fantasy. It is also dedicated to reality. Indeed, it seeks to demonstrate that fantasy (so-called) is reality while reality (so-called) is fantasy. Awakening could be defined as coming to that realisation.

INTELLECT AND INTUITION (WW)

A major factor behind the arrested spiritual development of the modern world is that we have failed to move on from an intellectual focus to an intuitive one. Intelligence is a good thing but if it is not supplemented by intuition it can turn against itself and work destructively. We can see this illustrated in the modern world where intelligent people are more likely to be atheists because their mental development is lop-sided. In a properly ordered society they would be encouraged to develop intuition so they would not get lured into cul de sacs of abstraction and theory. The old saying that the mind is the slayer of the real contains much truth.

Our world view today is formed by reason. Theoretically, at least. In actual fact, emotional reactions are far more prevalent than usually admitted. Prejudice and wishful thinking are everywhere but reason is still meant to be our guiding star in the sense that it is the highest we are prepared to acknowledge. Let us, therefore, assume that we really do live by reason in the 21st century.

Now, to live your life on a rational basis is certainly better than to live it according to unthinking automatic reactions based on physical or emotional responses because it is more or less objective and takes many different factors into account. But reason is still very limited because it is a mental activity and the mind as we currently experience it is restricted in its field of operation to the material level, the level of form. This means that reason, on its own, is a quite inadequate way of appraising reality in its totality. Unsupported, it is unable to see that there is anything beyond the material level and, as a result, will often deny there is.

But there *is* a transcendent dimension to life and knowledge of that puts everything else in an entirely different perspective. We don't normally experience this higher dimension (the adjective is correct since it is a dimension of greater insight and freedom) because we are so identified with our material selves but, if we allow ourselves to do so, we can sense it, and we also have it revealed to us through religion. The expression that revelation takes may not appeal to the modern mind, precisely with its focus on the rational, but an unbiased sensibility should be able to see that the truth is there behind the possibly out-moded presentation. The question is, how can we move beyond simple faith and access that truth ourselves? Not through reason which largely relies for its data on input from the senses so cannot see behind the appearance of a thing to the thing in itself. We must try some other way.

There are really only two ways. Experience is one. Those who have been fortunate enough to have had a spiritual experience find that it takes them beyond the view of the world as described by reason alone while in no way conflicting with what is sane or rational. The other way is through the intuition, taking care to differentiate that from gut instinct which is a non-conscious response to external stimuli. Intuition, on the other hand, is fully conscious. It is the light of God reflected in the human soul and it is that faculty in us that enables us to know by direct perception.

The person limited to reason will usually deny the existence of direct perception or else claim that what is called that just falls into the hunch or vague feeling category. Hence, that it is purely subjective. However, the fact that such a person may be right about this in many cases does not invalidate the reality of true intuition. It simply means that in our current state of spiritual ignorance imitations of it abound, and the lower is regularly mistaken for the higher.

Reason is always dualistic. There is always the thinker and the thought, and the thinker thinks his thought. But the intuition is not like that. It comes into being seemingly independent of the person in whose consciousness it appears. It is not born of experience, either personal or collective, for it is not the product of the past but arises spontaneously out of the living present, the ever-existing moment. It links the individual to the universal and the source of all things. It is objective, whole and illuminating. Reason seeks to dispel darkness bit by bit and never succeeds totally but the intuition lights up the mind with complete clarity, revealing truth in its pristine purity. Furthermore, what we know through reason is always external to ourselves but with the intuition knowing is part of being for it comes from identification with what you truly are.

Once we accept the reality of the spiritual intuition we will naturally wish to know how to develop a proper response to it. It's quite simple. Intuition will open up to the degree you coordinate your being to the reality of the higher worlds; that is to say, to the extent you bring yourself into harmony with the intrinsic quality of those worlds. This requires a radical reassessment of your life's purpose followed by realignment of all the levels of your being. Thus, it is not simply a question of believing in spiritual things and hoping for the best but of truly perceiving what is higher and of God and what is lower and of man, and then living according to the former. It is not a matter of passively sitting in meditation or 'just being' and waiting for insights to pop into your head nor does it involve 'raising your consciousness'. It is an active thing and it requires first purifying yourself of worldly desires and ambitions, and then doing a similar thing on the spiritual level. Many aspirants to the divine mysteries merely transfer the focus of their egotistical attention from one plane to another but it is still the ego seeking reward for itself and no spiritual benefit will come from that. I don't wish to sound harsh here but the first requirement for any serious spiritual aspirant is honesty. If you aspire to truth, you must start by being truthful with yourself. Anything less and you are wasting your time.

Just as we identify thought with the head and instinct with the gut so we can identify the seat of the intuition as the heart. The heart is the centre of our being. It is where we are joined to all creation and, symbolically speaking, where spirit is anchored in the body. The sun can also be regarded as a symbol for the spiritual intelligence with the moon, shining by reflected light, standing for the ordinary mind. Taking this analogy further, we can compare the darkness of night with our current state of spiritual unawareness, illumined only by a few pale shafts of light here and there, while the dawning of the day foreshadows the awakening of spiritual knowledge. But mark this. In the same way that there is a real and an imitation intuition so taking the heart as the centre associated with the intuitive faculty does not mean it is an emotional thing. Emotional is personal. Intuition is not.

All aspirants to the sacred mysteries need to develop intuitive sensibility but this is not the work of a few months or even a few years and during that time they should bear in mind that, while we should learn to trust our intuition, we must also be careful to distinguish between that and wishful thinking. Those who have started the climb out of this world into the next need to be alert to the fact that, while they may be becoming more sensitive to spiritual truth, they are still limited by their mental attachments and conditioning. They still have their desires, fears and prejudices, and their intuitive awareness will not be perfect until they have surmounted these. Remember that the intuition is not personal. It will enable you to see the truth but, as long as you are identified with the lower self, it comes to you filtered through the mind.

Reason is a God-given faculty which helps human beings to make sense of this world and shape it to their will. But it tells us nothing about ultimate things. It knows nothing about the world beyond this one and cannot reveal where we have come from or where we should be going. A person limited to reason is spiritually blind and ontologically ignorant and will remain so until his inner eye starts to open. This is the eye of the Intuition, the organ of spiritual vision, and only when the mind is illumined by the light from that eye can it be said to have truly awakened.

But what if it doesn't awaken? Our failure to develop intuition has serious consequences. It has led to the rejection of God and when that happens it is not long before the natural order of creation is rejected too. If it comes from nothing then it has no inherent meaning and you can give it any meaning you wish which is what we, in our unawakened state, are doing.

In an era when rational intelligence is prized and people are educated to think human intellect is the highest way to perceive reality, something quite odd happens. Unless this intelligence is balanced by faith it, as it were, goes rogue. People think in increasingly abstract ways. They embrace thought-constructed ideologies and abandon instinct which is perceived as a form of ignorance, superseded by mere braininess. This leads to a separation of the mind from reality. It is on its own, cut off by itself from its deeper source.

Human beings are meant to evolve from instinct to intelligence to intuition. The intellect is, therefore, a more advanced form of mind state than instinct. However, instinct is tied to reality in a way than rational intelligence is not. It falls in with truth (on its own level) unconsciously but it does fall in with truth. The intuition responds to truth consciously and is more advanced still but the intellect is severed from reality and has to approach it dualistically meaning there is always a separation from the thinker and his thought. This is not the case with instinct and intuition. There is no separation and therefore there is accommodation to what is. The human mind without instinct or intuition to guide it is on the outside of reality and cannot know it.

Intellect is purely human. Instinct is shared with the animal kingdom and the intuition is the mode of cognition in the true spiritual world. If we develop intellect but fail to develop intuition then we are at the mercy of all kinds of craziness. I mean that literally. Instinct keeps the ignorant on the right track. Intuition brings us into conscious harmony with God and the universe but intellect on its own risks a kind of insanity if we define insanity as an inability to see and live according to reality. In the past we were told that reason needed to be balanced by faith and this is wise counsel for those who are developing mentally but have not yet grown into intuitive ways of understanding. Faith keeps you sane. But when faith is rejected and reason or, it must be said, so-called reason because much modern reason is unreasonable, assumes complete authority then the trouble begins.

Why have we not started to develop the intuition in any serious sense? Some people have but many more have not and many of these unfortunately set the agenda and run the world nowadays. The answer is these people don't want to. There is a pride and self-will in them that rejects the idea of God and so they make no attempt to open their minds to higher things which is what you have to do if you wish to grow in intuition. If you want light to come into the room, you have to draw open the curtains. It seems that many people don't want spiritual light to come into their minds, at least not on the terms required. And that is down to pride. They refuse to open their minds to God so they remain in self-created darkness.

MERE CHRISTIANS (WW)

If there had been patrons, as in guiding lights, of the blog from which this book originated they might well have been C.S. Lewis and J.R.R. Tolkien with an honourable mention in Bruce Charlton's case of Owen Barfield. The stories of Lewis and Tolkien were an inspiration to us when growing up as they have been to countless others in a world starved of spirituality and real imagination. In my case I know, and in the case of my co-conspirators here I suspect, they were a real lifeline to something beyond the mundane, and their power has not diminished with age or familiarity. My opinion of Lewis and Tolkien has not changed. In fact, the more time goes by, the more respect I have for them and their achievements, all the greater for being made against the flow of contemporary thought.

Now, it is interesting to note that all three of these men were Christians but they were different sorts of Christians. Tolkien was Catholic, Lewis was Anglican and Barfield, while a follower of the anthroposophist Rudolph Steiner, was certainly orientated to the full reality of Christ. Funnily enough, this is reflected in the three of us in that John Fitzgerald was born and raised Catholic, Bruce Charlton is a Christian who leans towards Mormon theology, and I was raised in the Church of England and now don't have any official affiliation but am definitely Christian in that I acknowledge Jesus Christ as supreme Lord and Saviour. Some may regard a Christian universalism of this sort as a weakness but I see it as a potential strength insofar as it can actually enable one to go more deeply into the vastness of spiritual truth. I have argued about this many times and don't want to go into it here. Suffice it to say that it is neither the much and justly derided pick and mix version of religion nor is it an 'anything goes' attitude. The fullest truth is in Christ but official Christianity does not contain everything of Christ. It is, of course, quite enough for salvation (if observed properly) but it does not exhaust the wholeness of truth. Moreover, there are solid grounds for thinking that the Christianity of the past, based predominantly on faith, is no longer adequate and that we now need to seek a more direct insight into the nature of things. This does not deny the past but moves it forward, and I will go into it a little more further on.

Anyway, the point is that the three of us involved in Albion Awakening are all Christian but differ in externals, and probably in some beliefs as well, just like the Inklings mentioned above. I am not comparing us to them but it might be fair to say that we are standing on their shoulders and trying to follow in their footsteps if you'll forgive the rather clumsy mixed metaphors there. Quite frankly, the world is in such a sorry spiritual state at the moment that it is time for anyone who can to put his or her hands to the pumps. We write for those who see the disastrous spiritual condition of the modern world and often feel isolated or that there is nothing that can be done about it. We write to support such people and, at the same time, ourselves since it is a truism that getting stuff down on paper helps the writer himself to understand it better. That's true in my case certainly. The world can be a very lonely place for anyone who sees through its falseness and knows that what it calls good is often anything but. I think of people like that, among whom I number myself, as exiles, and exiles who are often not even sure if their dreams of home are real. One of the purposes of this book is to affirm, categorically and without ambiguity, that these dreams are not fantasies or wishful thinking but solid and real intuitions of truth.

As I say, all three of us here value the Christianity of the past but at the same time believe that, as it stands, it is no longer enough for the future. Times change, consciousness evolves and we are not the same now as we were in the Middle Ages. The roots of our religion remain the same but there needs to be new growth from those roots. We are now called upon to realise some of the inner truths of religion directly and for ourselves. This is not a matter of redesigning the basic picture but of making it more real by adding depth and perspective, maybe even some extra dimensions that will bring it to greater life. The fundamental truths are the same but we should now be going more deeply into them. Imagine that truth can be represented by a tree. We start off with a crude drawing of a straight line, the trunk, and a few more lines sticking out above that, the branches. As time passes we can develop that and fill in more detail. The trunk becomes more recognisably a trunk with bark and so on; the branches grow and sprout leaves. We add colour, perspective and maybe some fruit and flowers. Eventually the picture becomes real. We start to climb.

Christ is the living embodiment of truth. When he said "I am the Way, the Truth and the Life" that is what he meant. He does not teach truth like any other spiritual teacher. He is truth. Therefore, opening oneself up to him as a person is all that is required to bring one to the fullness of eternal life. But we can only receive as much of him as our own spiritual unfoldment allows. We are vessels waiting to be filled. Once we remove the cork of ego we can be filled but only with as much spiritual light (spiritual wine is light not liquid) as we are able to take. That is why anyone at any level of spiritual development can turn to Christ and be fulfilled spiritually. Nevertheless, the more spiritually aware we are ourselves, the more we can gain. A saint and an ordinary person can both go to heaven but the saint will be able to get more out of it because he can respond to it at deeper levels. At the same time, the ordinary person will be completed in his way too, and maybe, I don't doubt, develop further so that he can eventually get to where the saint is now.

I am a Christian but I am not an exclusivist. I think that some people from other religions can be closer to Christ than nominal Christians, even many nominal Christians, if they live by the highest truths in their religions. They may be following Christ even if they don't know it for, after all, Christ is not just the historical person. He is also the spiritual reality that is stamped on our hearts and which we have to learn to respond to and then become like. Some people may not give this reality the name of Christ but, if they follow it faithfully, then they are serving him.

This doesn't mean that all religions are equally efficacious. Some express Christ better than others and, it goes without saying, he is to be found revealed in Christianity while in other religions, if he is there, he is veiled. But the Incarnation spread a new spiritual force throughout the entire world and this could be sensed and picked up by individuals or cultures not necessarily Christian and expressed in various ways. The outer form would not be Christian but the inner inspiration might be. Christ is universal. He is the only saviour but it is my belief that he can operate through religions that do not bear his name in addition to the ones that do. That being said, it should be obvious that he can operate best and most effectively where he is most acknowledged.

What saves us? To begin with, what are we being saved from? I would say it is identification with matter. This means we are being saved from identification with our own little selves. Sin is born of this identification. If we associate ourselves with our material being, we are trapped in matter. Our material being is not just our body. It is also the self-centred mind and 'my' feelings that I regard as me. If they are happy, I am. If they're not then I am not. But this is all part of the self-enclosed personality. Salvation is liberation from this personality into the broader world of divine truth which is the God-centred world. Now, God is a Person. In fact, he is the Person, the Divine Archetype from which our personhood is derived. Recognition of this truth is salvation. It is release from the little self into the greater Self. That does not mean the little self is abandoned or destroyed. Rather it is transformed by its union with its Parent and it is transformed into something rather like that Parent.

What this means is that real salvation demands something more than simple belief though that is an essential beginning. It demands love. So, to answer my question of the previous paragraph, I would say that what saves us is love, love of God. This is not an emotional feeling but a deep recognition of God within one's heart. It is only this love that can take us out of ourselves, and that is what we must be saved from. You might argue that we are saved by faith not love. I don't disagree but in that case I would differentiate true faith from mere belief. Real faith in God necessarily means love of God. If you don't have this love of God then your faith is probably intellectual only. You need to work on it to deepen it but then that applies to all of us.

I don't think those who are not saved in this way go to hell taking that to mean a place of perpetual torment. Some particularly rebellious souls may find themselves in something corresponding to hell after their death in this world. This will be a reflection of their own state of consciousness. Hell is separation from God and, if that is what you want, no doubt that is what you will get. But most neither too good nor too bad people will probably find themselves in a world which is a continuation of this one, though non-physical in nature. They are not saved, that is to say, saved from matter, and they carry on in an environment that, again, is an externalisation of their own consciousness. God has given them what they want, or what they think they want, but they might also have the chance to want something more as Lewis depicts in his short novel The Great Divorce in which dwellers in hell are sometimes given the chance of a trip to higher worlds and the opportunity to change if they are willing. Who can know for sure but a God of love would presumably want to give his erring children, at least those who might still awaken, the chance to mend their ways and reorient their minds. Whether they do or not is up to them.

Before concluding let me return to the theme of this post. Mere Christians. I believe that Christianity needs to evolve. From being a communal religion with a central authority, it needs to move into something in which every man must learn to become his own authority though within the general framework of Christianity. When I say that I know alarm bells will instantly go off. People will point to heresies and illusions and false trails and deceptions and so on, and they will be right. These are all the very real risks of the approach I have just outlined. But, if we are to grow spiritually, we need to make the truths of the spiritual life our own, and this means following the inner path. That path will be individual for each one of us. It must be if it is to be ours. But that does not mean that it will be individualistic. It must be individual but it must also be grounded in truth. The former without the latter leads to the heresies of which we have seen many examples throughout history. The individuality required is that of the soul, the inner spiritual self, not the outer personality, the material separate self. Therefore, to be individual in this proper sense requires a genuine spiritual sensibility. But that sensibility has to be grounded in Christ. If it turns away from Christ it becomes severed from its roots and this is where the heresies and spiritual falsehoods come from. We can only discover our true self when we look for it in Christ.

The Christianity of the past was that of Peter. But there is a deeper Christianity, one which has always been there but was only followed by a few. Now the time has come when many people must discover this more mystical Christianity which is that of the apostle John. The religion of authority and obedience is to be superseded by one of love, vision and intuitive insight but, and it's a big but, you cannot move on to this new religion unless and until you have fully absorbed the lessons of the old which are not dismissed but built on. If you try to construct the new without basing it on the foundation of the old your edifice will collapse as so many have over the last hundred years. They responded to the inspiration of the new light dawning on the horizon but they did so from the perspective of the unreconstructed lower self and sought to eat the fruits without tending the roots. Those who reject tradition will have to relearn it before they can advance beyond it.

NATIONALISM AND PATRIOTISM (WW)

What's the difference between nationalism and patriotism? This has been in the news recently with the ex-New Labour politician Peter Mandelson commenting on the motives of people who voted to leave the EU. He clearly belongs to the ranks of those who claim to love their country but are happy to see it disappear. Surely if you really love something, you want to preserve it? Growth and organic change are fine but you don't want to radically overhaul it. Would you say to your wife, "I love you darling but I just need you to look completely different and get a new personality"? Would you appreciate it if she said that to you?

Nationalism and patriotism are often (deliberately?) confused by people who style themselves progressive and who prefer the abstract to the particular. (Note: the abstract doesn't actually exist). However, it's very easy to define the difference between the two. The patriot respects or even admires patriots of other countries but the nationalist does not. The patriot loves his country. The nationalist does not really love his country, at least not in his mode of nationalist. He merely identifies with it personally and from that he dislikes others who do not share in his identification. And then the nationalist is more likely to see his country as his while the patriot reverses this distinction seeing himself as part of the country. It's rather similar to the difference between the individual and the ego, and the two should not be confused since the latter is actually a perversion of the former.

The person who does not love his country is probably incapable of loving anything to any degree. Far from being the last refuge of the scoundrel (Dr Johnson was actually referring to false patriotism not the genuine article when he said this), patriotism is the mark of a healthy human being. Your country is like your family. Unless it has become radically corrupted, it is right and natural to love it which does not mean you dislike other countries any more than you would expect their natives to dislike yours.

This was all illustrated by CS Lewis in one of the key works behind the blog that was the origin of this book, That Hideous Strength, when he wrote that just as there is a Logres (or Albion in the present context) behind Britain so most countries have a hidden ideal counterpart behind their mundane outer self. As far as I remember, he specified France and China but you could add India, Russia, America, Greece,

Italy, Egypt, Japan and many others. But not, I would say, all others. I don't think that all countries are divinely inspired but some clearly are and they are the ones that leave an evolutionary mark on the world. However, one can be a patriot of any country because all countries have their land and their national character, and this is what one loves, real things, actual qualities, not theories or nebulous abstractions. And this is what distinguishes the patriot from the nationalist on the one hand and the internationalist or globalist on the other. He loves.

WOMEN READERS (WW)

I don't know how many women readers there were of the Albion Awakening blog. My guess is relatively few which is a pity and I want to try to look at why that might be so.

I suppose most women are not attracted to writings that view modern feminism as an aberration and not the progressive philosophy the contemporary world insists it is. But the criticisms of feminism here amount to the fact that it is not only anti-human but fundamentally anti-woman, seeking to remake her as an imitation male instead of something good and true in her own right. This is close to the traditional view of men and women but tradition seen in a pure and original form without any decadent accretions in which one sex seeks to dominate the other for its own advantage. Equality between the sexes is rejected because the sexes are not the same and the attempt to make them so has resulted in modern woman losing touch with her inner femininity which is damaging her, the family and humanity as a whole. Spiritually speaking, feminism is a false friend to women but it is attractive to the worldly self because it seems to offer more power and autonomy.

Well, there it is. People will point to the supposed good feminism may have done in certain areas but this is like saying Mussolini got the trains to run on time. It's the overall effect of something that matters not its hypothetical benefits taken in isolation. It is also its spiritual effect that is important and this is not obvious to those who do not see the world in spiritual terms and who therefore don't see the damage an ideology might do to individuals on a level above the obvious material.

Women incline more to the love aspect of spirituality than the truth aspect than do men. In a world orientated to truth this can have a salutary softening effect. In a world such as ours that has turned away from truth, it can be disastrous because what it does, or potentially does, is give truth and falsehood equal recognition. This is also why women are more comfortable following the distortions of the left these days. They see it as more compassionate than the right, which superficially it may be, but they miss its real foundation in adversarial destructiveness. I dare say that men are generally more able to see this even though, of course, it is men who have created these monsters in the first place.

Women are more conformist than men. This goes along with them being less risk-taking. They are more likely to toe the consensus line and less likely to look behind communally accepted things to deep reality. So a blog like Albion Awakening, which essentially exposes the modern world as a nightmare from which we need to wake up, is not going to appeal to women so much as the more adventurous male who is more likely to want to dig down into the whys and wherefores of things, and not accept what is told him just because authority says it. None of this means there aren't women who do this and men who don't. That's an individual thing and there is no reason why anyone should be the slave of their sex. But, in general terms, this is how men and women are. Like it or not, men are usually better philosophers just as women are usually more interested in people and therefore more likely to respond to the human angle. This is just a fact, hard-wired into reality which no amount of ideological theorizing can alter.

The writers here are all male but so are most writers pointing out the insanity and nihilism of the modern world, and the spiritual vacuity where any attempt at spirituality exists. Women are more likely to take to a doctrinally amorphous sort of spirituality which is more about pleasing or comforting the feelings than one which seeks to engage with reality. Again, not all women by any means but go to any New Age type gathering and women will be much more in evidence.

So much for some general points. But I'd like to make another observation on why there might be a greater number of men than women who see through the deviant state of the modern world and are therefore attracted to positions such as those represented in a book like this. Over the last few decades men have lost power and women have gained it. When you have lost power, you want to find out why and look for some kind of compensation. When you have gained it, you may well be happy with how things are and not open to being told that your new power derives from a world that has gone wrong. This is just human nature.

I have this phrase in my mind which I think I read somewhere but I can't remember where so forgive the plagiarisation, if plagiarisation it be. Men expand the horizons while women maintain the status quo. Men innovate while women imitate. This may not be a popular thing to say nowadays but it really just echoes something I have written before about how, in cosmic terms, the masculine is the expanding force while the feminine is the contracting one. Alternatively, you could say that the former relates to the transcendent and the latter to the immanent. Obviously, we need both and, though one might be seen as primary (transcendence does come before immanence), they are still two sides of one whole. The modern world has lost the sense of transcendence and I would suggest that it is men who are more likely to want to restore that and better able to do so as well.

It's hard to write about a question like this because the topic is sensitive and who can be sure that subjectivity is not interfering with his or her vision? But I think that humanity will only start to make real advances when men and women start playing for the same team and in their correct positions. That, and when they both see that the contemporary world, with its denial of God, is on the path to self-destruction. This may mean a healthy dose of humility for both sexes but that's never a bad thing.

I believe that the demons behind many of the modern transgressions have specifically attacked women through attempting to corrupt womanhood because they know that when woman is true to her inner self she correctly orientates man to God's immanence and love (just as he does her to God's transcendence, law and truth). When she deserts her post, as it were, he does not have her influence to put him on the right path in that respect. She softens and civilises him but only when she fulfils the trust laid in her femininity. In Christian terms you might say that Christ could not have been born if Mary had not been pure of soul. Modern women need to start recognizing what their spiritual duty is, and purity is central to that which is why the devil has targeted the idea of feminine purity and tried to make it a badge of weakness.

AN ENGLISH VIRTUE (WW)

A virtue that used to be associated with the English was reticence which included modesty. Even if this was not always practiced to perfection, it was respected and aspired to. You did not draw attention to yourself and, if praised for a particular out of the ordinary action, you shrugged it off as the sort of thing anyone would have done. This attitude went hand in glove with a self-control, understatement and emotional restraint which could be mocked as buttoned-up suppression but was actually a sort of humility and understanding that giving way to emotion was ostentatious and self-indulgent. In my opinion, these characteristics were based on a true spiritual understanding, though unlikely to be expressed as such, which had its origin in an awareness of the right manner for a created being to behave in the light of the reality of its Creator.

I don't think this approach as to how to behave exists very much anymore. It has been ridiculed too many times and, since the 1960s, rejected as insincere and false not to mention repressive or even inhuman. It was none of these things though, as most things have the defects of their qualities, it may have tipped over into those occasionally. But, essentially, it had a dignity and a sense of honour that are very much missing nowadays. It was based on both self-respect and a respect for others that you rarely find now in this age of vulgarity and self-expression.

Most people behave according to the standards of the society in which they find themselves. It takes a rare soul to stand apart from the conventions of their time. But these conventions, like the stars, incline, they do not compel. The great value of this traditional English virtue was that it strove to rise above emotion, not in an unfeeling way but in a way that saw the over-expression of emotion as behaviour centred on 'me'. Self-control is control of the self. It is the refusal to see yourself as the most important thing there is or life in terms of your own feelings. That is why I say it is a form of humility.

Since the English have lost touch with this quality they have become a second-rate people. I say this as a lover of my country but also as someone who recognises that it has been the object of a relentless attack over the last several decades and this attack has corrupted it. It's a familiar pattern. The people who build up a strong and unique culture leave heirs who take what has been won by their forebears for granted and fritter it away. They cannot make the sacrifices their ancestors made because they already have the status and comfort that has been won for them by those ancestors. They become sophisticated, and sophistication practically always leads to decadence as what you might call the pioneer spirit is replaced by urbanity. As I say, it's a pattern that has been acted out time and time again in many places. The energy of the English that created their Empire has dissolved into loss of confidence and self-indulgence. No doubt in some ways we are better than our forebears, but it seems to me that our virtues are often the virtues of weakness rather than strength.

The past is gone and cannot be revived. Nor should it be. But a healthy future is more likely if some of the traditions of the past are respected and not just discarded as old-fashioned and redundant. Not all traditions, of course, but it doesn't take much intelligence to sift the good from the bad. For the English, foremost among the good was their old virtue of dignified self-restraint which nevertheless stood firm in the face of adversity and opposition. If we could start to recapture that we might become worthier successors to our ancestors than we currently are.

WHERE WE ARE NOW (WW)

I wonder if future historians will look back at the last decade and conclude that this was the time when the Western world finally went insane. I can only hope so as it will mean that some form of sanity has been recovered. Will they note that the condition had been building up for more than a century but in this period the evil seeds planted in (for the sake of argument because actually the real seeds go much further back) the 18th century when faith began to be lost, finally flowered?

It is the loss of faith that is the root cause of the insanity. More precisely, for the West it is the loss of Christianity which entails the loss of belief in an underlying spiritual reality, a foundation of truth. When this sense has gone then there is no truth and we are free to make our own reality. But that is not real, not really real. It only depends on the whim of the moment. You're a man who wants to be a woman? No problem. Nothing is real so anything can be. Mind you, when a society has taken this attitude why should it stop there? I'm a cannibal. Why should I not be? Because you can do what you want as long as you'd don't hurt someone else. But why shouldn't I hurt anyone else? Is there a real reason, other than the purely utilitarian one, why I shouldn't? If it's just so that society can run smoothly without self-destructing, why should that concern me? I make my own reality. I can do what I want because, for me, there is no other reality. This can be taken to even more absurd lengths. There is no logical reason in a materialistic universe why I should not rob, rape, kill and so on. If there is no sub-stratum of reality, this should not be a problem, certainly not a moral problem. When nothing is real, nothing matters and this is the course we have set ourselves on. The denial of spiritual truth is the denial of any truth at all. When the human mind has no bedrock of truth in which to establish itself, it becomes deranged. We are only at the beginning of that period now because we have only just reached the point at which the legacy from our Christian inheritance has finally begun to run out. Previous generations may have, as they would have thought it, moved on from Christianity but they still operated in a world formed by Christianity and adopted many of its tenets. No more.

The real Christian influence is no more, or vastly reduced, but this means that a fake Christian influence can be introduced. Because Christianity is part of our history everyone has at least a superficial notion of what it is. But we no longer have any deep idea as to its proper meaning. Thus, we take its tangential elements, the ones that can relate to a materialistic world, and apply them, separating them from their spiritual origins and thinking we are taking the essential and just dropping the superstitious bits when we are actually doing the reverse. But because we don't acknowledge the spiritual, we simply ignore it. So, we can take love your neighbour and use that to create the kind of society in which proper qualitative differences and standards are erased. But we ignore love God which is the first and primary commandment from which all the others grow and without which the others are meaningless. We can take the idea of oneness in Christ, a spiritual unity of souls raised to a higher level, and distort that into egalitarianism, a kind of materialistic unity, a unity outside Christ, which denies the hierarchical nature of truth.

I have written on more than one occasion of how in the present age the devil is using the idea of love (love your neighbour, love your enemy) to destroy truth, and how the fact of oneness is used to deny the fact of difference. Many people are fooled by this and go along with it because they have no solid metaphysical foundations. Their beliefs are weak since they abandoned God and with Him the sense of an absolute reality. This means they can be herded in any direction chosen by the powers that seek to manipulate reality. In the past humanity has been led astray by hatred. That is still the case, of course, even though the hatred is generally disguised and presented as something good. However, in our day we are also led astray by a false idea of love. This is used to dismantle traditional societies with their basis in spiritual ideals which often have a separative element in them as there must be a separation between good and evil, right and wrong, truth and lies, the higher and the lower etc, and then rebuild in a completely materialistic form. It is a levelling down for materialistic oneness can only be on the most basic of levels, that of simple unformed matter.

What this amounts to is that Christian ideas that relate to this world are now used to subvert real Christian values which are rooted in the transcendent. This is like cutting down a tree and then presenting rotting apples lying on the ground as though they were fresh fruit on the bough. Christian ideas separated from God become in a short space of time these rotting apples.

All this having been said, it is nevertheless true that we did need to move on from the past view of Christianity as a religion of rules and outer authority to a new one in which faith, understanding and authority transferred from the outer world to the inner. We should have made the truth of Christ our own, progressing, as I said earlier, from the world of Peter to that of John. Our understanding of Christianity should have deepened to incorporate the idea of ourselves as sons and daughters of God, called to express that relationship in the fullest way. This means that Christ is not just up in heaven. He is also within ourselves and our job is to fit ourselves as a worthy receptacle for his light. This is all in the traditional understanding of Christianity but was rarely brought out into full view and shown to be the whole point of the religion. But we had reached the stage at which we should have started to become spiritual adults, leaving the childhood of faith. Faith is good and necessary at all stages of the spiritual path but it can develop into something more than simple belief into a deeper intuitive understanding.

Western Man has reached a critical point in ego consciousness and needs to advance from that. He has developed his individual ego, separating himself from an instinctive group consciousness, and with that the rational side of his nature. Now what he should be doing is start to progress to a conscious creative union with the Father, spiritual responsibility. Unfortunately, what he actually appears to be doing, in the mass and as things stand anyway, is falling back into the amorphous spiritual immaturity of the Mother, an unconscious union or return to Chaos, the state of undifferentiation. There are reactions against this but they are mostly on the ego consciousness level itself. We need to create a world in which the mature ego is able to transcend itself while retaining full individual integrity. That is the path laid out for us by Christ taking him as a kind of spiritual template.

We had to fall away from one form of spiritual belief in order to develop another in which inner understanding replaced outer acceptance. This should have involved a brief period of individualism, materialism even, quickly superseded by a higher spiritual life in which Man and God combine as they did in Jesus. Obviously not on such a high level to begin with but we should have embarked on that path. This is not what has happened. The individualism has become more entrenched because we have preferred self to God. That is what this is all about. We have preferred the little shrunken enclosed world of the separate self, the rebellious ego, to the greater world of our Divine Creator. And why? Because we have no love in us, no love for what is beyond us, a reality without which we would disappear as though we had never been. The only way to move out of the insanity of the present time is to develop this love and that means to forget ourselves and return to God, seeing ourselves this time as sons and daughters of the Father, able to grow into ever deeper communion with him. But recall what he said through the one he sent to bring us back to him. "If you love me, keep my commandments."

Great Britain at the beginning of the year 2020 looks further away from a spiritual revival than ever. There are occasional green shoots, reactions against materialism, leftism, the whole nihilistic ethos of the age, but they all seem to shrivel up in the harsh frost of the post-modern world. Albion can only awaken if a sufficient number of people cry out "Enough! We have been lied to and deceived for too long. But we have also succumbed to weakness and egotism like the children of Israel who danced around the Golden Calf, abandoning Moses while he went up to Mount Sinai." This means an awareness of the false views inflicted on us by politics, religion, science, the media, education and so on, basically every institution. But it also means an acceptance of our own complicity in all this. We have turned away from God. Awakening demands, as it always must, full knowledge of our own failures. Then we can face the future with confidence because all God really requires of us is the opening of our heart towards him. He will do the rest.

THE ROBIN HOOD OPTION (JF)

One can never be certain. We are dealing, after all, with a 'God of Surprises.' But it seems increasingly unlikely, to my eyes at least, that there will be a mass, instantaneous awakening in (or of) Albion any time soon. Things are too far gone for that. What has been set in motion needs to run its course. We will have to drop down a bit further, it seems - like Dante descending the circles of Hell - before we can start to look upward again.

'Lantern Bearers' is a phrase I have often used to describe our role and vocation in this age of civilisational decline. Now, however, I am beginning to feel that 'seed planters' might be more apposite. We are probably at the outset of a centuries-long endeavour, but what is absolutely crucial - right here and now - is that we make a start on the renewal of our culture, refreshing it at its deepest wellsprings, radically reorientating it towards the Sacred, the fount and source of everything true and good.

Our immediate problem is that the times we live in appear more and more inimical to any notion of the Sacred or Divine. Secularism is becoming strident and militant. Liberalism is growing increasingly illiberal. Christians are squeezed out of the public square and are finding it harder to work with a clear conscience in fields such medicine, law, government and education. How to respond to this burgeoning intolerance has been a topic of much debate, spurred to a great extent by Rod Dreher's book, *The Benedict Option* (2016) and his pugilistic column for *The American Conservative.*

I have been reflecting on these matters during a recent reread of Roger Lancelyn Green's, *The Adventures of Robin Hood* (Puffin, 1956). As well as some superb storytelling, Green gave me several springboards for thought pertaining to the themes of resistance and renewal and where the two meet and intertwine. Green portrays Robin as an Arthurian figure, bringing succour to Saxons suffering under the Norman yoke as, centuries before, the original Arthur had inspired the Britons to resist their invading ancestors. As Green evocatively puts it:

> Then, in that wild and lonely glade, while the owls screeched over the dark forest, and an occasional wolf howled in the distance, they all knelt down together and swore their oath - a pledge as high and as sacred, though they were but outlaws

> and escaped felons, as that sworn by the noblest knight who, in the days when the Saxons themselves were the conquerors and oppressors, had sat at King Arthur's Table.

'We take for the general good,' Robin declares, 'and it shall be as much our duty to seek out the poor, the needy, the widow, the orphan and all those who have suffered and are suffering wrong, and minister to their wants as far as we can.' This going out to the poor and needy is, I feel, of central importance to our predicament today. Robin's merry men have bigger fish to fry than mere self-preservation. They are engaged on a societal mission. Their rapport with people outside their group earns them kudos and affection and saves them from the hot-house insularity which often bedevils focused, intentional communities and can lead, at best, to a climate of gossip and backbiting and, at worst, physical and spiritual abuse.

Robin Hood is an intensely charismatic figure. So are his closest followers - Maid Marian, Friar Tuck, Little John and Will Scarlett. They radiate goodness and nobility. People see and feel those qualities in them, and their hearts are lifted. Can we say that truly about ourselves? Does the Gospel show itself in our body language and demeanour? Do our faces shine with love of God and love of Albion? If not, why not? Are we spending too much time mulling over culture wars and not enough time in prayer and contemplation? I think often of Karol Wojtyla in this respect who, as Archbishop of Kraków between 1964 and 1978, began each day with an hour and a half's silent adoration before the Blessed Sacrament. From a worldly, administrative point of view, this is time which would have been better spent breakfasting with colleagues, arranging meetings or answering correspondence. But Wojtyla, like Mary of Bethany in John's Gospel, chose the 'better part', simply spending time with Christ. I am convinced that this practice gave him that palpable aura of holiness that helped him to play such a decisive role on the world stage when he became Pope John Paul II in 1978.

We also have to take into account the nature of our particular era. What might have been an appropriate response to spiritual and cultural crisis in former times might not be so today. We don't live in first century Palestine, for instance, where religious questions were of paramount importance across all strata of society. Nor are we trying to convert fifth century European pagans either, who were already, in their own way, open and responsive to the Sacred. Our post-Enlightenment epoch is entirely different - desacralised, deracinated and disenchanted. The supernatural has been safely walled off and the numinous banished to the *demi-monde* of fancy and subjective imagination. We need to see ourselves, therefore, not so much as 'Preachers of the Word' but 'Evokers of the Sacred.' Without this basic receptivity to the Sacred, the Word will fall on barren soil.

This is important because twenty-first century Westerners still experience encounters with the Holy; as much, if not more so, than in the past. But the post-modern world has divested itself of the religious terminology which sets them in their proper frame. My experience, talking over these things with friends, tells me that they often take place in childhood. As the years pass the visitation fades from the conscious mind but remains embedded in the heart, waiting for the right moment and the right person, perhaps, to reinvoke it and call it back to life.

That person could be your or I. With this in mind, we should posit a Christ who holds the keys to a wider, richer realm of possibility than that offered by the currently dominant paradigm. Materialism does not satisfy the deepest longings of the human soul. Those trapped in its limiting vision, whether materially well-off or not, are truly the 'poor and needy' of our day, robbed of their spiritual heritage and the deepest knowledge of their hearts, just as the English of Robin Hood's day were defrauded of their ancestral homes and lands by the Norman aristocracy.

So, what would a 'Robin Hood Option' church actually look like? Something like this, I feel - Michael De-la-Noy's account in his book, *Church of England* (Simon and Schuster, 1993), of an evening visit to St. Patrick's Anglican Church in Hove in the late 1980s, at a time when the local bishop had recently invited a nearby monastic community to help reinvigorate the Liturgy:

> I wandered into church at 6.45. An assortment of tramps, alcoholics and the mentally ill were all jumbled up with parishioners in pews arranged around a free-standing altar in the nave, and vespers was underway, the plainchant being led by a young estate agent. Father Sharpe, in alb, sat in the centre...
>
> No account of the liturgy could by itself convey the

> unselfconscious devotion of the service. For the consecration everyone gathered in a strange intimacy around the altar, within feet of the celebrant. A home baked roll was consecrated; the patten and chalice were modern earthenware. Yet there was nothing folksy about the occasion. At the peace everyone moved round to kiss or shake hands. Everyone, including many of the down and outs, received Communion.
>
> It was a gentle, moving experience, which seemed by the nature of those present - unwashed, wearing mittens, unpatronised and essentially unimpressed and at home - to offer a glimpse of what worship may have been like in the Middle Ages, a rediscovery of a marriage of reverence, impressive ritual and sensitive simplicity.

The church has here become a piece of holy ground - a place of encounter, meaning, depth and possibility - a fount of living water, from where right thought and action flow into our lives and the lives of those around us, re-baptising and renewing the world without any strain or anxiety on our part. St. Patrick's, in those days, was a *clearing* - a free and open point of intersection between the human and the Divine. In an epoch like our own where there is no set guidance for restorative actions, the first restorative task is to start fashioning such spaces. This is what Robin Hood did with his 'wild and lonely' glade and what people found in Mother Julian's cell in Norwich at the other end of the Middle Ages. Let us leave the last word to that fine representative of the English contemplative tradition. May it act as a reminder that our spiritual foe has nothing to offer men and women, and that with our encouragement, faith and discernment they may find this out sooner rather than later and turn once again to that great Sun that lit up their faces when they were new to this world:

> This is the cause why we are not at rest in heart and soul: that here we seek rest in things that are so little there is no rest in them, and we do not know our God who is all mighty, all wise and all good. For he is true rest ... There is no end to our willing and longing until we know God in the fullness of joy.

REDDITOR LUCIS AETERNAE (JF)

I am currently reading *The Anathemata* by David Jones, a book-length poem, published in 1952 by Faber and Faber, exploring the cultural and spiritual history of Britain. Here is a brief extract. The speaker is 'The Lady of the Pool', a kind of Medieval tutelary spirit of London:

> And then, as if he perceived a body - coming
> as if he hails a personage
> where was but insentience
> and baulk of stone
> he sings out and clear:
> REDDITOR LUCIS AETERNAE
> These, captain, were his precisive words - what sentiments I can't construe - but at which, captain, I cried: Enough!
> Let's to terrestrial flesh, or
> bid good-night, I thought.

And here is a footnote provided by the poet to illuminate the Latin phrase:

> REDDITOR LUCIS AETERNAE - 'Restorer of the Eternal Light'; this is inscribed on a gold medallion found at Beauvains near Arras, struck to commemorate the relief of London in AD 296 by the Emperor, Constantius Chlorus, the husband of St. Helena (and father of Constantine the Great). He is mounted and with a lance, his horse stepping down from the gang-plank of a boat at a turreted gateway inscribed LON, where a female figure kneels with welcoming arms. The words, 'Redditor, etc.' are inscribed above the figure of the Emperor. Although this may but commemorate a chance victory in a war of rival generals, none the less Constantius, at that moment, was the outward sign of something and was himself the implement of what he signified, namely: in the domain of accidental fact, the saving of London from immediate sack; in the domain of contemporary politics, the restoration of Britain to unity with the West, and in the domain of perennial ideas, the return to Britain of the light of civilisation.

In AD 296, the Roman naval commander, Carausius, usurped control of Britain and northern Gaul and declared himself joint-Emperor. The Imperial government found him a difficult opponent and Britain remained under localised, independent rule until Constantius' expedition ten years later. The episode (known as the Carausian Revolt) is superbly dramatised in Rosemary Sutcliff's 1957 novel, *The Silver Branch* (Oxford University Press, 1957). Here, Carausius sets out his stall before the two young soldiers, Justin and Flavius:

> 'The Wolves gather,' Carausius said. 'Always, everywhere, the Wolves gather on the frontiers, waiting. It needs only that a man should lower his eye for a moment, and they will be in to strip the bones. Rome is failing, my children.'
>
> Justin looked at him warily, but Flavius never moved; it was as though he had known what Carausius would say.
>
> 'Oh, she is not finished yet. I shall not see her fall. My Purple will last my life-time - and nor, I think, will you. Nevertheless, Rome is hollow rotten at the heart, and one day she will come crashing down. a hundred years ago, it must have seemed that all this was for ever; a hundred years hence - only the gods know ... If I can make this one province strong - strong enough to stand alone when Rome goes down, then something may be saved from the darkness. If not, then Dubris light and Limanis light and Rutupiae light will go out. The lights will go out everywhere.'
>
> He stepped back, dragging aside the hanging folds of the curtains, and stood framed in their darkness against the firelight and the lamplight behind him, his head yet turned to the scudding grey and silver of the stormy night. 'If I can steer clear of a knife in my back until the work is done, I will make Britain strong enough to stand alone,' he said. 'It is as simple as that.'

Unfortunately for Carausius, and perhaps for the country, he did not escape a knife in the back. He was assassinated in AD 293 by his finance minister, Allectus, who clung onto power until the Roman reconquest.

The Carausian revolt erupted just a decade after the end of the so-called 'Gallic Empire', where, between AD 260 and 274, the usurper, Postumus, had assumed control of Britain and Gaul in an almost identical manner. It surprises me greatly that none of this history, so far as I can tell, has been referred to in the endless media commentary surrounding Brexit. Carausius, in many ways, can be seen as the first Euro-sceptic. His revolt shows that in some sense Britain is indeed 'set apart', as William Wildblood cogently argues in his 'Albion Set Apart' chapter.

Britain, on this view, is temperamentally unsuited to life as one cog among many in a giant European power-bloc. Geographically, the UK stands at one remove from the continent and that needs to be reflected in the way the country is governed. Britain, as Carausius intuited, is a nation that needs to find her own way in the world. She is independent by nature and it would be going against the grain to corral her into compliance with a supra-national, overseas authority, especially one perceived to be 'hollow rotten at the heart.'

So far, so straightforward. But there is more going on here. Jones talks about the 'restoration of Britain to unity with the West' and the 'return of Britain to the light of civilisation.' For him (and the designer of the Beauvains coin), the restoration of direct Roman rule is clearly a good thing. But that is because Constantius openly declares himself the representative and restorer of a higher principle - the 'eternal light' of civilisation, heaven and the gods. The contrast with the European Union, jumping to contemporary times, couldn't be starker. One of the great misjudgements of the Remain campaign, in my view, was to conflate Europe with the EU. Europe is a civilisation - at least 3000 years old - and a vast physical space, stretching from the Mayo coastline to the Ural Mountains. The EU is an institution, no different in essence from any other institution - Barclays Bank, for instance, or Her Majesty's Revenue and Customs. It exists to maintain and perpetuate itself. It is grey, bureaucratic and faceless, with little of the romance, glamour and rebel-chic some Remainers project onto it. It has no links with any higher principle, as symbolised by the EU flag, twelve yellow stars in a circle on a blue background with absolutely nothing in the centre. You would get extremely long odds on a functionary like Jean-Claude Juncker styling himself *Redditor Lucis*

Aeternae. Juncker himself would be appalled at the thought, and that says everything, to my mind, about where his institution stands spiritually and philosophically. Nowhere at all, in brief.

The EU's big problem is that it has no spiritual dimension whatsoever. It doesn't know how to connect with people on the level of spirit and imagination. It has no spark, no fire, and has, in recent years, become increasingly hostile to the Gospel despite the religious faith of its founders and its roots in post-war Christian Democracy. More sobering than the EU's shortcomings, however, is the sad fact that were a Restorer of the Eternal Light to turn up at a British port tomorrow he would most likely be deported straightaway. It is someone or something on this level, I believe, that 52% of the British people were, perhaps unconsciously, voting for in the 2016 referendum. Something essentially spiritual. But this has been not been understood, acknowledged or reflected in all the debate that has gone on since in Westminster and the media. Pro-Leave circles are perhaps the worst. A paper like *The Daily Telegraph*, for instance, views Brexit exclusively in terms of its potential for economic growth and increased global trade. It doesn't see it as an opportunity for spiritual and cultural renewal. It doesn't even go there, and this, I feel, is emblematic of a stunning lack of imagination and independent thought running right through the UK establishment.

The Brexiteers would be better advised to start forging links with the EU's Central and Eastern European members, particularly the 'Visegrad Four' of Poland, Hungary, the Czech Republic and Slovakia. These countries have displayed a fierce national pride and a feisty independence of spirit in their recent dealings with Brussels. Decades of communist tyranny have taught them the value of their own national patrimony and also the preciousness and precariousness of European civilisation as a whole. They are also (with the possible exception of the Czech Republic) profoundly Christian in outlook and orientation. In November 2016, for example, the Polish government officially placed the nation under the patronage of Christ the King, while Hungary's President, Viktor Orban, recently said this:

> Ever more frequently nowadays I hear that sixty years ago the European Union's founding fathers marked out the route. Europe, as Robert Schuman said, will be Christian or it will be nothing. The year 2017 has presented European countries with

> a historic task. A new task has been given to the free nations of Europe and the national governments elected by free citizens. We must protect Christian culture. We must do this not to oppose others, but to defend ourselves, our families, our nation, our countries and Europe, 'the homeland of homelands.'

Now, I'm not naive enough to think that the V4 don't have challenges and temptations of their own, but they are at least facing in the right direction, which is probably more than can be said for the UK at this moment. The only thing that can reorient us, I believe, is something that will never happen because the world today is so addicted to restlessness and ceaseless change. Britain needs to step off the wheel, in short. She needs to take a break and gather her thoughts, pressing the pause button for as long as it takes, so her inhabitants can start to feel their way into the essence and soul of the country, beginning to think seriously about what British identity is and what kind of relationships we would like to have, first of all between the UK's four constituent parts, then towards Europe, and finally to the world beyond.

Such a space for quiet recollection will never be officially sanctioned, as I say, but there's nothing to stop us engaging in it ourselves as individuals or groups. Whatever we choose to do, it is less opinion and debate that is required and more thought and reflection. We have become fixated, to a degree, on political procedures and solutions. But there is a pre-political level of myth and intuition which drives the direction a society takes at a more fundamental level. It's all about the kind of stories we tell ourselves and the stories we believe to be true or false. We need to return for a while to the primal, archetypal level of things, then tune back in to the land we have become alienated from, and listen to the story it's telling us. Where does it want to go? What does it want us to do? Then we can step forward into the future in confidence and clarity of mind.

Maybe what emerges from our time in the wilderness will appear strange and unsettling. The Russian Orthodox priest, Fr. Andrew Phillips, has proposed on his blog (www.orthodoxengland.net) the dissolution of the UK and its replacement by another acronym, IONA - The Isles of the Northern Sea. He wants Westminster to become the site of a devolved English Parliament and for central government to relocate to the Isle of Man, an island rich in British mythological lore and within sight, as it were, of all four countries.

It could well be that such a radical reimagining of who we are is exactly what is needed to propel us out of the current impasse. But nothing authentic or original will come to the surface without contemplation and stillness. We have to get beyond the head level - into the heart, the imagination and the guts. Argument and counter argument will get us precisely nowhere. We'll be stuck at the level of cliché forever, more and more dependent on the market and the state (and increasingly technology) to provide us with answers to problems we don't have the imaginative capacity to deal with anymore.

Silence is the key. As Cardinal Robert Sarah points out in his recent book, *The Power of Silence* (Ignatius Press, 2017):

> Mankind must join in a sort of resistance movement. What will become of our world if it does not look for intervals of silence? Interior rest and harmony can flow only from silence. Without it, life does not exist. The greatest mysteries of the world are born and unfold in silence. How does nature develop? In the greatest silence. A tree grows in silence, and springs of water flow at first in the silence of the ground. The sun that rises over the earth in its splendour and grandeur warms us in silence. What is extraordinary is always silent.

The still small voice that Elijah heard on Mount Horeb is there for nations just as much as it is for individuals. And it is that still small voice - more than any Emperor, military commander or referendum result - which is the true *Redditor Lucis Aeternae.*

THE GREAT RETURN (JF)

The Welsh writer and mystic, Arthur Machen (1863-1947), has become without doubt a highly influential figure. Artists as varied as H.P. Lovecraft, Jorge Luis Borges, Alan Moore, and the late Mark E Smith, creative mastermind behind Manchester post-punk pioneers, The Fall, have all claimed inspiration from him.

Machen is most widely seen these days as a purveyor of 'weird fiction', with stories like *The Great God Pan* and *The White People* viewed as early, and very unsettling, examples of the horror genre. He is also famous for his short story, *The Bowmen* (1914), which tells the tale of a phantom squadron of bowmen saving the British Army from destruction in France. Machen was a fine journalist, and he wrote the story in a journalistic style, which was taken as fact by many readers and gave rise to the legend of the Angels of Mons, who were said to have appeared to retreating British forces in September 1914.

Machen's most interesting books, in my view, are his novels, *The Hill of Dreams* (1903), *The Secret Glory* (1922), and the novella which is the subject of this post, *The Great Return* (1915). Machen's recognition of a deeper, richer reality behind the surface phenomena of daily life comes across particularly strongly in these stories. In this respect, as in others, Machen can be considered a precursor to Charles Williams. Like Williams, he was a High Anglican with a deeply mystical bent and a fascination with occult lore. His father was a clergyman, and the young Machen would have followed the same path but for a financial crisis which necessitated him leaving the family home and relocating to London to earn a meagre living through a variety of odd-jobs. Machen writes exceptionally well, as does Williams, about that city. This passage from *The Three Imposters* is especially reminiscent, I feel, of the perambulations around London Williams describes in *War in Heaven* and *All Hallows' Eve*:

> Before me was the long suburban street, its dreary distance marked by rows of twinkling lamps, and the air was poisoned by the faint, sickly smell of burning bricks, deserted as that of Pompeii. I knew pretty well what direction to take, so I set out wearily, looking at the stretch of lamps vanishing in perspective: and as I walked street after street branched off to right and left, some far reaching, to distances that seemed

> endless, communicating with other systems of thoroughfare, and some mere protoplasmic streets, and ending suddenly in waste, and pits, and rubbish heaps, and fields whence the magic had departed. I have spoken of systems of thoroughfare, and I assure you that walking alone through these silent places I felt fantasy growing on me, and some glamour of the infinite.

Machen was born in Caerleon, South-East Wales. The town's Arthurian heritage and its Romano-British ruins made a strong impression on his imagination. *The Great Return* is also set in Wales, in a small village on the South-West coast called Arfon. The narrator, at one stage, climbs a hill and sits among the ruins of an ancient fortification called the Old Camp Head, which looks out over the sea '*towards Cornwall and to the great depths that roll beyond Cornwall to the far ends of the world; a place where fragments of dreams - they seemed such then - might, perhaps, be gathered into the clearness of a vision.*'

Machen is not a great prose stylist and his stories are often constructed in quite a clunky fashion. In my view, however, it is passages like this which show why he is so compelling and influential. There is a real sense of the British Mysteries in his writing, and he has the ability (like Williams again) to bring those mysteries alive in a memorable and evocative manner.

In *The Great Return*, the Holy Grail appears in Arfon, bringing healing, transformation, joy and peace to all who come into its presence. That's the plot in a nutshell. The Grail comes and the lives of men and women are transformed. Spring morning consciousness, to borrow Colin Wilson's phrase, is the order of the day. That's all there is, and at this level of spiritual and imaginative encounter, that's all there needs to be.

I think this is also how it will be at the end of time. I really do. Sure, there will be wars and revolutions, earthquakes and tsunamis, totalitarian régimes, and economic and social meltdown. We will look at all these phenomena and see them as 'signs of the times' and so they are, but they are also nothing to be afraid of. Not ultimately. Not fundamentally. In his 1945 masterpiece, *The Reign of Quantity and the Signs of the Times*, the French metaphysician, René Guénon (1886-1951) delineates with pinpoint accuracy the headlong erosion and inversion of values which mark the times in which we live, the final stages of the

Dark Age, or *Kali Yuga* as Guénon calls it, following the Indian terminology. According to the Hindu doctrine of the Four Ages, which Guénon subscribed to, the Dark Age will cede place, as surely as night gives way to day, to a new Golden Age (*Satya Yuga*).

Our difficulty, here and now, is that we do not know how much further the Dark Age has to run. We might already be close to the nadir or, conversely, our fall - like that of Milton's Satan - may still have dizzying fathoms to come. We might conceivably have to plunge all the way down - to a self-created Hell - enslavement to an Artificial Intelligence demanding worship and obedience like the bodiless 'Head' in C.S. Lewis's, *That Hideous Strength*. We are not in charge of the timescales. Guénon teaches us that the Dark Age has to run its course as per the parameters set down for it at the foundation of the world. The world grows increasingly materialised until it is as far from its spiritual source as mid-winter is from mid-summer. Then the switchback occurs and the spiritual becomes once again the dominant paradigm. The transhumanists view this kind of pabulum as outmoded superstition, of course, to be outgrown at the earliest opportunity, but they have tunnel vision and are merely acting out the roles pre-ordained for them as men of the Dark Age. Their fall is as inevitable as the changing of the seasons and the rising of the sun. It will be as spectacular and comprehensive as the fall of Numenor or Atlantis.

Guénon also explains how, as we get closer to the Golden Age, some of the light from this era to come will find a way of shining into the darkness of this present time. We should remember as well, as Christians, that the Golden Age for us is not just a block of time but is in fact the coming of a Person who, like the Grail in Machen's story, brings healing, transformation, joy and peace.

The signs of His approach, as with His first advent, are likely to reveal themselves in a manner we have not anticipated and at a time and place we do not expect - a provincial backwater, not unlike Nazareth, perhaps - a place passed over and left to rot by the shifting tides of politics, finance and fashion - a run-down industrial estate, let us say, on a ring road just outside Middlesbrough. People turn up for work on a Monday morning, and already by lunchtime a thousand unobtrusive miracles have taken place. Old feuds are forgotten, horizons are widened, workplace politics are recognised as irrelevant, broken families are made whole, and faces shine with light, laughter and joy. No-one knows how or why this change has happened. No-one cares either. All the workers know is that it feels good, right, natural and true. 'It's always been this way,' they say to each other. 'It could never be any other way. We just forgot it for a while.'

It wouldn't surprise me if a tremendous act of healing, bordering on resurrection, also occurred in the locality - on a nearby council estate, maybe - very similar in its details to Machen's account of the moment Olwen Phillips, a sixteen year old girl in the last stages of consumption, begins her recovery:

> She said she woke up in the deep darkness, and she knew the life was fast going from her. She could not move so much as a finger, she tried to cry out, but no sound came from her lips. She felt that in another instant the whole world would fall from her—her heart was full of agony. And as the last breath was passing her lips, she heard a very faint, sweet sound, like the tinkling of a silver bell. It came from far away, from over by Ty-newydd. She forgot her agony and listened, and even then, she says, she felt the swirl of the world as it came back to her.
>
> And the sound of the bell swelled and grew louder, and it thrilled all through her body, and the life was in it. And as the bell rang and trembled in her ears, a faint light touched the wall of her room and reddened, till the whole room was full of rosy fire. And then she saw standing before her bed three men in blood-coloured robes with shining faces. And one man held a golden bell in his hand. And the second man held up something shaped like the top of a table. It was like a great jewel, and it was of a blue colour, and there were rivers of silver and of gold running through it and flowing as quick streams flow, and there were pools in it as if violets had been poured out into water, and then it was green as the sea near the shore, and then it was the sky at night with all the stars shining, and then the sun and the moon came down and washed in it. And the third man held up high above this a cup that was like a rose on fire; "there was a great burning in it, and a dropping of blood in it, and a red cloud above it, and I saw a great secret. And I heard a voice that sang nine times, 'Glory and praise to the Conqueror of Death, to the Fountain of Life immortal.' Then the red light went from the wall, and it was all darkness,

> and the bell rang faint again by Capel Teilo, and then I got up and called to you."

This is the Great Return. It is also the way the world ends, not with a whimper, nor with a bang, but with a high and holy chant, the ringing of a bell, a vision of goodness and purity, and a soft, warm light which grows and swells until the whole world, from the North Pole to the South, is suffused with its radiance. The fetters of the Iron Age snap and fall asunder. The Great Restoration is at hand. The dream, as Lewis writes in *The Last Battle*, is ended. This is the morning.

BEYOND THE GREY HAVENS (JF)

And thus was the habitation of the Children of Ilúvatar established at the last in the Deeps of Time and amidst the innumerable stars.

J.R.R. Tolkien, *The Silmarillion*

There are a wealth of creation myths to be found in the world, both now and throughout history. The best known, perhaps, is the one given in the Book of Genesis. But every religion has a creation myth, as does every mythology. There are scientific creation myths too, the Big Bang being the most obvious example, a transposition into scientific language of what other creation myths use poetry or stories to convey.

This multitude of accounts offer different approaches to the same mystery. They tackle the big question - why is there something instead of nothing? Viewed this way, all creation myths are worthy of respect. They are all laudable, all noble attempts at translating into human terms an act of creation on such a spectacularly large scale that it defies our minds' ability to comprehend it. None of us were there, after all, 'in the beginning', so it's impossible to say with the degree of certitude required in a court of law, for instance, that one myth is true and another false.

What I would say, however, is that some myths *feel* truer than others, and that what feels true for one person might feel less true for another. This sense of truth - this 'inner compass' - could well be subjective, therefore, coloured by our ancestral past and our religious and cultural upbringing. But that is no reason to distrust or disbelieve it. Quite the reverse. That very subjectivity is what makes it most real and true for us as unique, unrepeatable individuals. It connects us with the deepest part of our being, that secret chamber where the still, small voice points the subjective self towards the objective truth of God. Our deepest desire, as Ignatian spirituality emphasises, is also God's deepest desire for us.

The creation myth which speaks most powerfully to me is undoubtedly J.R.R. Tolkien's, *Ainulindalë: The Music of the Ainur*. Ever since I first read *The Silmarillion* at school in the 1980s, I have wished that this was the official Christian creation story. The Genesis account, if I'm honest, has never sparked my imagination or inspired any deep thoughts or feelings, whereas Tolkien's myth energises me on all levels. This, I believe, is due to the simple fact that Genesis is a Jewish creation myth, and I am not Jewish but Anglo-Irish. When I say this, I don't mean any slight on the Jewish people, who were and are a remarkable race who bring so many good things to the world. But the fact that Tolkien was attempting to write what he called 'a mythology for England' speaks volumes here. His writing is geared towards the European (and particularly British) imagination in a way that the Old Testament, through no fault of its own, is not. Maybe on some level Tolkien saw a gap where a native creation myth should be, and *Ainulindalë* is his attempt to fill it.

Some might find the high, remote style of *Ainulindalë* off-putting, perhaps, but there's a spaciousness and depth to the writing, I feel, which brings a real sense of the timeless and archetypal to the page. There's a warmth and musicality at work as well which tempers the text's severity and brings an extra dimension to a narrative which might otherwise come across as somewhat dry and abstract.

Ilúvatar, Tolkien's creator God, fashions the Ainur first of all, mighty angelic intelligences, 'the offspring of his thought.' He proposes a musical theme and commands the Ainur to take it up and develop it. They respond in some style, making a music so beautiful that Tolkien says it will not be equalled until the end of the world. As the music proceeds, however, it is marred by the discordant motifs introduced by Melkor, the most powerful and gifted of the Ainur. He wants to bring in his own ideas, rather than those suggested by Ilúvatar. There is a clash, and many of the Ainur become disheartened and lose their way. Ilúvatar introduces a second theme, which is spoiled again by Melkor's innovations. Undeterred, Ilúvatar launches a third theme, and this time, no matter how hard Melkor strives for mastery, he cannot drown it out. On the contrary, his discordance is taken up into the wider music and becomes part of that very theme which Melkor is trying to undermine. Ilúvatar brings the music to a close and shows the Ainur what they have created with their voices. They see the newly-minted Earth spinning in the void and the unfolding of its history. 'Behold your Music!' says Ilúvatar. 'This is your minstrelsy; and each of you shall find herein, amid the design that I set before you, all those things which it may seem that he himself devised or added. And thou, Melkor, wilt discover all the secret thoughts of thy mind, and wilt perceive that they are but a part of the whole and tributary to its glory.'

There are echoes of other creation myths here, of course, most notably Aslan's singing Narnia into existence in *The Magician's Nephew* and the Gaelic story known as *The Earth-Shapers* or *The Shining Ones*. In the Irish tale, it is the Earth itself that does the singing. Unformed, misshapen, and tormented by primordial monsters (a little like those in the stories of H.P. Lovecraft), the Earth dreams of beauty and expresses its longing in the form of a song which reaches the ears of Brigid, 'the keeper of the sacred flame', who resides with the other Lordly Ones in Tir-na-Moe. Brigid convinces her brethren to descend with her to the Earth and save it from its distress. They bring with them the four Hallows - the Sword of Light, the Spear of Victory, the Cauldron of Plenty, and the Stone of Destiny. With the aid of these sacred objects, they drive back the monsters, heal the wounded Earth, and create a fresh, new world.

Evil is active in each of these three creation myths (as it is in Genesis, of course) - the fallen angel, Melkor, in *Ainulindalë;* the corrupted queen, Jadis, in *The Magician's Nephew;* and the primal monsters in *The Shining Ones*. Tolkien's depiction of evil is subtly and skilfully done. Melkor falls by degrees - from frustration at not being able to use his talents the way he wants, to a fixation on following his own way rather than Ilúvatar's, to a flat-out refusal to countenance the good and a determination to destroy not just Ilúvatar's music but the whole new world the Ainur are labouring to build.

It didn't have to be this way. It remains a mystery what greatness Melkor might have achieved had he chosen to use his gifts as Ilúvatar intended. He falls into the trap of thinking that 'his way' and 'Ilúvatar's way' are different and that Ilúvatar wants to thwart and stymie his potential. Nothing could be further from the truth. Melkor's deepest desire for himself and Ilúvatar's deepest desire for him are one and the same thing. But through pride and arrogance, Melkor turns his face from truth and sets out on a path of destruction - of the world around him, of others, and ultimately of himself.

It is a futile endeavour though. Ilúvatar's third theme shows us that the machinations of evil only serve in the long run to give rise to new and undreamt of forms of good. Ilúvatar hides the Flame Imperishable in the secret heart of the world. Melkor searches for it, but in vain. He is looking in the wrong places - in self-promoting fantasies of power, glory and domination. But we can find it. All we need do is stay true to ourselves and our creator. It's easier said than done, of course, but we should remember that the final destiny of men and women - 'the Children of Ilúvatar' - is hidden even from the Ainur who sang the world into being and is known to God alone.

This tells us that the work of creation is still ongoing and that we have a special, as yet unknown, part to play in its unfolding. We are called to become co-creators with the Divine. Nothing less than that. We are not there yet, perhaps, but the grandeur and suggestiveness of J.R.R. Tolkien's creation myth (together with the whole of his *oeuvre*) certainly helps point the way.

THE RETURN OF CONSTANTINE (JF)

Image - www.yorkcivictrust.co.uk

I have been reflecting recently on the statue outside York Minster of the Roman Emperor, Constantine the Great (above). Constantine was acclaimed as Emperor in that city by the British legions in 306 AD. He emerged victorious in a series of civil wars against his rivals Maxentius and Licinius to become sole ruler of both the Western and Eastern Roman Empires from 324 until his death in 337. At the Battle of the Milvian Bridge against Maxentius in 312, Constantine claimed to have seen a vision of a great cross arising from the light of the sun, bearing the inscription, *In Hoc Signo Vinces* - 'By this sign you will conquer.' Constantine converted to Christianity shortly before his death, the first Roman Emperor to declare himself a Christian. He had already played a key role in the Edict of Milan in 313, which proclaimed tolerance for Christianity throughout the Empire, and had also called the First Council of Nicea in 325, which saw the Nicene Creed adopted by the Church.

Constantine is venerated as a saint in Eastern Orthodoxy and Byzantine Catholicicism. The Russian Church hails him as the first ruler of the Christian Empire, an Empire which was transferred to Byzantium after the deposition of the last Western Roman Emperor in 476, and then on to Moscow at the fall of Byzantium in 1453.

Moscow, on this view, is seen as the 'Third Rome', with Tsar Nicholas II (1894-1917), who was martyred along with his family by the Bolsheviks in 1918, considered the last Christian Emperor. Russian eschatologists expect the Christian Empire to reappear in the future, however, just before the rise and fall of Antichrist and the Second Coming of Christ. The Emperor, in this scenario, will do what he has always done, acting as a *Katehon*, as St. Paul puts it in the original Greek - a restraining hand against the power of evil - he who 'holds back' as the New International Version has it:

> And now you know what is holding him (Antichrist) back, so that he may be revealed at the proper time. For the secret power of lawlessness is already at work; but the one who now holds it back will continue to do so till he is taken out of the way. And then the lawless one will be revealed, whom the Lord Jesus will overthrow with the breath of his mouth and destroy by the splendour of his coming. (2 Thessalonians 6:8)

Evil has certainly been revealed, and many would say has prospered, both in the East and the West, since the Emperor was 'taken out of the way.' The Holy Roman Empire, turning our attention to Western Europe for a moment, was dissolved by Napoleon in 1806. The Empire, many believe, lived on in Vienna and Budapest until the last Austro-Hungarian Emperor, Blessed Charles of Austria (1916-1918), reluctantly relinquished his responsibilities in the same year that the Tsar was executed. A prayer for the Roman Emperor was included in the Catholic Missal until 1955, but the Imperial throne, to all intents and purposes, has been vacant in Russia and the West since the end of the First World War. It is an absence keenly felt. As Valentin Tomberg writes in *Meditations on the Tarot* (1984), 'Europe is haunted by the shadow of the Emperor. One senses his absence just as vividly as in former times one sensed his presence. Because the emptiness of the wound *speaks*, that which we miss knows how to make us sense it.'

None of this is to say that the Emperors were always good - Constantine himself committed many dubious deeds - or that the system worked worked perfectly in all times and places. But the principle, to my mind at least, is admirable and even essential - the establishment of an earthly counterpart to the spiritual authority represented by the Patriarchs in the East and the Pope in the West.

The aim was never (or never should have been) a stultifying theocratic dictatorship, but rather a form and style of government that gave priority to the sacred and set out first and foremost to protect and cherish the good, the beautiful and the true. What a contrast to the dissolution and fragmentation - the lawlessness and formlessness - we see around us in so many realms today, the end product of failed attempts to plug the Imperial gap - first by Communism, then Fascism and, most recently, by economic and social liberalism.

The Emperor, when he returns, will have to be something of an all-rounder. He will need to bridge the spiritual and political divide between Russia and the rest of Europe for a start. He will also be required to combine a deeply felt Christian faith with an understanding and appreciation of the continent's pre-Christian heritage. His Christianity should be grounded in the primordial spiritual tradition which all the major religions share, confident and spacious enough to incorporate religious and cultural minorities, finding the optimum fit for them which Europe has struggled for so long to find. France, for instance, relies on a hardline secularism which all too often breeds alienation and resentment. Britain's cut-throat consumerism provokes mindless hedonism followed by spiritual despair, while the bland humanism of the Scandinavian countries serves to marginalise traditional native values, creating a civilisational vacuum rather than fostering authentic integration.

The Emperor, more than anything else, will need to inspire his people and engage their hearts and minds, as Aragorn does on his return to Gondor in *The Lord of the Rings*. This, in my view, is the single biggest failing of the European Union and the root cause of its probable demise - its inability to connect with ordinary Europeans and speak to the imagination and the emotions.

How can such an archaic figure as an Emperor possibly have a role to play in our hyper-modern world though? The prevailing materialistic mindset will surely render his return out of the question. It would take an astonishing sequence of events to turn the hands of time so far back. Sometimes it feels that nothing short of a war or an almighty economic crash will give us the shake up we need to pierce the veil of linear time and perceive again the abiding, archetypal truths about the human condition and the right and proper relationship, in the political and social realm, between the two poles St. Augustine called the City of God and the City of Man.

Our prevailing mindset neither grasps nor comprehends the whole story, however. There are vast areas of reality existing beyond its ken. The big, seismic changes - the paradigm shifts that trigger the rise and fall of civilisations - tend to take place at the periphery rather than the centre, the birth of Christ being the prime example. Britain, at the time of Constantine's acclamation, was a remote, windswept province at the North-West edge of the Empire. I would like to imagine, consequently, that the great wheel of the Christian Empire might turn full circle here. The country has some pedigree. The British, in Medieval times, regarded Constantine as one of their own kings, with particular links to Caernarfon in Gwynedd. (Prince Charles, as a matter of interest, was invested Prince of Wales at Caernarfon Castle in 1969). Legend also has it that Constantine's mother, Helena (also a saint in the Orthodox Church) was the daughter of Old King Cole of Colchester.

So, maybe the next paradigm shift will set itself in motion on this island - quietly and unobtrusively - far from the media's clatter and din. Perhaps even this very night. We are in early May, after all, the start of the 'bright half' of the Celtic year. The veil between worlds is thin. I see, in my mind's eye, a ruined abbey high above the North Wales coast, waves breaking against the rocks below and the peal of a church bell, blown on the wind from over the mountains, slowly chiming midnight. Six men and six women stand in a circle between the broken columns of the nave, some in sweeping green garments holding bugles and horns, others dressed for battle in chain mail and helmets, starlight glinting on their swords and spears. In the middle is a silver chair, with a boy - far from manhood still - siting there in a purple robe with a white cross emblazoned on the front and the words *In Hoc Signo Vinces* inscribed beneath. He has a golden crown on his head, a globe of the world in his left hand and a little tree with many leaves and branches in his right.

The church bell sounds for the twelfth time. A shout of acclamation rings around the abbey, followed by a crescendo of brass and the ding-ding-ding of spears on shield rims. Then comes the silence. Just the wind, the waves and the sharp, briny tang of the sea air. The first Emperor in a hundred years hops down from his throne, looks around, smiles shyly, and addresses his people for the first time, speaking to hearts and minds with warmth, intimacy and grace ...

4th May 2017

THE SLEEPING KING (JF)

'The Kingdom of Heaven lies within'. Endless repetition might have dulled our senses somewhat to the significance of this phrase, so it's worth re-iterating that in the last analysis all things of value lie within the human heart and imagination. This isn't to imply that there is *only* the human heart and imagination. Far from it. The inner and outer interlink and dovetail together, a prime example being our latent sense of Royalty, this intangible but seemingly inbuilt human awareness of a Royal principle at work through the vicissitudes of the historical record.

Monarchy, seen in this light, is a natural and organic form of government, understood intuitively by individuals from widely varying backgrounds and levels of intelligence. Legitimacy is conferred from above (the Divine) rather than below (the people), but Monarchy remains part of the natural order and stands at a substantial remove from random and artificial systems of government imposed on pliant, submissive populations. The Monarch is a symbol of his or her people's liberty - a guarantor of freedom of conscience and speech - existing not so much to rule as to serve. This Christological function finds expression in, among other places, the tales of King Arthur and his Knights, where we find a body of lore and a central mythological motif common throughout Europe and beyond - that of the Sleeping King, destined to wake at his country's hour of need.

The hold of Monarchy on the human imagination is markedly weaker today than at any time in the past. Since the Reformation and Renaissance, the focus and dynamism of the West has revolved around the external world, to the detriment of the inner *milieu* that animated Medieval mystics such as Julian of Norwich and inspired the construction of the great cathedrals of Canterbury, Wells, York, Durham, etc. Society has been de-sacralised and rationalised to such a degree since that it has become increasingly difficult for supra-rational concepts like Monarchy and religious mysticism to gain any degree of purchase in the contemporary imagination.

This link between Divinity and Royalty is a crucial one. In a well-ordered polity the Sovereign acts as God's regent; so when, for example, the Medieval French kings abrogated power from the Pope, they unwittingly undermined their own legitimacy and *raison d'etre*. Their lust for hegemony only succeeded in tipping the balance of the natural order askew and sowing the seeds of their own destruction.

Once this natural harmony is thrown out of kilter it becomes very hard to restore the balance. The French Revolution and the bloodbath which followed are suitable illustrations of the chaos which results from a shaken hierarchy. In the 1790s, however, matters had not yet descended to such a pass that the situation was wholly irretrievable, and Napoleon's more or less principled autocracy restored a little of the equilibrium and saved France from unmasked brutality. But by 1917 the world had been de-spiritualised to such an extent that the fall from revolution to tyranny was able to take place largely unimpeded. A semi-Arthurian figure like Bonaparte would have been unable to make an impression on post-1917 Russia simply because he belonged to a different era where the Royal principle still commanded a central (if somewhat diminished) position in hearts and minds.

C.S. Lewis famously remarked that 'one can tell the extent to which a man's tap root to Eden remains intact by his attitude to Monarchy.' Inner and outer harmony begin to disintegrate when this tap root, this intangible and utterly mysterious quality, is weakened and subsequently severed. If Man - the microcosm - falls into step with natural hierarchical patterns, then the outer world - the macrocosm - flows likewise in a harmonious fashion. The human heart is the point where microcosm and macrocosm meet, and it is here that the future of Monarchy - our own future as free and independent persons, in other words - will be decided. The heart is the throne of the Sleeping King. We will flounder and struggle to restore kudos and depth of meaning to Royalty in the outer world unless we come to acknowledge this Royal aspect within.

It will be a stiff task. Ours an obtuse, chatter-filled, technologically-driven age, where talk of 'hidden kings' and suchlike will inevitably appear obscure and inaccessible. Nonetheless, the responsibility and challenge is ours to start setting a creative, imaginative agenda, through our thoughts, words and deeds. There are forces arraigned against us, powers of iron and stone, seeking to rob us of vision, reducing us to impotent cogs in a vast collective machine or, failing that, to mindless, zombified consumers, the *hungry ghosts* of Buddhist iconography.

It isn't good enough. Not for ourselves - the inheritors of Arthur and inhabitants of his holy realm. We are more, much more, than economic units shuffling around like atoms in some demented free-market disco. Our lives are more, much more, than a shapeless, rough and tumble scramble for comfort and security. Life is, or ought to be, an adventure, an exercise in nobility, and the traditional job of Monarchy is to serve as role-model and exemplar in that respect.

As for us - as for the future - well, Restoration starts from within, with a heightening in our level of consciousness and a deepening of our perception. Our task, our mythological function and responsibility, is a twenty-first century quest for the Golden Fleece - to unveil the Monarch within and awaken the Sleeping King.

WHEN BRITAIN FELL (JF)

This, as I wrote last Sunday, is my final post for this blog. And I'm writing it from the future - 7.15 am on Wednesday November 20th 2019. A lot has happened since that last Sunday of 2018. Britain has fallen for a start. It was conquered a month ago and officially ceased to exist last week. French, Russian and American forces occupy vast tracts of the country. The areas outside their control (including my current location on the North Wales coast) are wild and lawless, but also abuzz with a sense of possibility and renewal which did not, it has to be said, exist anywhere in the former UK before the upheavals of September and October.

No-one saw it coming. We were preoccupied all summer long with Brexit and King Charles's coronation. Rumour has it that Charles insisted on a quick investiture so he could take charge of Brexit and bring an end to the uncertainty and division that had so weakened the body politic. Speculation abounded as to his intentions but instantly became yesterday's news when Russia and Turkey attacked Europe on September 3rd in a pincer movement that caught us all cold.

The Russians, as far as I can tell with the internet being so unreliable, have borne the brunt of the fighting thus far. They swept through the Baltic states in seven days but had a torrid time in Poland in a three week campaign that has cost something like 20,000 Polish and Russian lives. Even now, the country is far from subdued, but the Kremlin's goal was simply to reach Germany - nothing more than that. Once the Russians set foot on German soil, Berlin surrendered straightaway, as Vladimir Putin had hoped, and now his forces are massing on the French border. Two weeks ago Russian troops occupied Scandinavia, and last week news came through that Austria, Hungary, Slovakia and the Czech Republic had also fallen. So things are going very well for President Putin. It only remains to be seen whether he'll choose to consolidate his gains or press on towards Paris.

The Turks have played a smaller but no less significant role. They annexed a handful of Greek islands and used them as bases to attack Italy, seizing on the country's political and economic woes and fully occupying the peninsula after a month's pretty straightforward fighting. They too are now threatening France, and the world is currently holding its breath, watching for President Macron's next step.

I say 'next step' because Macron's first step astounded everyone.

Rather than meet the threat head on as the Poles had done or seek immediate terms like the Germans, Macron had withdrawn France's military presence in Africa, then invaded Britain, capturing London in just three weeks. He is now busy integrating the former UK's armed forces into his new EU Army and acquiring ownership of our nuclear arsenal.

It's been a shocking defeat. Stunning and brutal. We were outclassed, outgunned and outmanoeuvred in every department. Years of spending cuts and political correctness had clearly knocked the stuffing out of Britain's military capability far more than anyone, apart from a few professional Cassandras, had imagined. The French, as a character points out in Michel Houellebecq's *Submission* (2015), have never made that mistake. No matter which President occupies the Élysée Palace, they have never compromised or cut corners on their armed forces. And that, in the last analysis, was the difference between the two nations in the Second Battle of Britain.

The Royal Family had declined President Trump's offer of refuge and had been taken captive by the French. They're being held, it's said, in a château just outside Grenoble. So at least we've some idea of where they are, unlike Pope Francis, who similarly refused to leave Rome and was dragged off by the Turks. No-one knows where he is or whether he's alive or dead. As a Catholic, that's been the most disquieting thing for me in all this. I'm fortunate, however, in that I don't have immediate family to worry about. My wife and children are safe in Australia, while my Mum - who lives in Manchester - is in the American Zone, which is probably the best (or least worst) place to be right now.

There's a Russian Zone as well, and all these spheres of rival influence have come about since the fall of London. The French have little authority as yet outside the South East. In the Midlands and the North a motley crew of gangsters, madmen, religious fundamentalists and self-styled warlords have scrambled to fill the vacuum. An opportunistic Russian flotilla recently took advantage of the chaos, sailing up the Humber and occupying Hull, York and Leeds. And that's what's finally goaded President Trump into action. Within days Ireland had become an American protectorate and shortly afterwards both Liverpool and Manchester were swarming with GIs.

It's a dreadful situation in short and it's been well-nigh impossible to know what to do and where to turn. But I'm here in Bangor at Neuadd William Blake (William Blake House) because of one name that's kept cropping up for me these past few weeks. Not a name you'd expect to hear in this context. Not a name you'd associate with resistance or national revival. I'm talking about Simon Hennessy, the ex-footballer. Let me fill you in on his CV if you're unfamiliar with the name.

In a peripatetic career, Hennessy decorated the midfield for Aston Villa, Leicester City, Sheffield Wednesday, Burnley, Bournemouth and Sunderland. He had a few other clubs as well and only stopped playing ten years ago when he was 41. He was a gifted, mercurial playmaker, with the vision of Glenn Hoddle, so they said, and the touch of Paul Scholes. He was a fine header of the ball too, I remember, but like many before him he squandered the best of himself in bookies, bars and sub-standard nightclubs. He had a fair old temper too and collected more than a few red cards on his Odyssey through English football.

I never held any of that against him though. I always liked Hennessy, as a player and a man. He was moody and intense, for sure, but football for him was an art and his post-match interviews made wonderful watching - for his passion, sincerity, poetic flourishes, and the personal warmth he exuded. I had the distinct sense of a man of depth and sensitivity looking in the wrong places for a meaning and significance which he desperately wanted and needed but which for some reason had so far eluded him.

It's fair to say, given all this, that Hennessy never became the player he could have been. He only played for England twice, for instance, but he enjoyed a memorable career nonetheless. He was hardly ever injured, played over 800 league games, and was widely respected for his thought-provoking insights into the game. He was studying for his UEFA coaching badges when he had some kind of religious experience on St. Michael's Mount in Cornwall. I forget the details now but the papers were full of it at the time, around 2010/11. They called him the 'new David Icke', but the story quickly faded as Hennessy gave up football altogether and trained to become a Catholic priest. But that had gone wrong too, just a few months ago, in a blazing row with the Bishop of Salford over Hennessy's insistence on quoting from Dion Fortune's *The Magical Battle of Britain* in his sermons. In typical Hennessy fashion things had escalated very quickly as he turned the air blue in front of the Bishop and found himself banished, at least temporarily, from the priesthood.

Such was the character and history of the man who people, for some reason, kept talking to me about. 'Hennessy's the only one with any style', muttered the woman rooting for food in the bins. 'Hennessy has to take over', said the old man walking his dog on the beach. 'Hennessy can set this whole bloody country right,' roared the beggar with the red hair and beard in Conwy. 'He's got balls, he's got soul. If he gets enough followers he'll turn the whole f****** shambles on its head.'

So that's how I came to be here. I'm due to fly to Australia in a couple of weeks and I've been looking forward to it, but I couldn't possibly leave without seeing what all the fuss is about. I'm lucky too that Hennessy's base - overlooking Anglesey and the Menai Straits - is very close to where I live. So yes, here I am. I heard him speak yesterday evening, stayed the night, and am writing this over coffee the next morning. I've no idea what I'm going to do next - whether I'll stay or go - but let me at least 'set my lands in order' as Eliot says in *The Wasteland* and make a start on the future, whatever that may be, by telling you what transpired last night and this morning.

Neuadd William Blake is an ivy-clad Victorian mansion perched high on a hill above a spectacularly rocky cliff-face. It was almost dark when I got here, but lights blazed in the windows and I had a good feeling about the place straightaway. I hadn't intended to stay over, I could happily have slept in the car, but Hennessy's staff offered me a room 'on the house' and for as long as I wanted, and I was so taken aback that I immediately accepted. His workers, both men and women, wore royal blue shirts and trousers with white collars and cuffs. Leicester City colours, I thought, and that was fitting as Leicester was Hennessy's home town and it was there that he enjoyed his finest years as a player in the mid-90s.

The house has a calm, contemplative feel. The carpet is orange and the wallpaper a soft, subtle silver. There are lots of icons on the walls - images of saints, kings and queens. All the saints I've seen so far have been British or Irish, such as Cuthbert, Bridgid, Hilda and Kevin. There are several monarchs I'm familiar with too - Alfred the Great, Athelstan, Harold, Charles I, etc - but also many others I've never heard of - Mark V, Joseph the Noble, Sophia I, and more.

The house feels much bigger on the inside than it looks from the outside. The corridors are long, with numerous staircases leading up and down at various points, and a wealth of spacious, lamp-lit chambers lined with tapestries and books. Hennessy addressed us in the Great Hall. There were about forty or fifty of us present. Ordinary working men and women mainly. A couple of professorial types. A smattering of teenagers. One or two old punks. A log fire leapt and crackled in the hearth. After supper (roast turkey with veg), Hennessy's staff took the tables away and we gathered our chairs in a loose horseshoe shape around a candlelit table draped with cloth of gold.

Hennessy stood between the table and the hearth. Behind him, on the wall, stretched a huge banner - a red dragon on a gold background. The long haired will o' the wisp of football yore, by the way, is long gone now. Hennessy has filled out considerably and has short brown hair and a stubbly grey-flecked beard. Last night, interestingly, he was wearing the same blue and white uniform as his staff. I also saw a look of firmness and resolve in those famous green eyes that made me wonder if his spat with the Bishop had been less a case of him throwing his toys out of the pram and more to do with a reluctance to suffer fools gladly.

He spoke for about an hour. Gestures were minimal but there was eye contact aplenty. His tone was warm and eager. It felt like he was addressing me personally, but I'm sure we all felt like that. I remember every word he said. I don't have space or time to record it all here, but I'll do my best to paraphrase. What he said went something like this:

"When the Angel of this Island appeared to me on St. Michael's Mount he showed me all these disasters which have now befallen our land. But I also saw - like a spark of gold on a field of black - how this self-same ignominy can and will become the seedbed for a radical transformation which will restore the holy realm of Logres and rouse and inspire the world.

"For it was from Great Britain that the darkness grew and spread and engulfed the whole Earth. Four centuries of mercantilism and shrunken vision have banished God, the saints and angels and the whole supernatural order from our lives. We no longer feel or sense the presence of a spiritually-charged universe. We have traded the deep and holy mystery of the human person to those who hate the numinous and fight against profundity - economists, sociologists, media men and bureaucrats. Our imaginations have wound down to nought and we are paying the price now for our spiritual blindness. It is right and just that we do so.

"That is only half the story, however, and not the most important half at that. Because the truth, brothers and sisters, is that Logres never disappeared, it was just that our eyes became too obtuse to see it. For there have been many kings and queens of Logres since that dark day at Camlann - an unbroken chain - some names known to history and others not. Once established by Arthur and Merlin, the Holy Kingdom could never cease to exist, and now that the wheel of involution has run its course, men and women will start to perceive it again. From Albion's shores it will shine out like flame, in compensation for the centuries of constriction, and restore all that is high, noble and pure in all corners of the Earth.

"The word, my friends, is spreading about the seeds we are planting here at Neuadd William Blake. Personnel and equipment are arriving every night, but that again is not the most important element. The most tremendous fact, as most of you know, is that right beneath our feet, at the bottom of this very house, Arthur and his Companions lie sleeping, waiting for the signal to rise and retake the land.

"This Great Hall, it seems to me looking about, is around a quarter full tonight. When the British start to really see, when they feel drawn to this place, when there is standing room only in this room, that is when Arthur and his men will rise up and the radiant dawn of renewal shine forth upon this land. That day, brethren, is close at hand. Until then, apart from those who have arrived tonight, please continue in your roles, some remaining here to prepare, others going into the world to announce the good news of liberation - a liberation which will be so much more than the expulsion of foreign powers, a liberation to unchain and unleash those aspects of our national life which have been kept captive so long - emotional, mental, imaginative, spiritual - everything that William Blake, the patron of this house, fought for in his words, pictures and deeds."

It was stupendous stuff - a speech for the ages - met with cheers and raucous applause. I appreciate, however, that for some of you reading this on a page Hennessy's words will come over as delusional nonsense or the ramblings of one grown soft in the head through too much booze or the repeated heading of a football. You had to be there, I guess. But I was won over like the others, and I'm not easily swayed by purple prose and standing ovations. As with his TV interviews back in the day I was touched by Hennessy's warmth and sincerity, but also by his audacity - the sheer *chutzpah* of it - in taking this national crisis and making something deep and mythic and metaphysical out of it. The woman rooting in the bin, the old man walking his dog, and the beggar with the wild red hair and beard were all spot on, I saw. They had all seen in him the one thing needed to meet and match the crushing gravity of national collapse. Hennessy isn't trying to fight fire with fire like the Poles, you see. Nor does he want to make a quick peace like the Germans and pretend the conquest never happened. He's after something deeper and more far-reaching. What he's offering is a national rebirth - a return to the source - at the most primal, archaic levels of our being. He's a priest after all, not a politician, and a sportsman to boot, playing with the great British archetypes - Arthur, Albion and Logres - as twenty years ago I saw him ping forty yard passes around Old Trafford, silencing the crowd and seizing the game by the scruff of the neck. He's like a more creative version of Donald Trump. In a world where rational argument has disintegrated into jargon and post-modern babble, Hennessy bypasses all that and engages with the roots of British consciousness. He's connecting with hearts and minds and firing up imaginations, giving people the mythic food they need and have been starved of for so long. He's doing it in a positive and constructive manner too. Nothing dark and sinister like the Nazis. The future, my intuition tells me, could be his if he continues in this vein.

I still have one or two doubts, however. I wasn't convinced, for instance, by the background noise during his speech of vehicles parking up outside and feet stamping on gravel. It seemed a bit staged and could easily have been a recording designed to persuade us that troops are mustering at Neuadd William Blake.

I wanted to go to my room and have a good think about it, but beer and wine had appeared and people were mingling merrily in the Hall. It was all very pleasant and convivial. Reassuringly old-school in many ways. A few of the 'brethren' were smoking and Hennessy himself had a bottle of Moretti in his hand. So in some ways at least, he was still the *bon viveur* of old!

I didn't get chance to speak to him and I disappeared after twenty minutes and went back upstairs. I lay on the bed and began to reflect but must have fallen asleep straightaway. When I opened my eyes the room looked and felt very different and I knew that we were deep into the night, possibly not far from dawn. A bell tinkled faintly somewhere, high up and far off. I tried to ignore it and go back to sleep but it was like the bell - quiet but insistent - wouldn't allow me. I felt compelled to find out where it was coming from. So I got up, opened the door and looked along the corridor to the right. A gentle golden light was shining on the carpet at the far end. I walked down and saw a door wide open on the left. The light shone on a spiral stone staircase leading up. The bell carried on chiming, directly above my head now.

I started to climb. The bell stopped ringing but the light grew stronger, until I stepped out a few minutes later into a small stone chapel with two thick candles burning on the altar and a large picture on the wall behind it which I couldn't see. There was a small window-niche to my right and a candle glowed there too, but even then it was still too dark for me to see the image clearly. I could make out blocks and shapes of green and white and gold, but nothing more distinct than that.

There were no pews, just little kneeling boards dotted around the floor. That was when I saw Hennessy, kneeling at the front and gazing at the altar and the painting. It was strange that I hadn't seen him before. He was certainly hard to miss, dressed in a dazzling white robe - probably the brightest thing in the room - with what looked like a golden circlet around his head. Part of me wanted to go back down and leave him to his prayers, but the atmosphere in the chapel was so still and the sound of the waves crashing on the rocks below so refreshing that I took one of the kneeling boards and knelt down on it at the back of the chapel.

After a while, Hennessy stood up, bowed low towards the altar, turned around and walked slowly towards me. He had a purple cross sewn onto the front of his robe, and I thought he was about to say something profound, but all he said was, 'Remember to keep the candles burning. Don't blow them out. Not even when dawn comes.'

'Yes,' I replied. 'Of course.'

'Thank you,' he said. His eyes sparkled for a moment in the half-light, then he was past me and gone, out of the room and down the stairs.

I stayed where I was for a long time. I had a lot to think about. Purple, white and gold, I reflected, are royal colours. Hennessy clearly believes he's some kind of king - the current representative, no doubt, of that 'unbroken chain' of kings and queens of Logres he referred to last night. But how can I evaluate such a belief? What does believing such a thing signify? There are three possibilities as I see it: either Hennessy is mad, bad, or telling the truth. He's definitely not a bad man. But he could easily be mad. Almost certainly, some would say.

But deep down, you know, I have to say I don't think so. I've developed quite an effective 'bullshit detector' for fantasists and would-be gurus over the years, and even though I've no empirical evidence I sense some level of truth and integrity to what's happening at Neuadd William Blake. But what if that's just wishful thinking on my part? Or symptoms of trauma triggered by the events of the past three months? Who can say? But it's important that I decide on a course of action quickly. There are people depending on me, on the other side of the world and elsewhere in the country. I haven't been given a 'role' yet either. Maybe that will become clear over breakfast. I will have to wait and see. Not long to go now.

Gradually the chapel grew brighter and the seagulls started to squawk and squabble outside. I could see the picture on the wall at last. It was an icon, a depiction of the holy women arriving at the tomb and the angel telling them that Christ has risen and gone before them into Galilee. It set me thinking about the word 'resurrection' and what that might mean in an individual and a national context. I meditated too on all those weighty words beginning with 'r' - restoration, renewal, renaissance, reanimation, rejuvenation, rebirth - which I realise I have used so often in these Albion Awakening posts these past two and a half years.

The smell of coffee roasting downstairs broke the spell. I stood up, bowed low as Hennessy had done, descended the staircase, took my IPad from my room, ordered a macchiato from the little espresso bar in the drawing room and sat down to write this piece.

And there's the bell for breakfast! Time to add my pictures, press 'publish' and walk forward into the future, knowing that Christ, as in the icon upstairs, has gone before me and before us all into Galillee, to Jerusalem and Rome, and out around the globe - in times of war and times of peace, in times of grief and times of joy - *Urbi et Orbi* - to the City and the World.

ΑΙ ΜΥΡΟΦΟΡΟΙ

Yet some men say in many parts of England that King Arthur is not dead, but had by the will of our Lord Jesu into another place; and men say that he shall come again, and he shall win the holy cross. I will not say it shall be so, but rather I will say: here in this world he changed his life. But many men say that there is written upon his tomb this verse: *Hic jacet Arthurus, Rex quondam, Rexque futurus.*

Here Lies Arthur, Once and Future King

ABOUT THE AUTHORS

John Fitzgerald is a writer from Manchester, currently living in North Wales. His writing revolves around themes of spiritual and cultural renewal and the resacralisation of the contemporary world. John's website is www.deepbritainandireland.blogspot.co.uk

William Wildblood was born in London and, after spending time abroad in India and France, has returned there. He is the author of three books, *Meeting the Masters*, *Remember the Creator* and *The Spiritual Crisis of Modern Man.* William's website is www.meetingthemasters.blogspot.com.

For those who might wish to explore further the ideas behind this book please see www.albionawakening.blogspot.com

Printed in Great Britain
by Amazon